Hanging On and Rising Up

Princeton Theological Monograph Series
K. C. Hanson, Charles M. Collier, D. Christopher Spinks,
and Robin A. Parry, Series Editors

Recent volumes in the series:

Steven C. van den Heuvel
*Bonhoeffer's Christocentric Theology and Fundamental
Debates in Environmental Ethics*

Andrew R. Hay
God's Shining Forth: A Trinitarian Theology of Divine Light

Peter Schmiechen
*Gift and Promise:
An Evangelical Theology of the Lord's Supper*

Hank Voss
*The Priesthood of All Believers and the Missio Dei:
A Canonical, Catholic, and Contextual Perspective*

Alexandra S. Radcliff
*The Claim of Humanity in Christ: Salvation and
Sanctification in the Theology of T. F. and J. B. Torrance*

Yaroslav Viazovski
*Image and Hope:
John Calvin and Karl Barth on Body, Soul, and Life Everlasting*

Anna C. Miller
*Corinthian Democracy:
Democratic Discourse in 1 Corinthians*

Thomas Christian Currie
*The Only Sacrament Left to Us: The Threefold
Word of God in the Theology and Ecclesiology of Karl Barth*

Hanging On and Rising Up

Renewing, Re-envisioning, and Rebuilding the Cross from the "Marginalized"

Patricia Cuyatti Chávez

☙PICKWICK *Publications* · Eugene, Oregon

HANGING ON AND RISING UP
Renewing, Re-envisioning, and Rebuilding the Cross from the "Marginalized"

Princeton Theological Monograph Series 235

Copyright © 2019 Patricia Cuyatti Chávez. All rights reserved. Except for brief quotations in critical publications or reviews, no part of this book may be reproduced in any manner without prior written permission from the publisher. Write: Permissions, Wipf and Stock Publishers, 199 W. 8th Ave., Suite 3, Eugene, OR 97401.

Pickwick Publications
An Imprint of Wipf and Stock Publishers
199 W. 8th Ave., Suite 3
Eugene, OR 97401

www.wipfandstock.com

PAPERBACK ISBN: 978-1-5326-5158-8
HARDCOVER ISBN: 978-1-5326-5159-5
EBOOK ISBN: 978-1-5326-5160-1

Cataloguing-in-Publication data:

Names: Cuyatti Chávez, Patricia, author.

Title: Hanging on and rising up : renewing, re-envisioning, and rebuilding the cross from the "marginalized" / Patricia Cuyatti Chávez.

Description: Eugene, OR : Pickwick Publications, 2019 | Princeton Theological Monograph Series 235 | Includes bibliographical references and index.

Identifiers: ISBN 978-1-5326-5158-8 (paperback) | ISBN 978-1-5326-5159-5 (hardcover) | ISBN 978-1-5326-5160-1 (ebook)

Subjects: LCSH: Christianity—Latin America. | Jesus Christ—History of doctrines. | Jesus Christ -- History of doctrines—20th century. | Liberation theology. | Peru—Church history—20th century. | Matto de Turner, Clorinda,—1852–1909.

Classification: BT83.57 .C89 2019 (print) | BT83.57 .C89 (ebook)

Manufactured in the U.S.A. 06/25/19

To Victoria and in her to all women and men who struggle for life daily. Her presence, like the strong and delicate wind, continues to be an inspiration.

Raise your words, not your voice.
It is the rain that grows flowers, not thunder.

—Rumi

Contents

Acknowledgments | ix
Introduction | xi

1. Conquest, an Encounter with Another God —Christ Arriving in the New World | 1
2. The Latin American Christology: Resurrection of the Body of the Poor | 29
3. Christologies from Latin American Women's/Feminists' Perspective | 59
4. Christ in Peruvian Evangelization | 92
5. Suffering and Salvation in the Novels of Clorinda Matto de Turner | 113
6. Who Do You Say that I Am? A Relationship Christology | 131

Conclusion | 155

Bibliography | 159
Index | 169

Acknowledgments

I BEGIN THIS SECTION giving honor to the thousand women and men who have touched my life. The first Victoria Chavez, my *mamina*, and with her also my family. Mamina's strength and passion is a beautiful combination that taught me how to face life. She moved me to pursue my dreams and, to a certain extent, her loving courage remains as soft breath that continues to refresh, making this journey alive in heart and mind.

I am thankful to the Lutheran Church of Peru for trusting this process and for allowing me to be part of an inclusive ministry. I am grateful to the Evangelical Lutheran Church in America for their commitment in leadership, humbly walking with men and women and the growth through what is, from my experience, a heartfelt companionship. Special gratitude to the Rev. Dr. Raquel Rodriguez and the Rev. Rafael Malpica-Padilla for their profound sensibility and their engagement in the development of women leaders. I recognize Gustav-Adolf Werks' commitment to the churches in the diaspora and the gracious opportunity to learn German. That singular experience nourished my understanding of the Lutheran heritage and caused me to reflect on what it means to live faithfully in a secular context.

The Lutheran School of Theology at Chicago remains home to me. Embracing students from different parts of the world promotes learning and mutual growth. This journey has been an mission growing and harvesting fruits guided by Rev. Dr. Vítor Westhelle. His interest in the research, his trust in this "caminata" and doing theology in the "conversa" has inspired and motivated strongly. My gratitude is also for professors who inspired me to continue my studies like Dr. Antje Jackelén, Dr. Linda Thomas, Dr. José David Rodriguez. My gratitude to Dr. Luis Rivera-Pagán for his deep insights related to theology and literature. My especial recognition is to T. H. and Ruth Rossing for the honor of being the first recipient of the T. H. and Ruth Rossing Scholarship at the beginning of my doctoral studies.

I am thankful to Armando Del Valle, friend-husband-committed partner. His simplicity in doing theology is a great source that made me land in the reality of the simple and meaningful. Armando not only motivated me during times of disinterest in this research, he also danced and warmly inspired me to reach my goal. I acknowledge Rob Worley who walks with international students and makes relevant our voices, experiences, and dreams. Big thanks to the Rev. Dr. Katharine Bergbusch for her honest presence as my pastor, tutor, and friend. Katharine was present at times to discern with me whether to pursue doctoral studies and during my studies. Katharine, thank you for reading the entire research trusting your knowledge of years of pastoral ministry in Peru and for your deep insights!

This book is the fruit of inspiration on pastoral care; a topic that I developed alongside my PhD studies on Clinical Pastoral Education. My gratitude to Barbara Sheehan for encouraging me to follow this dream and to the Department of Religion and Health and Human Values of Rush University Medical Center where I was a Resident Chaplain for one year. My gratitude goes out to my supervisors Mark Tabbut, Mary Altenbaumer, Jo-Ann O'Reilly. The lively parish in chaplaincy gave me the opportunity to nourish my soul while engaging in my personal healing with care and love. Part of that community are patients with their families who are the image of God that daily taught me of the meaning and power of being resilient.

Introduction

THE TASK OF RE-IMAGING Christology asks us to consider two approaches: first, engagement in dialogue about the nature of Jesus Christ, which implies a return to the Christological debates of the early church in order to reaffirm what has been determined as dogma; and second, recognition that in Latin America, people confess Jesus as the Christ. This research follows the second approach but its purpose is to understand the concrete reality of suffering in which the confession takes place.[1] To confess that Jesus is Christ implies knowing what the confession means. Knowledge about Jesus the Christ comes from revelation, from the divine initiative to the place of a divine–human relationship. Even though Christology bases its reflections on that relationship, the confession of faith as fact comes from daily life experience between humans and the divine. The experience of faith uncovers *ordinary knowledge*, knowledge that is based in trust, a "depth of relationship."[2] Marginalized women and men who believe in Christ as the Lord know what they confess; that truth[3] is discovered in their daily struggle. Through their suffering, they act hoping that their relationship with God may impact their reality that negates life.

---

1. Ritchie asserts that to confess Jesus as the Christ depends on the reality in which the confession is made. That Jesus is the Christ "is a truth to be discovered. A name translated into words and actions will gain its historical veracity, its liberating force" (Ritchie, "Mujer y Cristología," 84).

2. The knowledge of Christ constructed and objectified goes hand-in-hand with ordinary knowledge. "I will argue that for Luther these realms of knowledge are related . . . 'knowledge of God' and 'ordinary knowledge' . . . are related because, from the perspective of Luther's theology, they set each other off: They help to define one another, to some degree, by spelling out what each is *not*, at least as much as they do so by spelling out what each *is* or deals with. They also make each other possible, in the sense that each has its proper bailiwick . . . it also requires and enables epistemological responsibility: Humans knowers must and can act responsibly in the world, in relation to others" (Solberg, *Compelling Knowledge*, 100).

3. Ritchie, "Mujer y Cristología," 120.

Centuries of suffering and exploitation placed uncertainty before the profession of faith that Jesus was the Christ. The Messiah who came to liberate his people from oppression and to strengthen them was used to maintain their silence and to enforce control. In the context of conquest in Latin America and the Caribbean, Christ was used to support conquest. Today, the reality still needs change to affirm the truth of Christ that liberates and affirms life.

In 2002, when invited to speak in some congregations of the Texas-Louisiana Gulf Coast Synod, the companion synod for the Peruvian Evangelical Lutheran Church—ILEP, I considered deeply the Peruvian reality in which the ILEP was being developed and serving God. To consider poverty as one of the main characteristics of the Peruvian reality was unavoidable. Poverty was not a novelty for the audience, but the new element that made it important, as a consequence of the economic shock,[4] was the growing percentage of the population living in extreme poverty.[5] Even given this scandalous reality, the good news to be revealed was that marginalized people, especially women, had the capacity to struggle to survive. Economic survival, as an expression of hope of the crucified people, is an everyday experience among thousands in Latin America. From and in their struggles, people confess "I do believe in Christ" as a deep expression of struggle and determination, identified in this research as crucifixion. Crucifixion does not eliminate hope; in the midst of suffering, women and men have the strength and the capacity to celebrate making resurrection possible.

---

4. In July 1990, during his visits to the United States and Japan, it was made very clear to Fujimori that unless Peru adopted a relatively orthodox economic strategy and stabilized hyperinflation, there would be no possibility of Peru's re-entry into the international financial community or no international aid. His financial shock was more extreme than the most orthodox IMF economic procedure recommended at the time. Privatization of several state industries and liberalization of the trading system were in place. Overnight, Lima became a city which had, in the words of several observers, "Bangladesh salaries with Tokyo prices" (Hudson, "The Fujimori Government").

5. Poverty is defined considering the family income. Families living in poverty cover the basic needs to subsist. However, families living in extreme poverty expend the entire income to provide a meal per day using basic ingredients but without the capacity to cover expenses for gas. Extreme poverty is measured considering the population that is economically active but is underpaid and overexploited. They are mainly street merchants or work in agriculture. Agriculture has a quantitative relevance, it covers the 75% of the population economically active considered in extreme poverty. This reveals that the majority of the population are in rural and agricultural areas. Bravo, "La Pobreza y Extrema Pobreza."

In order to understand better this reality of faith and the Christology that arises in Latin America, it will be necessary to go back to the historical roots of the arrival of Christ. Chapter 1 centers on the encounter between Christ the Savior and God the Creator present in the Peruvian culture. The methods that the conquerors employed to evangelize are rooted in the period of expulsion of Muslims and Jews from the Iberian Peninsula. The Roman Catholic Church in exile within its own territory recovered Toledo in 1085. The turning point: abandonment of the "Rito Mozarabe" to return to the Roman rite.[6] The Muslim and Jewish expulsion was a political and religious decision against infidels.

The perception of infidelity worked well to recover the southern areas of the Iberian Peninsula. In 1492 arriving in the new lands and realizing that the Indigenous had strong beliefs, Spaniards charged them with infidelity and idolatry. According to the conquerors, the Indigenous populations were people who worshiped idols and therefore needed to receive and accept the Christian faith and the authority of the Spanish King. Assuming a messianic character, the conquerors believed that God had chosen and favored them in that enterprise. Even though the conquest clearly was a political move, their triumphant view of God was represented by their King and Queen.

The encounter between the two different religious worldviews was complex. The language was a problem itself. Even with the use of native interpreters who learned the conquerors' language, it was difficult to translate culturally determined concepts. However, the conquerors did not conduct a genuine dialogue; instead, they imposed their ideas through a monologue. The research uses monologue as metaphor to confirm the imposition of the Christian faith. The two relevant dialogues between Moctezuma and Cortés in Mexico, and Atahualpa and Pizarro in Peru, illustrate this tension. In each one, the Spaniards try to convince the Indigenous that their gods were idols and should be disregarded.

Some strategies in this monologue impacted the life of the Indigenous. These included the change of their native names to Christian ones, the establishment of churches in their sacred places, the "encomienda" system that turned the conquerors into saviors of the native people, the "repartimiento" that made more obvious the possession of the lands, and conversion that was linked to the "encomienda" system and worked in a political and economic manner. Colonization and

---

6. López Lozano, *Precedentes de la Iglesia*, 41–47.

Christianization were the two faces of the same coin in the new world but did not kill the Indigenous beliefs. As José Carlos Mariátegui argues, native beliefs survived in the sub-soil of a religious culture that superficially had a Christian face.[7]

Chapter 2 dives into Latin American Christology after considering the arrival of Protestantism on the continent. During the Republican period, the Protestant movement had two characteristics: a) protestants arrived with the Bible, not with the sword; b) European protestants immigrated bringing their culture and religious traditions. During the period that Protestantism became established in Latin America, reading and propagation of the Bible and education were promoted. Protestant churches celebrated and worshiped their faith and, at the same time, established the spirit of Christ through schools, hospitals, and farms. One of the most influential aspects of their presence in the continent was education.[8] Protestant Christians were creative and helped to "rediscover religion as faith, as relation between person to person . . . which life is never based in codes and commandments but in the power of God that recognizes in Jesus the Lord of earth and heaven."[9]

In the eighteenth century, the quest for the historical Jesus began in Europe. Hermann Samuel Reimarus denied the miracles written in the scriptures. The historical and academic research that this quest promoted motivated German theologians to write Jesus' biography as a critical interpretation of Jesus' life and actions. After fifty years of research, a new quest arose with the article "The Problem of the Historical Jesus" by Ernst Käsemann. His conclusion consistently affirmed that the Christ of faith was the Jesus of history proclaimed by the first communities of faith. Käsemann addressed the relevant aspects of Jesus' life that give a sense of continuity to his ministry. For Latin American theologians, faith based on historical information about Jesus, these studies were relevant to Christology.

Latin American theologians used the sources developed in Europe to emphasize the unity between the confession of Christ and Jesus' acts. The historical Jesus helped to clarify the mission and destiny of Jesus of Nazareth;[10] therefore, his ministry became the methodological beginning

---

7. Mariátegui, *Siete Ensayos*, 136–37.

8. Mackay, *El Otro Cristo Español*, 275–76, 284.

9. Mackay, *El Otro Cristo Español*, 304.

10. The reality of Jesus of Nazareth, his life, mission, and destiny is known as the historical Jesus. Sobrino, *Jesucristo Libertador*, 59.

for Christology.[11] The reality of Latin America is one of marginalization, oppression, and poverty. To follow Jesus, in the middle of this reality, implies to act in solidarity with the poor. The poor constitute a key element. God is incarnated in the poor and feels their suffering. The poor people were elevated to the suffering servant of Yahweh to affirm that the crucified people are a place of salvation. The poor de-center[12] economically privileged people from individualism and egoism and invite them to participate in their world.

The emphasis on justice helps in adressing the disparities created by colonialism and economics. It wants to eliminate these contradictions that negate life, contradictions that crucify thousands of poor people. Understanding that Jesus did not rest before injustice, his active presence takes the crucified people from the cross. This hopeful expression of love is a sign of the Kingdom of God and is in tension with the anti-kingdom expressed as structural and personal sin. The Kingdom of God finds its continuity through the ministry in favor of the poor.

In the context of suffering, women develop theology together adresing their identity as women whose bodies are "in dialogue with Christ."[13] Chapter 3 considers Christology contextually where women theologians discovered that, despite the great impact that the concept of the poor developed in relationship to theology, there are specific and diverse humans whose experience of faith and suffering are singular. Women "prophesy with the denunciation of their suffering, not through words but through their own bodies."[14]

Women theologians' *caminata* has been one of struggle in patriarchal oppressive contexts denying them access to leadership and ministry. In dialogue with feminists and theologians from Europe and North America, Latin American theologians flourished in their theological reflection using knowledge linked to women's particular experiences. It is a way to justice[15] because knowledge of God is concrete through embodiment.

---

11. The circularity between Jesus and Christ has a strong emphasis in Latin American Christology. To understand the divinity of Christ it is important to consider Jesus' humanity. Jesus' ministry makes visible the Christ of faith. Sobrino, *Jesucristo Liberador*, 76–78.

12. Sobrino, *Principio Misericordia*, 103.

13. Althaus-Reid, *From Feminist Theology*, 46.

14. Althaus-Reid, *From Feminist Theology*, 56.

15. Knowledge brings "the power of our dreams, of our deep faith, the thread that weaves together the entire elements of our life and helps us to make sense of our existence." See, Gebara, *Intuiciones Ecofeministas*, 37.

God was embodied and continues to be embodied in challenging realities. Embodiment considers a God who feels and knows the pain of women. In the lovely motherly–fatherly God expression, the incarnated breaks religious and social norms. The concrete actions of Jesus toward women allow women to transgress the social, cultural, and religious norms inscribing new hope[16] to women. The recovery of Jesus' humanity makes sense in contexts of women's daily experiences of terror and death. As a locus of revelation, the marginalized bodies reveal multiple oppressions guiding to enrich theology in an interdisciplinary way.

Chapter 4 explores the development of mission that informed Peruvian Christology. This chapter will focus on three documents.[17] The *Plática para todos los indios* and *The Christian Doctrine for the Instruction of the Indians* were written by the evangelizers in Castellano/ Spanish and translated into Quechua. The aim was to introduce terms and concepts that were completely new to the Indigenous' culture and religious experience. The evangelizers used Quechuan concepts to explain Christian concepts deeply rooted in Platonic-Greek concepts and to establish Christianity. The third book, *Pasión y Triunfo de Christo*, is a collection of ten prayers developed by Pedro de Peralta, who demonstrates the relevance of the triumphant Christ in his faith and the importance of glorifying Christ's suffering.

The official Christology imposed during these centuries of conquest followed the Christological dogmas that recognize Jesus Christ as the savior and Lord. From the official perspective, Christ came to be worshiped in the Roman Catholic manner by substituting Christ for the gods that the Indigenous had venerated. The worldview of the Quechua was based in a dual way that considered the opposites and complementarities as phenomena present in the community. In that communal reality, Christ was welcomed and venerated. The cosmic bridge, or chakana, connected the Indigenous with their divinities, a belief that remained.

Syncretism spread rapidly in the combination of the different religious beliefs that was detected as another dangerous element for the Roman Catholic Church. In their need to control it, the Third Council of Lima in 1582 and 1583 established pastoral guidelines to stop

16. Tamez, "Women's Lives as Sacred Text," 62, 63.

17. The *Plática para todos los indios* written in 1560 by Domingo de Santo Tomás and *The Christian Doctrine for the Instruction of the Indians* written in 1584 were written in Castellano. The book *Pasión y Triunfo de Christo* is the collection of ten prayers written in 1738 by Pedro de Peralta Barnuevo.

syncretism and idolatry; nevertheless, the ancestral gods and the Indigenous rituals survived in the subsoil of official Christology.[18] That reality made the Peruvian Christology not really Christ-centric[19] but ritual centered. This religiosity is syncretic because people embraced Christ, the cross, the Virgin, and other Christian elements into their rituals. For instance, the Indigenous began to worship Christ, but they also continued to hope for material miracles.

Chapter 5 discusses the Christology of the Peruvian writer Clorinda Matto de Turner as expressed in her novels. Considering the customary syncretism within the Andean Indigenous communities, *Aves Sin Nido* explores the relationship between the foreign Marin family and the ancestral and Christian divinities.[20] The novel narrates the Yupanqui family's misery as a consequence of the bad use of power by the local Andean authorities.

My choice of the writer Clorinda Matto de Turner has six reasons. First, Matto demonstrates a deep commitment to the suffering of the Indigenous. Second, Matto courageously denounces the religious, political, and civil authorities who conspire to exploit the Indigenous. Third, Matto, conscious of the social structures, proposes education as an alternative to make progress in life. Fourth, Matto knows that emigration is a phenomenon that will allow the Indigenous to develop; therefore, she made the Indigenous cross the borders of their own environment to enrich their own lives. Fifth, Matto addresses the Indigenous' suffering and marginalization, reminding the reader that faith needs to "pay attention to human beings' dilemmas (and enigmas) that literature reflects."[21] Finally, Matto introduces the marginalized women's reality. The use of the old mita system reveals the sexual abuse of the Indigenous women in *Aves sin Nido*, and in *Herencia* Matto touches on the struggle for survival of women of African descent.

---

18. La evangelización en la América española no puede ser enjuiciada como una empresa religiosa, sino como una empresa eclesiástica . . . Lo que tenía que subsistir [de la religión Inca], en el alma indígena había de ser, no una concepción metafísica, sino los ritos agrarios, las practicas mágicas, y el sentido panteísta . . . los pueblos de confesión católica han conservado instintivamente gustos y hábitos rurales y medio-evales. Mariátegui, *Siete Ensayos*, 143, 129, 140.

19. Marzal, *Tierra Encantada*, 323, 324.

20. Lucía is identified with the Virgin and Fernando is called Viracocha. Both the Christian Virgin and the Indigenous god are present in the mind of the Indigenous.

21. Rivera, *Mito, Exilio y Demonios*, 8.

In terms of Christology, Matto helps us to lift up and explore more concretely the white Messiah motif. In her novels, the Marins are the saviors of the Yupanqui and especially of the two orphans Margarita and Rosalía. Salvation happens through separate actions. First, the Marins economically save the Yupanquis from their debts, from the loss of their goods and from the loss of their second daughter. Second, through the payment of the Yupanquis' debts, the Marins supply their need and compensate the exigencies of the local authorities. The ransom atonement that Matto uncovers is based on a certain influx of patronage, largely practiced by foreigners in the Andean areas. Killac, the novel's town, illustrates the possibility of disobeying the local laws and disobeying the borders that Killac represents. Killac symbolizes the history of the suffering of the Andean people at the end of the nineteenth century and at the beginning of the twentieth century. *Aves sin Nido, Índole,* and *Herencia* were written between 1889 and 1895.[22] The drama depicted in these novels moves us to rethink the suffering of the body of Christ.

In Latin America, mythic-religiosity is very much alive and in Peru there were some efforts to keep this mythical consciousness alive. Chapter 6 enters into the Peruvian Andean religious context following the reading of novels like *Tayta Cristo* by Eleodoro Vargas Vicuña, *Todas las Sangre,* and *El Zorro de Arriba y el Zorro de Abajo* by José María Arguedas, and *Garabombo el Invisible* by Samuel Scorza. These novels help us to understand such expressions as "the real marvelous (to perceive) the extraordinary things behind the superficial epidermis of the ordinary things."[23]

Behind the superficial Christology, there are ancestral religious elements that survived becoming part of the religious view of the Andean populations. Arguedas dances with the foxes and brings, like Vargas, the invitation to be conscious of a reality where the myth persists and represents a return to the roots. Even though new experiences and events have enriched life, the return to the myth is to strengthen the capacity

---

22. In 1889 Matto became the director of the magazine *Perú Ilustrado*. In the publication of August 1890, when Matto was sick, the article entitled *Magdala* written by the Brazilian writer Enrique Maximiliano Coelho Neto related Christ's sexual attraction to Mary of Magdala. As a consequence, the Archbishop of Lima prohibited the reading of the article and of *Aves sin Nido* as well. At the same time, the bishop of Arequipa prohibited the reading and publication of *Aves Sin Nido*. In the middle of the social and ecclesiastical pressure, Clorinda continued her task as writer. See Tauro, *Clorinda Matto*, 16–18.

23. Rivera, *Mito, Exilio y Demonios*, 28–29.

to stay in contact with the community and the meaning of relationship. The mythological consciousness calls to consider syncretism as real in the Peruvian context. From the Lutheran Christological perspective, the incarnated reintegrates into the world of suffering, becoming one with the people who are different. Incarnation is an attempt to challenge what contradicts life.

Compassionate service and compassion for and with people in need becomes an invitation to mutual conversion. Conversion happens when a church welcomes, receives, and respects the particular cultural and religious traditions of the community that it serves and humbly is enriched for its own liberation.

The desire to renew, re-envision, and rebuild Christology cannot be done by a single person or from one side only. Conversion means resurrection because it is the marvellous awakening to justice. Considering the singular experience of the divine presence in each person, the multiple manifestations of marginalized people are relevant events and moments where God continues to be incarnated. In this reason of daily struggles and new starts, *Hanging On and Rising Up* become a motivation to understand how Christology is deeply rooted and re-imagined by people embraced by God's love. The daily experience informs how the sacred texts are approached and make sense in the incarnation of Christ's love and justice.

Conquest, an Encounter with Another God—Christ Arriving in the New World

THE CHRISTOLOGICAL REFLECTION OF this research is motivated by Latin American writers grasping daily life experiences that in a unique manner resemble God's incarnation. Their writings are sources of strength inviting to reimage God's holy presence especially among marginalized people. Life is a challenging event in contexts where the air spreads a sort of dry aroma of death. There, God's presence moves to active resistance affirming life as a gift to live: "Yes! Indeed, every morning . . . I say to myself 'I am alive!'"[1]

The meaning of being alive in a context whose disparities seem to destroy dreams and hope motivates us to understand the impact of evangelization and conversion. Before coming to conclusions, it will be relevant to reflect on some events that connected to Christology reshaped history. First, the encounter between Christians and Indigenous peoples whose two world views considered God in particular ways. During the encounter, the Indigenous' worldview was not considered by Spaniards; therefore, it is a responsibility to reread these components and enrich the understanding of Christology.

Christ the Savior and the Encounter with God the Creator

The arrival of Christianity to the Americas happened through imposition of culture, religion, and social organization by Spaniards. It included the appropriation of the land of native people. Observing the Spaniards' experience, eight centuries under the Arab empire, they found liberation after the expulsion of Muslims and Jewish from the Iberian Peninsula. Eight centuries of resistance was a fresh experience

1. Trigo and Chirinos, *I Love Life*, 22.

for those conquering and evangelizing the new world. Conquerors were openly opposed to idolatry and infidelity to God. These historical elements are relevant to understand the conquest.

Brief Historical View of the Iberian Peninsula before the Conquest of America

In the years prior to the conquest of America, the Roman inhabitants of the northern Iberian Peninsula reverberated in their desire to expel the Muslim and Jewish populations. In 1491, a secret "Agreement of Capitulation . . . between the last Nasrid named Muhammad XI . . . and the Catholic Monarchs,"[2] made Muslims abandon Granada after seven centuries of presence, as a result of the extension of the Muslim population from North Africa. The Jewish population settled earlier arriving

> around 300 CE facing discrimination and restrictive legislation under the conquering Visigothic Christian rulers from about the middle of the sixth century until the Muslim invasion of 711 . . . the Muslim conquerors . . . were considerably more tolerant toward the Jews, life was not always perfect and harmonious.[3]

Jews in Toledo moved later to Cordoba, Granada, Malaga, and Almeria.[4] The Arab Muslim presence altered the Iberian social-structure by taking control of vast and important areas of the Peninsula and configuring it through communities whose religious[5] dissimilarities encouraged further and rapid processes of conversion and domination. Their presence also influenced areas like literature, art, commerce, architecture, and religion.

> The Arabs decreed that all should speak a common language and adopt Arab cultural values. These values, however, did not necessarily come to reside on the Iberian Peninsula . . . we should remember that all one had to do to be considered Muslim was to recite the "Shahada," and that it was only with the passage of many, many years that Islamic culture truly penetrated enormous sectors of the population.[6]

2. Menocal, *The Ornament of the World*, 245.
3. Roth, "Coexistence and Confrontation," 1.
4. Menocal, *The Ornament of the World*, 25, 39.
5. Valdeavellano, *Historia de España Antigua*, 509.
6. Dias Farinha, "*Ahl Al-Kitab* or the People of the Book," 70.

The establishment of Arab Muslims in Al-Andalus in South Spain, created new social structures. The members of the Christian population who accepted the new faith were known as *Mozarab*. The Islamicized Jews were known as *deunmes,* and the group called *marranos* were Jews who remained in Christian lands and became Christianized.[7] In the religious sphere, Islam made its way into Spanish mysticism. The daily promotion and transmission of the law and prayers, the norms of life, the blessings and rituals moved populations to convert to Islam. The establishment of the Umayyad Caliphate transformed Cordova into a political and social center of faith. The social organization changed with the construction of Muslim temples. The newly converted had access in spaces of the ones with power and control[8]. Tolerance, as acceptance of different views, especially in religious and political matters, was not practiced during the initial period of Muslim presence in the Peninsula.

From the beginning, the encounter of the three different religious views was one of confrontation and struggle. Dominion through conversion was unavoidable. After the domination of the Roman-German and Jewish populations there was a period of great acceptance and easy contact between the three major groups. Acceptance from the Muslim side happened after most of the populations were converted, subjected, and dominated. Acceptance was a matter of control rather than a principle based on respect and recognition. The *capitulaciones,*[9] for instance, were agreements of submission to incorporate Christian and Jewish populations into the Muslim world. Even though Christians and Jews were allowed to work, maintain their beliefs, customs, and engage in mixed marriages; they were considered *dhimmins,* i.e., the People of the Book or "the protected ones" with the obligation to pay taxes.[10] Some were allowed to maintain their religious and cultural identity with certain administrative autonomy.[11]

During the period of peaceful coexistence between the three religious groups, the role of the *al-Mandaris al-Mushtarak*, institutions known as Common Teaching Establishments, played a key role for forums and debates attended by Jews, Christians, and Muslims. Simultaneously,

7. Casimiro, *Judeus e Árabes*, 11.
8. Menocal, *The Ornament of the World*, 67.
9. García Fitz, "Las Minorías religiosas," 30.
10. García Fitz, "Las Minorías religiosas," 24.
11. Bennani, "Fundamental Values," 81.

the interest in theological and philosophical Arab works grew among Christian and Jewish helping them to succeed in the Arab language and making the process of assimilation easier. At the intellectual level, tolerance happened by an acceptable peaceful coexistence. Alfonso X of Castile promoted cultural relationships between Christians, Jews, and Muslims. His interest in astronomy, geography, mathematics, medicine, philosophy, literature, and history moved him to support the translation of important material into Castellano.[12] Alfonso's admiration of Jewish and Muslim cultures had the purpose to enrich the Spanish culture but the translation of important materials appropriated learning resulted in cultural symbiosis[13] through the passing and obtaining of knowledge.

Dominion in the North

Now, during the reconquest of Toledo in 1085, the Muslim and Jewish populations were submitted to the Christian dominion. Muslim Mosques were changed into Christian temples; authorities annulled free expression of faith changing again religious and cultural aspects[14] and mixing them with economic strategies. The process of reconversion to Christianity affected common people's transactions. Taxes were imposed, creating again a sense of frustration.[15] In the middle ages, the Spanish population lived with the desire to expel the Jews and Muslims from their territories. The dream of the reconquest became real because it was supported by the crown, the church, and by the displeased masses.

The impregnated idea of reconquest permeated the crusader spirit. Aggression and war, especially at the beginning of the eleventh century, allowed the intervention of the Pope in the administration "to polarize this religious and cultural mosaic into two antagonistic blocks: the *Dominus Dei* and the *Dar-al-Islam*. The conflict reached its high point in the battle of Navas the Tolosa in 1212 binding the crown and the church together against the infidels.[16] Historians offer enough resources to believe that the campaigns against Muslims and Jews and their expulsion basically responded to the thesis that the Catholic sovereigns,

12. García Fitz, "Las Minorías religiosas," 41.
13. García Fitz, "Las Minorías religiosas," 46.
14. García Fitz, "Las Minorías religiosas," 31–32.
15. García Fitz, "Las Minorías religiosas," 48.
16. Dias Farinha, "*Ahl Al-Kitab* or the People of the Book," 71.

Ferdinand and Isabella, who came to power in 1474, made a political decision to expel unbelievers.

In that political circumstance, the rulers were "the repository of the national will and made the nation synonymous with the community of believers."[17] A different historical view demonstrates that Isabella and Ferdinand struggled "to control and to make use of powerful social forces in a deeply divided, frequently unruly kingdom that was just emerging from a long and disruptive series of civil wars."[18] Nevertheless, the authorities faced a huge obstacle: the assimilation of the populations to Christianity; therefore, based on Jews' proselytism Spaniard authorities found reasons to expel Jews from the Iberian Peninsula in 1492.[19] Not only Jews experienced hostility. The "*converso*s" or Christianized Jews, Christians who maintained links with the Jewish populations[20] were forced to abandon their cities or break connections with any kind of religious belief other than Christianity.

The power of the crown moved by the elite was connected and supported by popular movements such as the Holy Brotherhood.[21] Ironically, organizations like the Holy Brotherhood were against the elites searching for justice and sovereignty. Isabella and Ferdinand used the social momentum to gain support and build a strong alliance with the populace. The Papal Inquisition was added to this political deal. Established in 1233, the Inquisition had the purpose to persecute Muslims and Jews to eradicate heresy.[22]

---

17. Haliczer, "The Expulsion of the Jews," 237.

18. Haliczer, "The Expulsion of the Jews," 238.

19. Even though there were tax-farming contracts that Jews pay, the edict of expulsion of March 31, 1492 presents it as the end product of a long-meditated, carefully planned Jewish policy designed to prevent Christians from being exposed to the intense campaigning of proselytizing that was allegedly being carried on by the Jews. Haliczer, "The Expulsion of the Jews," 240–42.

20. Haliczer, "The Expulsion of the Jews," 146–47.

21. Santa Hermandad or Holy Brotherhood was based on a number of pre-existing leagues of cities and its role in providing Ferdinand and Isabella with the military support they needed to win the War of Succession—against French, English, and Australian army—and the real control was in the hands of local urban patriciates who governed the Hemandad through a *cabildo* composed of *regidores* and *jurados* but finally they were used to seat more firmly the aristocracy in power. Haliczer, "The Expulsion of the Jews," 238–39.

22. Menocal, *The Ornament of the World*, 221.

The political and religious campaigns against infidels were fresh in the life of the conquerors. It fueled intolerance and moved into long periods of discrimination that required the *corregidores'* presence. The *corregidores* or *assistants* royally appointed were municipal and provincial governors functioning as mayors and superior judges overseeing situations and causes related to Muslims and Jews.

> (When the) royal protection was withdrawal [a] gradual shift of instructions to the corregidores away from being protectors of Jews to becoming their persecutors, and from being adjudicators of the rights of Hebrews, to joining their foes.[23]

Historians see Isabella's three periods reign as follows: During the first period (1474–1484), her rule moved toward the control of the aristocracy bringing direction and promising justice and protection to the poor. The second period (1485–1594) related to a financial crisis as a consequence of her tax policies to continue handling the Granada war. Isabella moved the crown to practices of segregation against the remaining Jewish communities. Her policy included the suspension of Atlantic exploration which was controlled by the Portuguese authorities.[24] As a consequence of the socio-religious chaos, the expulsion of Jews and Muslims took place. The populations that remained in the Peninsula were forcibly converted and the promises to protect and develop justice for the poor abandoned. Her final period (1495–1504) suffered the consequences of the past and ruined the slight peace that had existed before her monarchy. [25]

The reconquest of cities like Toledo, Malaga, Murcia, Seville, Granada, and Cordova happened with the control of the Catholic crown and the internal struggle and divisions between Muslims fighting for political and religious legitimacy.[26] The Catholic crown reestablished the church in the Peninsula and the *encomienda* system in order to reorganize colonies which social circumstances were similar to those of the Muslim communities. The *encomienda*, a feudal and legal system practiced in Western Europe, established authorities, assigned lands, and restricted

---

23. Lunenfeld, "Facing Crisis," 254–55.
24. Lunenfeld, "Facing Crisis," 260.
25. Lunenfeld, "Facing Crisis," 253.
26. Especially the division between Berbers Muslims from North Africa and the Andalusians who developed their religious identity in al-Andalus. See Menocal, *The Ornament of the World*, 37.

property rights over a certain number of vassals who worked the land and produced crops to meet the empire's economic needs.

The dream of the Christian rulers to reassert control of the territories of the south, right after the Muslim dominion started growing in the eighth century was seen as "an act of atonement"[27] that finally was accomplished after centuries. How did the experience of reconquest influence the Conquerors' attitude upon their arrival in the Americas? Why did the connection between the image of the crown and Christ legitimize the conquest and the strong imposition of Christian faith? What made the conquerors faithful to their mission to evangelize idolaters in the new lands?

Dominion and Conversion: Two Faces of the Christian Empire

By the time of the conquest of America in 1492, the religious theme that dominated Castilian Spain was on the mind of Christopher Columbus. Columbus was commissioned by the royal governors to arrive in India, the center of power, raw materials and spices in the world. Columbus' commission was also intended to return from India to Spain. Nevertheless, he wanted to contribute to the colonization competition dominated by Portugal, England and Holland. In his letter to Queen Isabella, Columbus reveals his deep desire to convert idolaters. "So, having expelled all the Jews from all of your Kingdoms and Dominions . . . Your Highnesses commanded me to go, with a suitable fleet, to the said regions of India."[28]

The Colonial Messianism

It is not a coincidence that religious feelings among conquerors were connected to the royal commendation, with remarkable privileges and titles, received from the crown[29] to govern in the lands they arrived. As viceroys, they were political authorities designated by the crown ruling

---

27. Linehan, *History and the Historians*, 12.

28. This note is a reference to the diary of Christopher Columbus, see Lunenfeld, "Facing Crisis," 253.

29. Viceroys, governors in all the islands and main lands they should discover and acquire. Lunenfeld, "Facing Crisis," 260.

provinces or countries in the name of the monarchs. It was not a simple recognition; it signified being fully invested in the monarchical spirit and to be part, to a certain extent, of the royal elite. In political and religious terms, Columbus' viceroyalty was connected to a triumphant history where the king represented the divine will in the world. The conquest, as a religious enterprise, beyond conquering lands promoted evangelization by forcing people to accept the Christian faith. Conquering new lands was a political, religious, and economic project.

Columbus, like Cortés and Pizarro, felt that he was chosen by God. Providentialism, events on earth determined by God, was connected to the messianic sense of representing the crown and God in earth. It was a result of the blossoming marriage of state and the Church in Medieval Spain. Columbus, Cortés, and Pizarro believed that God had chosen them to discover, possess the lands, and to convert people to the Christian faith. They felt favored by God. They were liberating idolaters from their sinful conditions. Conquerors credit their achievements to God.

> "it pleased God," "it seems that God was fighting for us," "how God, our Lord gave us victory each day," "after having attending mass."[30]

The Church and State

Why was it relevant to convert idolaters and to rule over them? In 598, the doctrine of indissolubility established the principle where state and church were totally united.[31] The presence of Muslims, in the seventh century, raised a deep desire to develop a religious vitality and to unite the kingdom. Religious unity was a pillar for state and the church[32] and both played a consistent role. From the seventh century onwards, the church was a different entity among authorities and churchmen or nobilities.

> The real purpose of introducing a distinction between Church and churchmen, for example, is evidently to preserve the reputation of the former by exonerating it of responsibility for the notorious excesses of the worst of the latter. But even without

---

30. Rivera, *A Violent Evangelism*, 56.
31. Linehan, *History and the Historians*, 46.
32. At that time, bishops required personal qualities, qualification by age, literacy, and status, free election by the people and clergy. Linehan, *History and the Historians*, 45.

this refinement, the very concept is unhelpful. Beyond society itself there was no "Church."[33]

Bishops, present in the royal sphere, played a relevant role in uniting the kingdoms of Spain and informing the relevance of a Christian empire. A Bishop anointed Sisenard in 631, before his ascension, becoming "the first recipient of royal unction . . . kings in the future were to be elected by lay nobles and bishops in council."[34] Moving away from a hereditary legitimacy, kings needed to be elected by political and religious authorities. Another case is Julián's royal anointing in Toledo.[35]

The act of anointing was part of a legitimate process where the church sanctified the election and the elected one. By anointing and laying on of hands "gothic people had been brought into the Church . . . by anointing with oil, certain priestly functions had been bestowed upon their king."[36] These powerful religious acts secured the church into the political power. The king became a divine figure who not only was a sovereign with legitimate rights but also a ruler with religious functions.

The indispensable role of the church, securing and entrusting the political and religious power of the crown, carried the intention to protect people's faith. Thus, for the populace, it was their public and religious duty to obey the king who was directly accountable to God.[37] The monarch, seen as a mediator, was the last person who solved difficult situations that even the hierarchy[38] was unable to do. The task of sanctifying the king was a new duty for bishops thus ensuring relationships; that worked as concession within the concept of limited monarchy. Finally, the king stood at the summit of the social hierarchy,[39] moving bonds among the church and Empire. Bishops had a sort of divine authority now with political power.

The exercise of power during the reconquest resulted from the religious venture against the infidels and was inflamed by Muslim and Jewish proselytism. This strategy echoed in Columbus' mind after receiving

33. Linehan, *History and the Historians*, 37.
34. Linehan, *History and the Historians*, 41, 42.
35. Linehan, *History and the Historians*, 56.
36. Linehan, *History and the Historians*, 57.
37. "After God, it was to the king that honor, glory, and recognition of apostolic merit were due" (Linehan, *History and the Historians*, 62).
38. Linehan, *History and the Historians*, 45.
39. Linehan, *History and the Historians*, 44.

the command from the crown; a voice confirmed by the monarchs was the voice of God. Columbus carried that voice with the mission to put into practice in the lands where he arrived. As he was invested with power, entitled as viceroy, and authorized to acquire the lands, he acted through the divine role in appropriating and possessing[40] the lands that did not belong to his crown. The indirect idea of reconquest of the Iberia Peninsula strongly affirmed being servant to the Spanish Christian kingdom. He applied his authority and used juridical procedures to affirm sovereignty in the right of Christians and ignored the indigenous processes and their identities. Conquerors changed the indigenous' names[41] and were convinced that the Indigenous lands belonged to the Spanish kingdom.

> As a public act officially registered in the presence of a scribe, the expropriation was directed toward other possibly interested parties, the other European Christian sovereigns.[42]

This public and juridical possession declared that no other Christian nations could take them; therefore, upon the arrival crosses were placed meaning that "the territory thus marked belongs from then on to Christianity, and specifically to the Spanish Catholic Monarchs."[43] The cross used to mark territories symbolized the political and religious triumph among other Christian nations and especially over non Christian nations.

In this context, Christ arrived with the power of the cross transfigured in the Spanish image. Christ was projected over the royal figure dictating the possession of all goods. It was a triumphant act where Christians were struggling against the remaining evil forces of Islam and where the deity of Christ was present in the conqueror but more specifically in the form of the King. Columbus acted clearing the way for a triumphant and victorious Christ, for the victory of the Spaniard kingdom that represented God on earth. Arriving in the name of the crown and representing the Lord was enough to exert control over Indigenous ancestral cultures their divinity and kings. With that authority, the conquerors presented the Christian message to the natives in strange and unrecognizable language. Not being able even to understand it, the Indigenous slowly understood the conqueror's attitude as superior and egoistical.

40. Rivera, *A Violent Evangelism*, 7, 8.
41. Rivera, *A Violent Evangelism*, 9–12.
42. Rivera, *A Violent Evangelism*, 8.
43. Rivera, *A Violent Evangelism*, 8.

The Encounter: The Universal Christ Talks and the Native Gods Reply

Bernal Diaz, in his account of the discovery of New Mexico, addresses the inevitable religious impression that Indigenous' deities had on the conquerors. Bernal's writings give the impression that the native divinities were devils and idols. Bernal's narrative expresses the conqueror's view easily directing readers toward the conclusion that Indigenous were idolaters and sinners. For instance, when the Spaniards arrived at Yucatan, after being welcomed and invited to visit the town, they saw

> near the place of this ambuscade were three buildings of lime and stone, wherein were idols of clay with diabolic countenances and others with women's faces, and in strange unnatural postures, and several wooden chests which contained similar idols but smaller, some vessels, three diadems, and some imitations of birds and fishes in alloyed gold.[44]

This outsider's lenses describe rich elements linked to unknown religious expressions and appeared different and irrational. The so called idols did not provoke admiration among the conquerors in the way that Christian images would have done. The worshiped images were far different from the monotheistic Christian religion. Here, the notion of difference caused disagreement or fear and consequently the determination of the different religions as pagan, sinful, and evil. The presence of images did not allow dialogue in order to know more about them. It did not stimulate the desire to know the difference and their relevance for the Indigenous. With regard to relationships, the conqueror had the impression that natives were hospitable at the beginning. But according Columbus, they became savage and bellicose. Conquerors did not consider that the Indigenous realized that the conquerors claimed to own and to rule over their lands.[45]

Assuming the position of lords, the colonizers acted in condemnation, missing the opportunity to understand the Indigenous' beliefs and their own proper divinities. The opportunity to enter into dialogue was lost as well as the possibility to open paths for initiatives that perhaps could change a long history of wars and deaths. Instead of dialogue and attentive listening, the conquerors spoke their Christian language while

---

44. Díaz del Castillo, *Historia verdadera de la conquista*, 71.
45. Rivera, *A Violent Evangelism*, 12–13.

diminishing the relevance of other religious expressions and spirituality. Their mission to possess and expropriate lands had nothing to do with evangelism.

> central premise of the conquest *expropriation was conceived, from the beginning, as essential to the discovery.* When the natives resisted the vassalage imposed on them, the conquest is revealed as a violent act, and it then is presented as a theory of 'licit domination'.[46]

When the so called 'pagans' agreed to be in dialogue with conquerors, it happened through different channels because they did not speak the same language in terms of political conquest and evangelization. Why did Christianity have a different sense to the Indigenous while engaged in theological discussion with Spaniards? The dialogs offer insights to this question.

Between Words: Christians and "Idolaters" in Dialogue

The encounter of the universal Christ with the many gods of the Indigenous occurred, first, as a monologue. Conquerors developed a one sided dialogue directed to the aborigines. Second, the formal dialogue between the authorities, for example the dialogue between Cortez and Moctezuma or Pizarro and Atahualpa, derived in discourses of disagreements between the two parts, in different moments, and places in history.

Spaniards' Monologue

The monologue metaphor helps one to read critically the conquerors' actions and conversations that manifested as one sided speech. In the monologue, the Christian faith "played an exceptional role in imperial ideology."[47] The Christian voice was imposed over other existing voices. As the Spaniards considered the aborigines as barbarians, they concluded that the Indigenous would be "civilized"—Christianized and educated-through their conversion. The proposal was that the native population needed to be subject to the Spanish crown.[48]

---

46. Rivera, *A Violent Evangelism*, 13–14.
47. Rivera, *A Violent Evangelism*, 22.
48. Leon-Portilla, *The Broken Spears*, xxxiii.

The conversion was a religious, economic and political[49] proposal that happened mechanically after condemning and destroying the aborigines' deities. The colonizers, having received the instruction first to 'persuade' and then to 'instruct' native inhabitants in the Roman Catholic faith,[50] neglected the recommendation. Letters, royal orders, a portion of scripture, or preaching were presented to natives in the language of the powerful one. As soon as captive aborigines learned the colonizers' language, they were used as translators. Aborigines who translated faced problems with new concepts and words, especially from the religious side,[51] which affected the translation. For instance, the native of Puná origin, Felipe, failed while translating Friar Vincente de Valverde's argument to Atahualpa. When Atahualpa realized this situation, he responded to Vicente de Valverde in the language of the Puná[52] region so that it would be less difficult for Felipe to interpret.

Language, a powerful tool in the process of colonization, was imposed as a way of control and dependency in terms of being obligated to learn the conquerors' language. Aborigines themselves had different cultures, beliefs, experiences, tastes, abilities, rituals, and ways to understand life. They faced real difficulty in interacting with colonizers and by learning their language became vassals of the king and Lord Carlos[53] while being forced to abandon their language, divinities, sacrifices, and customs. The Spaniards did not consider the aboriginal political and religious authorities that had been established for centuries.

49. The Indigenous problem was rooted in the Spaniards' appropriation of the land and consequently in the agrarian regime mixed with the "protection" of the Indigenous who were subjected to the conquerors. The social regime named "repartimientos," the adjudication of land extension to a certain person to be economically administrated and "mitas," the forced work that the Indigenous assumed in mine, labor, and agriculture areas is these were central element for political and religious subjection. Mariátegui, *Siete Ensayos*, 27–31.

50. Rivera, *A Violent Evangelism*, 43, 45.

51. In Quechua for example, the word trinity did not exist. Later on, it was literally translated as *kimsakaychuya Tayta*, kimsa (three) kaq (is) chuya (clean, saint) Tayta (God), but the notion of three persons in one God was totally inconceivable. The word gospel never existed and until Quechuas used the Spanish word *evangelio*. Conversion and cross were other unknown words; later conversion was mixed between Spanish and Quechua ending as *almaganakuy* which means winning souls for God. The problem not only remained in the use of new words but in the theological notion behind them.

52. See Garcilaso de la Vega, *Comentarios Reales*, 332–33.

53. Díaz del Castillo, *Historia verdadera de la conquista*, 152.

Fray Bartolomé de Olmendo, for example, preached in March 1519, reinforcing Cortés' message and requiring aborigines to worship Jesus Christ as Lord, to follow the Christian faith, and to respect our Lady and the cross. Aborigines associated the images with their worldview and linked them to personalities. For instance, the image of our Lady, introduced by Cortés as the mother of the Lord who was in heaven, was connected to the "great tecleciguata" because it was how natives named the great ladies[54] at the time.

The monologic metaphors reveal practices of baptism, producing a change of identity and the establishment of churches generating changes in rituals. After being baptized, aborigines received Christian names. Mariana,[55] for example, recognized as a cacica or chief by the colonizers themselves[56] became a servant of Cortés and helped the conquerors to destroy the empire with her translations. The change of names was at the beginning "considered an honor; only later did (natives) discover that it was a subtle manifestation of the act of expropriation of which they had been the object."[57] Natives' lands, names, and identity were expropriated. The change of names, as part of the process of taking away the legacy and the uniqueness, formed part of the process of evangelization.

The establishment of churches[58] in places where aborigines had their gods or where they practiced sacrifices were dishonored the aboriginal sites and transformed them into Christian temples. In Cingapacinga, for example, Cortés ordered an altar built and placed on it the image of the

---

54. Díaz del Castillo, *Historia verdadera de la conquista*, 154.

55. Nahuas called Mariana Malintzin which suffix tzin denotes reverence and slave condition "noble prisoner or noble captive." The conqueror Bernal Diaz de Castillo recognizes Mariana's linguistic gift, therefore at the age of thirteen, she embarked with Grijalba to Cuba where she learned Spanish. As translator, Mariana was used to preach to the natives inviting them to abandon the idols and to accept God. Pérez Alvarez, "Teoría del Destino Manifiesto," 112–13.

56. Pérez Alvarez, "Teoría del Destino Manifiesto," 154–55.

57. Rivera, *A Violent Evangelism*, 11.

58. Later, the establishment of churches followed the extension of the royal patronage created in 1574 as Royal Ordinance Governing the Patronage. Friars in charge of Indian congregations received the jurisdictions from bishops rather than directly from popes; regulars could not establish new religious foundations without royal and Episcopal approval; and Indians had to pay tithes. These provisions opened the way of ascendancy of the secular clergy in spiritual matters except in frontier missions and teaching and charitable activities, thereby permitting a much firm exercise of the royal patronage. See, McAlister, *Spain and Portugal in the New World*, 426–27.

Virgin and the cross after destroying the Indigenous' divinities.[59] The conquerors did not consider native religions and divinities seriously. The latent Muslim and Jewish presence continued to echo in their minds. Spaniards were against other religious practices and judging from their religious frame, they condemned the natives as idolaters, denouncing indigenous for "human sacrifice, anthropophagy, and sodomy, which constitutes something of a [legend] against the natives."[60] But because natives were part of the possessed lands, conquerors changed their names to Christian names in order to distinguish the converted from the pagans. They also built up Christian temples over native ritual centers in order to make the traces of paganism disappear, a kind of expulsion of native spirits and divinities.

Dialogue between Spanish and Native Authorities

The formal dialogue between Native and Spanish authorities reveals the theological discrepancy between natives' divinities and the practice of proselytism developed in the name of the Christian king. Two dialogues will inform this topic; first, the dialogue between Moctezuma and Cortés in Mexico, and second, the dialogue between Atahualpa and Pizarro in Peru.

Moctezuma and Cortés in Mexico

Before his arrival to Tenochtitlan and passing through different towns, Cortés received news of a great chief called Moctezuma, who was rich and powerful. Throughout these territories, Cortés left cities in ruins and massacred their inhabitants. In his intention to meet Moctezuma, Cortés received Moctezuma's messengers and gold gifts[61] like Tezcatlipoca, the chief God of the pantheon with solar attributes, collars of fine shells, the finery of Tlaloc the God of the rain,[62] and other fine gifts. Moctezuma believed that the strangers were "Quetzalcoatl [the God of learning or the God of wind] and other divinities returning to

---

59. Díaz del Castillo, *Historia verdadera de la conquista*, 201.
60. Rivera, *A Violent Evangelism*, 158.
61. Rivera, *A Violent Evangelism*, 279–80.
62. Leon-Portilla, *The Broken Spears*, 23–24.

Mexico, as the codices and traditions promised they would."[63] Cortés arrived in Tenustitlan, Mexico on November 8, 1519. Being received by Moctezuma[64] Cortés initiated the dialogue,

> Are you Motecuhzoma? Are you the king? Is it true that you are the king Motecuhzoma?" And the king said: "Yes, I am Motecuhzoma." Then he stood up to welcome Cortés . . . The kings Itzcoatl, Motecuhzoma the Elder, Axayacatl, Tizoc and Ahuitzol ruled for you in the City of Mexico . . . You have come back to us; you have come down from the sky. Test now, and take possession of your royal house. Welcome to your land, my lords![65]

Moctezuma welcomed the Spaniards, believing that they were the returned divinities. Therefore, Moctezuma's publicly expressed respect and gave account of those who governed the territory before him. The notion of coming down from the sky refers to the eschatological return of one more powerful than Moctezuma. Cortés perceived the fear and therefore answered, "We have come to your house in Mexico as friends. There is nothing to fear."[66] The next day, Cortés decided to visit Moctezuma and after being received, Cortés initiated the dialogue again:

> What I come to say on behalf of our Lord God had already been brought to your knowledge through your ambassadors, Tendile, Pitalpitoque and Quintalbor, at the time when you did us the favor to send the golden sun and moon to the sand dunes; for we told them that we were Christians and worshipped one true and only God, named Jesus Christ.[67]

Cortés presented a refined theological speech centered in Jesus Christ and specifically in Jesus' work as savior and creator. Cortés concentrates on salvation, assuring that salvation only happens through

---

63. Leon-Portilla, *The Broken Spears*, 13–14.
64. Díaz del Castillo, *Historia verdadera de la conquista*, 316.
65. Leon-Portilla, *The Broken Spears*, 64.
66. Leon-Portilla, *The Broken Spears*, 65.
67. Díaz del Castillo, *Historia verdadera de la conquista*, 318–19. And it continues: "who suffered death and passion to save us, and we told them that a cross, when they asked us why we worshiped it, was a sign of the other Cross on which our Lord God was crucified for our salvation, and that the death and passion which He suffered was for the salvation of the whole human race, which was lost, and that this our God rose on the third day and is now in heaven, and it is He who made the heavens and the earth, the sea and the sands, and created all the things there are in the world, and He send the rain and the dew, and nothing happens in the world without His holy will."

Jesus Christ and no other god. His insistence on change, while diminishing Mexicans' divinities, assures that his lord and king will send men who live in sanctity, referring to priests, in order to teach them all things related to the Christian faith, Montezuma replied:

> Senor Malinche, I have understood your words and arguments very well ... We have not made any answer to it because here throughout all time we have worshiped our own gods and thought they were good, as no doubt yours are, so do not trouble to speak to us any more about them at present. Regarding the creation of the world, we have held the same belief for ages past, and for this reason we take it for certain that you are those whom our ancestors predicted would come from the direction of the sunrise.[68]

Moctezuma feels Cortés' provocation and his answer therefore stops Cortés intention. Moctezuma understands that Cortés tries to belittle their Gods and knows that behind Cortés' words resides the intention to change his people's minds with respect to his divinities. Moctezuma rejects the hostile and audacious decrying of the native divinities and without entering into the topic of salvation, Moctezuma understands that the three Gods and the cross do not invalidate the native Gods. Moctezuma concentrates and expresses his belief in creation, demonstrating the importance, goodness, and relevance of their Gods and making them equal to the three Gods and the cross. In this manner, Moctezuma agrees with Cortés in a splendid way, "regarding the creation of the world, we have held the same belief for ages past." In this high topic, Moctezuma not only points out the beginning of native history but also opens a line of agreement by giving value to the event of creation and even connecting the Spaniards presence to the predictions of the divinities' return from the place where Huitzilopochtli, the Sun god,[69] rises. The link made sense to Moctezuma but not to Cortés. Days after Moctezuma invited Cortés to his sanctuary and let him know of all the holy places with all their wealth, Cortés said with an ironic laugh:

> Senor Moctezuma, I do not understand how such a great Prince and wise man as you are has not come to the conclusion, in your mind, that these idols of yours are not gods, but evil things that are called devils, and so that you may know it and all your

---

68. Díaz del Castillo, *Historia verdadera de la conquista*, 319–20.
69. Leon-Portilla, *The Broken Spears*, 4.

> priests may see it clearly, do me the favor to approve of my placing a cross here on the top of this tower, and that in one part of these oratories where your Huichilobos and Tezcatepuca stand we may divide off a space where we can set up an image of Our Lady and you will see by the fear in which these Idols hold it that they are deceiving you.[70]

The aggression was clear and Moctezuma noticing the dishonor and intention to destroy their gods, replied, "Senor Malinche, if I had known that you would have said such defamatory things, I would not have shown you my Gods, we consider them to be very good, for they give us health and rains and good seed times and seasons and as many victories as we desire, and we are obligated to worship them and make sacrifices, and I pray you not to say another word to their dishonor."[71] As Cortés noticed that Moctezuma was angry and needed to offer sacrifice because of the sin in allowing Cortés to ascend to his great altar and dishonor the gods, he replied, "I ask your pardon if it be so"[72] because he did not want to miss the chance to lose all the gold and precious ornaments.

Atahualpa and Pizarro in Peru

After receiving news of a great, rich, and splendid kingdom, Francisco Pizarro made two exploratory travels to Peru, in 1524 and 1526 with the royal support and the "capitulación"[73] signed by Queen Isabella in July 26, 1529.[74] The destruction and atrocities made in Puná, Tumbes, and Piura made the Incas aware of Spaniards' hunger for gold and power. So, they doubted that conquerors were Viracocha's representatives.[75] When the conquerors arrived in Peru, the Tahuantinsuyo[76] territory was divided.

---

70. Díaz del Castillo, *Historia verdadera de la conquista*, 335–36.
71. Díaz del Castillo, *Historia verdadera de la conquista*, 336–37.
72. Díaz del Castillo, *Historia verdadera de la conquista*, 337.
73. The capitulación was a model of geographical accuracy, of prevision, and of organization to know what to do in the new lands and gave concessions to the Spaniards. Armas, *Las Lágrimas de Caxamarca*, 186–97.
74. Armas, *Las Lágrimas de Caxamarca*, 186.
75. Huayna Capac Inca, father of Huascar and Atahualpa, heard from natives of other regions that white bearded men were searching for his empire. He did not believe Spaniards represented Viracocha (the God creator). If sent by Viracocha; they would know Cusco, his name, and the places of gold. Carrión, *Atahualpa*, 52.
76. Tahuantinsuyo is the Quechua name of the empire that means the four regions: Chinchaysuyo in the north, Collasuyo in the south, Antisuyo in the east, and Contisuyo at the west.

Huascar and Atahualpa were engaged in military conflict. Huascar, in charge of the southern area, with Cuzco as its capital city, wanted to govern the entire empire. Atahualpa ruled the north area with its capital in Quito. Huascar was taken prisoner in the central highlands by Atahualpa as Pizarro crossed toward Atahualpa. After receiving the Inca's messengers, Pizarro replied with his desire to befriend and to develop a loyal relationship.[77]

On November 14, 1532 Pizarro arrived in Cajamarca and, knowing that Atahualpa was in Putulmarca, sent Fernando Pizarro and Fernando De Soto to meet the Inca. The Spaniards, recognized as "the sons of Viracocha," were welcomed. De Soto initiated the dialogue, with Felipe as translator:

> Most serene Inca . . . permit me to tell you that, of all the princes in the world, there are two who are more powerful than all the others. One of them is the Pope, who represents God among men; he administers and governs the guardians of divine law, and teaches the word of God. The other is Charles V, king of Spain and Emperor of the Romans. These two monarchs have been informed of the state of blindness in which the natives of these kingdoms have been living . . . and this is why they have sent our governor and Commander-General Don Francisco Pizarro, his companions and several priests.[78]

The Inca did not understand the entire message but seeing the offense replied:

> I am delighted, divine lords, that you and your companions should have succeeded in reaching such remote regions as these . . . How does it happen that, although you affirm your desire to discuss peace and permanent friendship with us, in the name of the two princes you claim to represent, you should have so severely handled and massacred the inhabitants of the provinces you passed through . . . before having discovered whether our intentions were good or bad? You must have acted, therefore, upon the orders of these two princes who, themselves act, in obedience to instructions given by the great Pachacamac.[79]

Atahualpa then addressed relevant questions considering the value of foreign people, but knew that fate, in terms of divine intervention, was on the conquerors' side. Knowing the Spaniards' cruelty, the Inca hold

77. Armas, *Las Lágrimas de Caxamarca*, 246.
78. Garcilaso de la Vega, *Comentarios Reales*, 326.
79. Garcilaso de la Vega, *Comentarios Reales*, 327.

the ancestor's predictions accepting that the conquerors were divine beings and gave him confidence to receive Pizarro the next day. During the encounter Friar Vincent de Valverde approached the Inca with a cross on one hand and his bible on the other. He had the intention to teach the 'genuine Catholic faith'[80] in two points. First, he presented the one God in three persons as the creator, the corruption of all human beings by common origin in Adam, the exception of sin in Christ who was born from the Virgin Mary and his entire work of salvation, the Apostolic succession pointing to the Pope as sovereign Pontiff of Rome, the great rights Charles V emperor had to conquer all nations to bring salvation, Francisco Pizarro as commander of the mission with whom the Inca was called to develop an alliance of perpetual friendship, and the empire will become subject and will offer tribute to the Christian Empire. Second:

> the Inca must obey the sovereign Pontiff the Pope in all respects, to accept the faith of Jesus Christ our Lord and to abandon completely and for all time your odious superstitions concerning idols: then you will be given actual proofs of how holy is our law, and how false and demon-ridden was your own ... For if you refuse, you must know that we will make merciless war upon you, that all your idols will be cast down, and that fire and sword and bloodshed will compel you, whether you will or not, to reject your false religion, to receive our Catholic faith[81]

Understanding the imposed obligation to reject his divinities, Atahualpa discerned the persuasion for his people to follow the five gods that the Spaniards were proclaiming: the god three in one that makes four, the second the father of all human species, third Jesus Chris, fourth the Pope, and fifth Charles.

> But then, if this Charles is the prince and lord of the entire world, how is it that the pope should have had to grant him permission to make war upon me and usurp my kingdom? ... For if this is the case; then, you have more gods than we have, for we worship no god other than Pachacamac, who is our supreme God, after whom we worship the Sun, whose bride and sister is the Moon ... You say that Christ is God and that He is death. I worship the Sun and the Moon, both of which are immortal. And what is your authority that God created the universe?[82]

80. See the two points addressed by Vincent de Valverde in Garcilaso de la Vega, *Comentarios Reales*, 330–32.

81. Garcilaso de la Vega, *Comentarios Reales*, 332.

82. Garcilaso de la Vega, *Comentarios Reales*, 334–40.

The two different understandings of God were well taken by Atahualpa. He was clear about the Spaniards' desire to impose over them their many gods and accept their worldview. Looking at the triumphant point of view, Spaniards did not consider the natives' perspective. Instead, they despised the fact they were different and used tactics of exaggeration "to manipulate religious symbols from both, the Christian and the indigenous ones"[83] judging not only the Peruvian but also Mexican and other cultures. It becomes impossible to find sources of Christology that engaged the native populations. As their ancient beliefs were disregarded, their only way was mixing them with the new faith in an amalgam of new expressions of faith.

Christ the Savior: the Triumphant God Framing the Colonial Christology

The mutual support between church and state during colonization was modified while the crown extended royal patronage and designated civil and religious authorities in their colonies. The establishment of the Church followed royal ordinances. The church in the service of the crown and the viceroyalty formed hierarchies, electing officials to establish mission's responsibilities and to design the kind of services that they will provide. Viceroyalty and provincial governors controlled and managed the finances including the ecclesiastic funds. For that, the *cabildo*, a municipal institution integrated by colonial authorities, became an extension directly connected to the crown.

> The crown likewise instructed more directly into the governance of the Indians, prompted by two inconsistent concerns: their protection and more efficient collection of revenues and services from them. Its measures included resettlements of indigenes in reductions, *resguardos*, and civil congregations; standardizing the base and rates of tributes; and increasing the numbers and authority of *corregidores de indios*.[84]

The crown transplanted to the Americas the Holy Office of the Inquisition. The Inquisition and inquisitor bishops were instituted in Lima in 1570 against idolaters and as consequence of "the appearance

---

83. Pérez Alvarez, "Teoría del Destino Manifiesto," 97.

84. McAlister, *Spain and Portugal*, 426. The *corregidores de indios* were local and administrative and juridical position in Spain and its colonies.

of Lutheran heretics, active *converso* communities, and an influx of heterodox literature."[85] The religious, economic, social, and political interest characterized the conquest; a triumphant history justified in the conviction to defeat infidels and based on the reconquest of southern Spain.

The Royal Christ

The encounter between "idolaters" and Christians in the native lands of the Americas was characterized by the battle between infidels—idolaters and the Europeans followers of the Lord Jesus Christ. The eternal adversary of Spain was confirmed: the different religions or spiritualties, gods. Then, Christians understood themselves as the chosen people to save and liberate infidels from idolatry. This messianic and providential notion placed them close to heaven developing Christianization and reinforcing the figure of a victorious Christ:

> The confrontation between Europeans and the natives of the Americas was perceived by the Europeans as a divine, transcendental, and cosmic battle in which the victor was God and the loser, Satan. "No matter how hard the devil tried, Jesus Christ vanquished him from the kingdom that he had here."[86]

Christ, transformed into the Spanish image and projected in the royal figure of a triumphant Lord, [87] became a vague figure of god in terms of Lordship and so was the King–the principal member of the aristocracy. The notion of lordship was understandable for natives because they were used to having noble figures that received authority from their creator. But, Christ presented as creator and savior, was not the equivalent to the always present natives' divinities like the sun or moon, because he died. How can a dead god vanquish his enemies? It clearly indicates two different notions about Christ's divinity, death, and life. Native populations did not have a notion of the cross and resurrection.[88]

---

85. McAlister, *Spain and Portugal*, 427.

86. Rivera, *A Violent Evangelism*, 162.

87. The Christ the Victor theory plays here a role because in the process of reparation, the struggle between God and the forces of evil, the deity of God is hidden in human form. See Migliore, *Faith Seeking Understanding*, 182.

88. Wañusqamantarikchariq, which is a composed and created word that literally means the death [is] awaked up or awaked up from death.

And the incarnated[89] Christ needed to be seen as a present figure. Therefore, while Fria Valverde talks to Atahualpa, the Inca understood that Jesus Christ was one more divinity among the king, the pope, the three in one god that makes four, and the father of human species which was equivalent to the creator Viracocha. Not only the Greek concept of the trinity and the person of Christ complicated the understanding, but also how it was presented and translated. In a world lacking certain theological concepts, the notion of a God triune was simply difficult to reconcile with the natives' notion of living gods.

The dialogue between conquerors and native chiefs illustrates the difficulty Spaniards had in bringing the notion of satisfaction[90] as a necessary condition in salvation. Here, the act of Christ's suffering on the cross relates to the idea of fulfillment and compensation. Christ, who is both divine and human, demonstrates perfect obedience and is the saint figure required to restore the sinner and to satisfy God's requirement.[91] This notion was totally absent in the native's spirituality and religious practices. Spaniards concentrated on salvation, convinced that natives were sinners, and they neglected the opportunity to know whether natives had a similar or different notion in relation, for instance, to sin. In every case, from their dialogues, we can affirm the different faith views. Moctezuma feels the need to offer sacrifice because of his own sin. Even though the one who dishonored his gods was properly Cortés, the sin was assumed by Moctezuma. He gave Cortés the opportunity to dishonor them by allowing Cortés to see his sacred temples and gods and discredit them.

Theology was fundamental for evangelization. Colonizers conquered, possessed, and exploited lands and the inhabitants through royal permission and support by the church. Under this understanding, *encomenderos* and other authorities subverted the message of life and freedom, exchanging God for gold and wealth.[92] The legitimating presence of Christ was at the end the legitimating desire of power.

---

89. This word does not exist in Quechua for instance. It was created using the Spanish root "encarna" and the ending quechua "korqa." Encarnakorqa is translated as "has been incarnated."

90. The Anselmian satisfaction theory refers to God's requirement of dignity and honor that could only be satisfied by the sacrifice of Jesus Christ. See McGrath, *Christian Theology Reader*, 356–57.

91. Migliore, *Faith Seeking Understanding*, 184.

92. Pérez Alvarez, "Teoría del Destino Manifiesto," 122–23, and Rivera, *A Violent Evangelism*, 259–60.

"Your Idols Are Not God"–Rejecting Idolatry

If infidelity was the religious topic during the reconquest of the Iberian Peninsula, idolatry became the banner to justify the conquest of America, and the *encomenderos* were turned into the saviors of native populations. Idolatry, the adoration of divinities that were dissimilar to the monotheistic deity, was used as the "excuse to destroy indigenous consciousness, and therefore, to legitimate the Spanish intervention."[93] Native deities had their value and theological perspective but in that realm differed from the Western one. Looking from a Western perspective, native religious practices were inconsistent and incompatible with the exclusivist, rationalist, and synthetic or dialectic discourse of the occident. The Hellenic-Christian came to the encounter of the pantheon of divinities that "do not know the separation . . . between philosophy and religion, knowledge and salvation, theory and praxis, and does not respond to the exigencies of exclusivist logic."[94] From the native perspective, their religious practices and expressions of faith were incomprehensible not because they were sophisticated but because indifference, centrism, and relativism were in the mind of the ones arriving from the place where the sun rises.

During the conquest it was impossible to address the native's religious phenomenon as different from a structure based on the duality between divine and mundane; a different world mediated by the myth. Belief and mythology run together and played a key role in pre-Incas' and Incas' view.[95] Spaniards indicted the Quechua spirituality and devotion as idolatrous. From that authoritative angle, both Mexican and Inca gods were considered false gods, products of superstition, and the devil. It was impossible to consider native gods as a source to understand unusual relationships with divinities that accounted for their apparition and interaction with humans in the Andean and Mexican territories.

The native communities' individual and collective experiences, including religious experiences, were transmitted and interpreted orally, without reference to written texts in the case of the Incas. Because of the reliance on oral tradition, the interpretation of the lived experience developed different graphic expressions like designs, rituals, songs, and pictures, or symbols like the quipus used by Incas. In contrast, the Christian culture arrived with graphic—written documents like the scriptures,

---

93. Pérez Alvarez, "Teoría del Destino Manifiesto," 102.

94. Estermann, *Filosofía Andina*, 42.

95. Lara, *Mitos, Leyendas y Cuentos de los Quechuas*, 12–13.

royal letters, official orders for the viceroyalty and *encomenderos*, and even legal document to possess territories. All these differences were reasons to consider natives as barbarians. Behind that argument, "the conquerors obscured violations, massacres, and unjust appropriation of natives' lands. Idolatry . . . constitutes an important excuse . . . that legitimates the Spanish intervention."[96]

The *encomienda* was a system to save the Indians and the idea of the *repartimiento* or apportioning was "to evangelize them, to teach them good and proper customs . . . and to give them the discipline of work."[97] By eradicating idolatry, the *encomenderos* became rescuers and sort of saviors of the ones condemned to die in pagan sacrifices and cultures. Based in the concepts of royalty/lordship, the conquerors had the task to eradicate idolatry by a violent imposition of the Roman Catholic faith. Behind the Christian element, the real element surrounding their violent salvific act was the economic one to increase the crown's income while depriving the native populations of their freedom.[98]

Conversion: The Religious Transformation

As indicated before, evangelization during conquest was a work developed by the church and the state through the royal patronage system. The Papal bull gave rights to the crown in order to develop a spiritual evangelization of native populations in the new lands. This concession was linked to the state's role in the expulsion of Muslims from the Iberian Peninsula. The state intervention in the process of evangelization tightened relations, especially economic support for Christianization,[99] from the revenue and wealth of the conquered lands. Concession during the evangelization developed under royal orders and regulations that continued through the viceroyalty period until the Republic period. In Peru, for instance, "Roma conceded in 1875 to the Peruvian President the patronage right . . . the right of intervening in the presentation of Bishops"[100] and other events.

---

96. Pérez Alvarez, "Teoría del Destino Manifiesto," 102.
97. Rivera, *A Violent Evangelism*, 114.
98. Rivera, *A Violent Evangelism*, 116, 118.
99. Nieto Velez, "La Transformación Religiosa Peruana," 87–88.
100. Nieto Velez, "La Transformación Religiosa Peruana," 90.

The royal patronage, with the *encomiendas* as the model of conversion, worked in the political and economic sense. Spaniards gained revenues through cheap labor while natives were governed and subordinated to the crown. Natives were massively converted and possessed, exploited, slighted and dehumanized. Since Columbus' second voyage, "some friars learn(ed) the language before the aborigines would be converted ... if the natives did not accept the invitation to become Catholics ... force would predominate over love."[101] The Spaniards believed that the Indigenous transformed or substituted their old beliefs for the new Roman Catholic faith. This triumphant vision did not consider that there was a juxtaposition of both beliefs. The Indigenous were faithful to idols and other gods and at the same time were sincere while going to the church because they did not see conflict[102] between the old and new elements of faith. They went to the church and completed the requirements and in doing so, they learn to dissimulate and to survive.

As conversion happened as the triumph of the conquest, this triumphant spirit connected to dominion makes us recognize that *encomenderos'* and *corregidores'* functions responded to a political and legal system[103] ending in a mission of subjugation. Even though the system controlled the reductions or places where Indigenous were located, there were missionaries and religious orders struggling against suppressive practices. The well-known defense of the Indians by Friar Bartolomé de las Casas happened at the legal, juridical, and theological level through letters and visits to Spain. In the colonies, missionaries who were conscious of their pastoral task tried to learn the language addressing the religious leaders through the catechist process. Missionaries were aware of the atrocities committed by *encomenderos* and *corregidores* and therefore, "there was concern and care by the religious orders. They did not permit Spaniards' entrance in the reductions because they were considered the true 'mouth' of evangelization and because the Indigenous established the contrast between what the priests said and what Christians did."[104]

---

101. Rivera, *A Violent Evangelism*, 218–19.

102. Rivera, *A Violent Evangelism*, 99.

103. The political reduction of belief to a certain dogma, one church and its rituals was intentional applied during the conquest after the conquerors realized that in the Caribbean and Latin American territories the population was political, religious, and cultural organized and seen as superstitious. Mariátegui, *Siete Ensayos*, 127–28.

104. Rivera, *A Violent Evangelism*, 97.

Among the natives in both Mexico and Peru, the idea that Spaniards were divinities was strong. The Indigenous in Peru believed in divinities[105] without strong religious or dogmatic bases. Priests struggled to picture that among Spaniards there were bad Viracochas.[106] This notion, instead of helping, brought a negative idea about the creator and supreme divinity among natives. Moctezuma wanted to explain that that negative idea was not true,[107] and they had a healthy and lively relationship. Transformation/evangelization in the sense of exchanging bad for good reinforced the idolatrous sense impressed by colonizers at the beginning of their Christian enterprise. Evangelization tried to maintain "the idea of a radical antithesis between Christianity and native idolatry"[108] which could enrich their own religion and culture. Conversion was a process of replacing the bad with the good through radical illegitimizing of the different. "What was never doubted by the Europeans was the need to make the autochthonous cults illegitimate, to destroy them, and to substitute Christianity for them."[109] Colonizers changed meanings and transplanted religious concepts that did not exist in the native world like the proper concept of conversion to the one only God.

Without recognizing the value of the indigenous' spirituality or myths, evangelization devaluated[110] their beliefs and practices. It reinforced the neglecting act to see creation as integral to life. Both the Maya and Inca leaders, in their dialogue with the conquerors, clearly manifested their rich conceptions about creation like relationality and dependence on the entire environment.[111] But because evangelization was an armed, political, economic, and religious task, the invasion of native lands was equivalent to winning the Indigenous' souls for the economic benefit of the Christian empire. Under this, it is possible to

---

105. Mariátegui, *Siete Ensayos*, 130.

106. Mariátegui, *Siete Ensayos*, 130.

107. See note 71 that refers to the dishonor of native gods.

108. Rivera, *A Violent Evangelism*, 161.

109. Rivera, *A Violent Evangelism*, 219.

110. The prevailing idea was that natives' religious, philosophical, and moral convictions were inferior and should be abolished. Rivera, *A Violent Evangelism*, 163.

111. In the Tawantinsuyo, the goal of religion was temporal. It was concerned on how to rule the land rather than the heaven realm; it was more social than individual insisting in the agrarian rites, magic realism, and in the pantheist feelings. Mariátegui, *Siete Ensayos*, 129.

understand how conversion was used as an ideological weapon distorting the good news and the message of life in Christ.

Evangelization was a means to facilitate dominion, if necessary by force, over Indigenous but the "*missionary action . . . consists of reasonable persuasion through convincing arguments and adherence of the will through attraction.*"[112] Nevertheless, persuasion was replaced by the military and religious crusade where "the death of Atahualpa . . . covered with religious reasons . . . appears as the first condemnation of the Inquisition in Peru."[113] The evangelization, an ecclesiastical enterprise, was strongly and historical rooted in the dominion of western ecclesiastical element.[114] Even that the Christological implications show that Christ has been historically projected through images determined by tensions and struggles, the Latin American Christology returns to Jesus' solidarity asserting love as expression of justice and mercy. The following section will focus on Christology based in liberation rather than oppression.

---

112. Rivera, *A Violent Evangelism*, 226.

113. Mariátegui, *Siete Ensayos*, 133.

114. Mariátegui, *Siete Ensayos*, 143–44.

2

The Latin American Christology

Resurrection of the Body of the Poor

THE FIFTEENTH CENTURY SERVES as a milestone to understand, in part, the present in Latin America. The consequences of the encounter of different cultures cannot be denied. Conquered, exploited, and possessed, the native population increased in poverty. The conquest endorsed the presence of new subjects, Europeans and Africans—slaves to replace indigenous slavery. In the following periods of the conquest, prosperity and subjugation were intrinsically present changing the social structure and adding levels of servitude. In the eighteenth and the nineteenth centuries, movements for independence awakened. The invitation to live in freedom was contradicted by the reality of servitude as absence [1] of life.

The dream of liberty, modernity, and democracy was imported from Europe becoming real for some but not for many. Liberty was an illusion,[2] a formalism that prolonged the colonial system especially in the rural areas of the Andes and the Amazon. After independence in 1928, the Indigenous did not gain rights; they were not citizens. Only years later, the legalization of their rights gave them rights to vote, to be elected, and to enter into legal transactions. But freedom, in such circumstances, was not innocuous. The Indigenous lost half of their communal lands[3] (their lands of connection and spirituality) to the capitalist system. Liberty brought along aggressive economic transactions and a dramatic change to the 'trueque'[4] practice.

Capitalism accentuated dependence in the nineteenth and twentieth centuries. Its methods and values were imposed and did not resolve

---

1. Tamez, *Bajo un Cielo*, 18.
2. Burga, "¿Cuándo se jodió el Perú?," 83.
3. Delgado, *En qué momento*, 55.
4. Trueque is a practice of interchange, in collective or communal societies, of services and objects without the presence of money.

problems linked to poverty. Additionally, technology, relevant for production, increased the costs, reduced the need for workers and made it difficult to produce and to compete in the international market. Production depending on modern technology and international investment pushed inflated more the external debt.

Democracy could not help overcoming the desire for supremacy between countries causing rivalries ending in wars. For instance, the "triple alliance"[5] (1865–1870) between Brazil, Argentina, and Uruguay against Paraguay resulted in the loss of a vast territory of Paraguay. The Pacific War[6] (1879–1884) between Chile and Peru resulted in the loss of territory in Bolivia and Peru to Chile. In both wars, the British Empire supported the conflict. In the twentieth century, most of the countries in Latin America democratically elected their governments, but the international cold war tensions between the USA and Russia brought a side effect. The United States tried to align the countries through economic dependence against communism. The USA, in negotiations with leaders in Latin America, prompted a period of militarism during the 1960s to the 1980s in almost all the countries. These actions reinforced financial and technological dependency. Theologians, in this context, started to touch the root meaning and cause of dependency and unjust domination. Analyzing the characteristics of commercial relations between the industrialized and poor nations, they recognized these adverse conditions as idolatry and vain promises of a better future in the poor continent. Aware of the economic disparities, theologians based on a dialogue between text/Bible and reality, set up bases to analyze Christology and the presence of Christianity in the continent.

Protestantism in the Eighteenth and Nineteenth Centuries

In the fifteenth century, Latin America experienced the arrival of Roman Catholic and non Roman Catholics in the continent. Protestants, moved by commercial and colonial interests, arrived in Venezuela around 1529, in Brazil in 1555 and on the coast of Florida[7] in 1562. To prevent a Protestant influx, Spain moved its Inquisition machinery, accusing the

---

5. Gaylord Warren, *Paraguay and the Triple Alliance*, 1978.
6. See Chirinos Soto, *Historia de la República*.
7. González, *Christianity in Latin America*, 186–87.

British, Dutch, and French of piracy and of being heretics.[8] Protestants settled sporadically, influencing the populations. The British and Dutch settled in the Caribbean, the French in Haiti, the British in Panama, and the French again in Brazil.[9] The Roman Catholic colonizers prevented the arrival of Protestants but could not prevent Protestants from engaging in commercial endeavors.

In the eighteenth century, the well-established Roman Catholic Church appointed bishops through the crown, according to the *patronato real*,[10] enhancing the nexus between the Pope and the Church in Latin America. In the eighteenth century, the Mestizo and Creole presence raised two levels up to the social structure, forming part of the elite leaving the Indigenous and African descendants at the bottom of the social structure. From 1810 to 1828 most of the countries in Latin America and the Caribbean, except Cuba and Puerto Rico, gained their independence from the European kingdoms. The Mestizo and Creole were involved in that struggle. The elite, divided into liberals and conservatives,[11] interacted in different ways with the church. While liberals challenged the socio-political, cultural, and economic structures, promoted human rights through reformist ideas, and opposed the continuing financial support that the state gave to the church, conservatives saw the church as a way to maintain control and gave continuity to the colonial structure.[12] After independence, stability was not the same within the Church. The anticlerical liberal governments wanted to transform the traditional church by promoting laws against their privileges. The church lost lands and some rights in some countries but never the relationship with the states.

To maintain its position of power,[13] the church engaged in social action, supporting upper class women's charity and becoming a "servant

8. González, *Christianity in Latin America*, 187.

9. González, *Christianity in Latin America*, 188,

10. "The Patronato, applied by Alejandro VI in 1493 Bull is the *right* to possess and the *duty* to evangelize" (Rodríguez, "Los Movimientos Misioneros," 64).

11. The conservatives mostly represented the interests of the landed, whose wealth was based on agriculture and cheap labor. The liberals came mostly from the new and growing merchant class, whose model was the rich industrialized nations of the North Atlantic and for whom an educated and skilled labor force represented greater wealth. González, *Christianity in Latin America*, 189.

12. González, *Christianity in Latin America*, 141–42.

13. In Peru, the patronage continued until the Republican period when the Pope conceded his intervention in the presentation of bishops but not in their election. See Nieto Velez, "La Transformación Religiosa Peruana," 90.

church" that legitimized regimes in Brazil and Argentina. Individual Catholics, conscious of the social, political, and economic challenges, developed social manifestations to respond to the societies' challenges in different countries.[14] After independence, leaders engaged in modernization, progress, and exportation. Countries in the south of the continent, that had the need to populate vast areas, welcomed immigration. Juan Bautista Alberdi in Argentina argued that "the nation needed immigrants in order to exploit the under populated and fertile lands of the interior, as well as to provide skilled labor for industry and a solid foundation for democracy."[15]

Leaders were Roman Catholics with "little theological sympathy toward Protestantism, who yet felt that religious freedom was both a value in itself and a necessary concession to prospective migrants."[16] Immigrants received the promise of freedom to maintain their culture and faith, but reality was different. Behind religious freedom, polarization between liberal and conservative leaders struggled between change or support to the Roman Catholic Church. The flag of religious freedom, raised by liberals to get support from Protestants,[17] brought an economic motivation to progress in the capitalist sense of overcoming colonial ideologies by improving the human condition in the expansion and population of lands and industrialization.

There was a period of colonization of many different areas. In 1555, French Huguenots started a colony in Brazil[18] and in 1567 they founded the city of Rio de Janeiro. Around 1626 to 1630 the Dutch, interested in taking Brazil from the Portuguese, controlled the northeast of Brazil. John Maurice of Nassau, a prince of the house of Nassau-Siegen built up the state of Pernambuco and rebuilt the city of Recife.[19] Immigrants arriving in Argentina, Uruguay, Chile, and the Southern areas of Brazil were English-speaking, Anglicans, merchants, and professionals. They settled in the cities. The Reformed Scots and mostly Methodist, Baptist or Congregationalist Welsh settled in the interior.[20] Waldensians found-

14. González, *Christianity in Latin America*, 149, 161–63.

15. González, *Christianity in Latin America*, 190.

16. González, *Christianity in Latin America*, 190.

17. Rodríguez, "Los Movimientos Misioneros," 77.

18. French Protestants inspired to form a Huguenot colony in Brazil. For that enterprise, two different projects were organized, the first in 1555 and the second in 1558. Mackay, *El Otro Cristo Español*, 275.

19. McCarter, "Protestantism in North and South America," 4, 7.

20. González, *Christianity in Latin America*, 191.

ed the first community in Uruguay in 1877 after the arrival of the first immigrants in 1856. Later groups moved from Uruguay to Argentina in 1901[21] without splitting as a church.

Lutherans arrived in Brazil, Argentina, and Chile from 1824 to colonize the territories or to work on plantations and in industry. The promises to respect their cultures and traditions were not kept. At the beginning, the government guaranteed full religious freedom to Brazilian immigrants but it only became real after the approval of the Constitution of 1891; seventy decades later.[22] Russian Mennonites arrived in Paraguay in 1926, creating four communities from 1930 to 1947.[23] Since their presence was promoted by the state, immigrants were recommended not to evangelize the Catholic continent. Missionaries maintained the link with their national churches back in their countries, without sharing their faith with their neighbor. Even though mission was illegitimate, Anglicans did it by starting Spanish-speaking Anglican congregations.[24] Progress, one of the ideas behind the Protestants' presence in Latin America, was preached, and pointed to social regeneration through "moral development but not by political changes."[25] Change did not come from the majority of Indigenous populations but from the ones in power and some who understood the moment and were engaged in the capitalist system.

Missionaries from the United States arrived in Latin America in the second half of the nineteenth century, organizing Bible societies and churches. Again, the utopian hopes for a new society proclaimed conversion to the true faith. In Chile, for instance, "David Thrumbul, sent by the Foreign Evangelical Union in the United States . . . began holding Protestant services in Spanish . . . organized the first Protestant Church in Chile . . . in 1868."[26] Penzotti founded the first Spanish-speaking church in Peru that joined the Methodist presence,[27] experience repeated in almost all countries. Protestants organized conferences to work in the area of international cooperation aiming at evangelizing the continent.

---

21. González, *Christianity in Latin America*, 192–93.
22. González, *Christianity in Latin America*, 196.
23. González, *Christianity in Latin America*, 202.
24. González, *Christianity in Latin America*, 218.
25. Rodríguez, "Los Movimientos Misioneros," 73.
26. González, *Christianity in Latin America*, 224.
27. González, *Christianity in Latin America*, 227–28.

Immigration and later missionary activity planted the seeds of confrontation between Roman Catholics and Protestants. The evangelized continent, a place where the immigrants progressed and missionaries proclaimed conversion, was impacted from both sides the life of further generations. Protestant leaders promoted the reading of the Bible influencing education.[28] The Roman Catholic Church maintained the colonial model of Christendom was, at the beginning, opposed to Protestants evangelism efforts. Protestants soon awakened to the apologetic tactic defending faith from the accusation of heresy and slowly gained respect, joined efforts with other Protestant churches growing in dialogue and ecumenism.

To inspire the air of a "solid foundation of democracy," as asserted by the Argentinian Alberdi, Protestants followed the values of Christianity without changing the idea that Western civilization was superior to the native ones. Certainly, immigration and mission were under the impulse of progress in terms of growing and developing economically. Protestants were, in religious terms, the bridge for a faith that had a "religious attitude more than institutional organization or a collection of dogmas."[29] The germ of freedom, progress, education, and democracy developed slowly at the time that poverty was becoming one of the principal realities on the continent. Protestantism slowly penetrated in Latin America "not because of its religious and spiritual power but because of its social compromise."[30]

Latin American Christology

In Latin America, two strong Christological emphases informed people's images with respect to Christ. First, the monarchical and celestial Christ supporting the heavenly incarnated Christ, reinforced by the empire, and linked to the Pope's authority. Consequently, this image promoted related images such as the crucified Christ, the suffering Christ of Good Friday hanging on the cross, and the resurrected, triumphant, and distant Christ. Second, the spiritual Christ coming to redeem sinners from bad

---

28. Diego Thompson, agent of the "Sociedad Bíblica y Extranjera" and member of the "Sociedad Educativa Lancasteriana," promoted the reading of the Bible and education in Argentina, Uruguay, Chile, Colombia, and Peru. Mackay, *El Otro Cristo Español*, 277–79.

29. Mackay, *El Otro Cristo Español*, 303.

30. Mariátegui, *Siete Ensayo*, 152.

habits; Christ became, in spiritual terms, a friend for those who changed their lives and followed Jesus in a consecrated manner.

These two emphases, present during the twentieth century, moved Roman Catholic and Protestant theologians to reconsider the images connected to the historical reality of mission. In this effort, Latin American theologians, influenced by the Historical Jesus concept which arose in Europe, began to see the life of Jesus through the lenses of Latin America's reality. Given this influence, it will be pertinent to consider the most relevant elements of the Latin American Christology developed by theologians in the twentieth century.

The Historical Jesus: Relevance for Latin American Christology

Latin American Christology matured in its interaction with Western theology.[31] This influence moved theologians to assert that the gospels are a confession of faith,[32] faith expressed after the historical reality of Jesus' life, the cross, and the resurrection. But Latin American Christology emphasizes salvation by looking at Jesus' ministry of justice and interpreting it in the light of the actual context. In Latin America, the ideological use of Christ[33] has been difficult for Christology. In a world that cries for liberation, it was not enough to confess Christ but to act as Christians. This reality challenged the churches and theologians because a Christology articulated in a soteriological way needed power to promote hope to liberate the poor. Jesus of Nazareth, as the methodological starting point of Latin America Christology, nourishes itself from the historical Jesus.

---

31. The dialogue of Latin American theologians with Western theological literature took place. Latin American theologians consider the Latin American context emphasizing the relevance of reflection based in the practice of love. See Sobrino, *The True Church*, 35. Boff, *Jesucristo el Liberador*, 58. "The Latin American Christology thanks the achievements of the European Christology (and) its methodological return to the Historical Jesus" (Sobrino, *Jesús en América Latina*, 96–97).

32. "The New Testament speaks of the resurrected Jesus as the resurrected Lord and when it speaks about Jesus of Nazareth, it does considering the faith in Jesus who is the Christ" (Sobrino, *Jesucristo Liberador*, 61).

33. Latin American Christology asks for the functionality of Christ and how it operates in the continent. There are two classic images of Christ, the "conquered," a suffering and passive Christ and the "celestial monarch," a powerful and assimilated conqueror Christ. Both are "the face of the Christology of oppression" in constant tension. See Miguez Bonino, *Jesús Ni vencido ni Monarca*, 10.

Relevant Facts in the Quest of the Historical Jesus

The quest of the historical Jesus was the attempt to reconstruct Jesus' biography and life through historical and literary criticism of Jesus' life, considering the contemporary Jewish world and the expectation of the messiah among Jews. The quest began in Europe with Hermann Samuel Reimarus. After his death, Lessing published Reimarus' seven *Fragments*[34] between 1774 and 1778. In his writings, Reimarus established elements to understand Jesus' intention to establish the immediate future and earthly kingdom of a kingly messiah. Jesus' intention was to advance the hope of Jews following the promise of the Israelites' deliverance from bondage. Jesus sent his messengers to propagate belief. John the Baptist acted by acknowledging Jesus as the Messiah before the baptism and preaching repentance because the kingdom of God was at hand. John confirmed Jesus' messianic role through revelation during Jesus' baptism and connected it to the long awaited kingdom of the Messiah. [35] For Reimarus, Jesus' intention followed a preconceived plan that involved Jesus' disciples to spread his deeds as signs of the kingdom of the Messiah.

Jesus' miracles were intended to make Jews enthusiastic about the worldly messiah. "It is not until thirty to sixty years after the death of Jesus, that people began to write an account of the performance of these miracles."[36] Reimarus disbelieved the miracles while discovering the "contradictions in their system of the Messiah, and in their unsatisfactory evidences of his resurrection and return."[37]

Reimarus affirmed that the messianic ideal Jesus proposed followed the political ideal of the son of David[38] who expected to free Israel from oppression. The expectation failed. Consequently, as Jesus did not expect to suffer and die, his hope was frustrated. Jesus' words on the cross were "a confession which can hardly be otherwise interpreted than that God

---

34. The fragments are: "The Tolerance of the Deists," "The Decrying of Reason in the Pulpit." "The impossibility of a Revelation which all men should have good grounds for believing," "The Passing of the Israelites through the Red Sea," "Showing that the books of the Old Testament were not written to reveal a Religion," "Concerning the story of the Resurrection," and "The Aims of Jesus and His Disciples." Schweitzer, *The Quest*, 16–17.

35. Lessing, *Brief Critical Reimarus*, 12–16.

36. Lessing, *Brief Critical Reimarus*, 73.

37. Lessing, *Brief Critical Reimarus*, 76.

38. Lessing, *Brief Critical Reimarus*, 39–44.

had not helped him to carry out his intention and attain his object as he had hoped. It was then certainly not the intention for Jesus to suffer and to die, but to build up a worldly kingdom, and to deliver the Israelites from bondage. It was in *this* that God had forsaken him, it was in *this* that his hope had been frustrated."[39] After the failure, Jesus' disciples invented the spiritual Savior to overcome "the failed first hopes,"[40] demonstrating that the Christ of faith was not the Jesus of history.[41]

Reimarus challenged the construction of Christ and moved to reconstruct theologically the life and ministry of Jesus. The historical Jesus, in Reimarus' reconstruction, tended to be eschatological with an earthly and political character.[42] Reimarus' *Fragments* failed in their attempt to discredit Christian belief and to establish a portrayal of Jesus as he was, even though the value in Reimarus' work resides in the distinction between the spiritual Messiah and the historical and political Messiah behind the Gospels.[43] It is right that Reimarus' works were "before their time"[44] initiating a variety of literary studies on Jesus' life, biography, historical studies, and psychological approaches ending up with different representations of Jesus' life.

Among the rich literature produced during the first quest, I will choose some theologians who emphasized different aspects of Jesus. Friedrich Schleiermacher (1786–1834) developed the notion of Jesus as divine redeemer. Faith in Jesus is the requirement to obtain participation in the Christian communion. His work "The Life of Jesus," dominated by rationalism, "is not in search of the historical Jesus, but of the Jesus Christ of his own system of theology . . . the historic figure which seems to him appropriate to the self- consciousness of the Redeemer as he represents it. . . . He comes to the fact with a ready-made dialectic apparatus and sets his puppets into lively action. Schleiermacher's dialectic is not a dialectic which generates reality . . . but merely a dialectic of exposition."[45] Schleiermacher found the authority in the gospels reflecting Jesus'

---

39. Lessing, *Brief Critical Reimarus*, 27.
40. Lessing, *Brief Critical Reimarus*, 28.
41. Lessing, *Brief Critical Reimarus*, 94.
42. Schweitzer, *The Quest*, 23.
43. Tatum, *In Quest of Jesus*, 94.
44. Schweitzer, *The Quest*, 26.
45. Schweitzer, *The Quest*, 62.

consciousness and developing the idea of the "divine Sonship."[46] He intends to explain Jesus' miracles and resurrection in a rationalistic way where Jesus' crucifixion is "a condition of reanimation."[47] But Schweitzer finds contradictions in Schleiermacher's authority of the gospels because he "avoids the scene in Gethsemane (inferred) in the silence of John (and avoids) the miracle of the birth and childhood."[48] As Schweitzer discovers Schleiermacher's difficult in writing the life of Jesus, Schweitzer understands that Schleiermacher speaks, only by accident of Jesus but consciously of Christ,[49] affirming that there are more possibilities to write a life of Christ.

David Friedrich Strauss (1808–1874) understood that the synoptics were permeated with myth and that prior to the baptism of Jesus everything was myth. There is nothing of history consistent in them. The gospel according John, compared to the synoptics, is "inferior . . . as a historical source just in proportion as it is more strongly dominated that they by theological and apologetic interest."[50] Myth, in Strauss' understanding, was the view that Jesus was a supernatural being who thought he was the Messiah that "should after his earthly life be taken up into heaven, and thence should come again to bring in His Kingdom."[51] Strauss was strongly influenced by Reimarus and used historical elements to establish a new system of dogma but the mythological explanations made more obscure his rationalization ending with a critical life of Jesus more obscure.

Ernest Renan (1823–1892) had a historical purpose and artistically developed the life of Jesus. For Renan, Jesus was a gifted preacher imitating John the Baptist and returning "to Galilee He became to have some knowledge of the art of preaching. He had learned from him how to influence masses of men. From that time forward he preached with much more power and gained greater ascendancy over the people."[52] As a great teacher, Jesus proclaimed the idea of a spiritual kingdom.

Schweitzer, in his critical role, pointed out the significance of "Jesus as spiritually arisen with men . . . not the historical Jesus, but the

---

46. Schweitzer, *The Quest*, 66.
47. Schweitzer, *The Quest*, 65.
48. Schweitzer, *The Quest*, 65, 66.
49. Schweitzer, *The Quest*, 67.
50. Schweitzer, *The Quest*, 87.
51. Schweitzer, *The Quest*, 92.
52. Schweitzer, *The Quest*, 184.

spirit which goes forth from Him and in the spirits of men strives for new influence and rule, is that which overcomes the world."[53] Schweitzer maintained an eschatological predestination. The kingdom established by Jesus cannot be earned; its imminent arrival was bringing a new age.[54] The Kingdom of God was connected to Jesus' suffering, a historic event, secretly revealed to his disciples where "He will go to Jerusalem, there to suffer death at the hands of the authorities."[55] Schweitzer found a difference between the Jesus portrayed in the Gospels and the Jesus of history. The Gospels reveal the disciple's faith mediated over time. Each critical attempt to set in time the genuine figure of Jesus caused scholars to enter into a deep reflection about the relationship between the historical Jesus and the Christ of faith.

In Schweitzer's comprehensive account of the first quest, he analyzed and critiqued most of the scholars who approached the historical Jesus, demonstrating a failure in their effort to recover Jesus as he really was in the nineteenth century. Schweitzer found too "artificial history with which (Jesus' life) had thought to give new life to our Christianity."[56] His critique demonstrated that scholars did not succeed in building a historical figure "designed by rationalism, endowed with life by liberalism, and clothed by modern theology in a historical garb,"[57] a figure in which it was impossible to find Jesus of Nazareth and his ministry of promoting the kingdom of God.

The continuity between the historical Jesus and the Christ of faith, portrayed in the Gospels, was still to be found. A period of silence of around fifty years took place. Rudolf Bultmann (1874–1976) had a different attitude toward the quest for Jesus. Bultmann renounced the historical Jesus under the lack of evidence to sketch the life of the Jewish prophet. The quest for the historical Jesus was superfluous in relation to the apostolic preaching or kerygma.[58] Through the kerygma one can an-

---

53. Schweitzer, *The Quest*, 399.
54. Schweitzer, *The Quest*, 355.
55. Schweitzer, *The Quest*, 386.
56. Schweitzer, *The Quest*, 399.
57. Schweitzer, *The Quest*, 396.
58. "This posture originates in Kähler who, after various attempts to recover Jesus' biography, was disappointed and delivered in 1892 a famous speech entitled 'the true Christ is the preached Christ.' Since then, terminology 'historical Jesus' and the 'Christ of the faith' was used distinctively. Under this distinction, the preaching of the kerigma became important for faith and to Christology" (Sobrino, *Jesucristo Liberador*, 66).

nounce that the Savior died for our sins on the cross and was resurrected by God. Bultmann encouraged interpreting and translating the apostolic message of Christ for today. The merit is that the preaching of the gospel "considers the actual reality –what happens in history– in Christology."[59] But preaching the apostolic message was necessary to demythologize the message of Christ from its Greco-Roman syncretism,[60] and to seek its meaning for our existence today.

To proclaim the gospel in faith, according to Bultmann, it was necessary to know that the Son of God lived, was crucified, and resurrected by God. The gospel is preached knowing that the one who saves is Christ. Bultmann concluded that Jesus was not a historical figure.[61] Belief in Jesus results from proclamation of the message. Christology then announces the kerygma inviting to have faith in the Christ of the gospels and receive redemption. Taking on here a soteriological character, Bultmann's Christology asserts the flesh becoming Word, not the inverse.[62] The kerygma, as the source faith, sets the power behind the preaching that moved Jesus' disciples to go back to Jesus who was a historic being who lived in a certain moment in history. The central role of the kerygma points to the essential requirement for faith, the decision to choose new life in Christ while being confronted with the proclamation. The exercise of demythologizing is to consider supernatural events (the resurrection, Jesus' birth, and miracles) as stories recovering faith in the cross that is proclaimed.

Research on the historical Jesus took on a new phase aiming at searching for unity between the historical Jesus and the Christ of faith. Ernst Käsemann in his lecture in 1953, later published under "The Problem of the Historical Jesus," gave some background to Christology and the reason for the historical reality of Jesus "as the continuity of the Gospel within the discontinuity of the times and within the variation of the kerygma."[63] The continuity and discontinuity was not based on Jesus' biography; rather in the stability between the Christ of faith and the Jesus of history where the first community lived a new moment that inspired

---

59. Sobrino, *Jesucristo Liberador*, 67.
60. Boff, *Jesucristo el Liberador*, 22.
61. Boff, *Jesucristo el Liberador*, 23.
62. Boff, *Jesucristo el Liberador*, 25.
63. Tatum, *In Quest of Jesus*, 101.

writing the gospels. Ascording to Käsemann, Jesus reinterpreted the Law of Moses in two ways:

> First, Jesus regarded himself as a new Moses, with messianic authority to reinterpret the old Moses. This is most clearly seen in the "antitheses" of Matthew (5:21–22, 27–28, 43–45). Second, Jesus welcomed sinners to his meals and to his student family. He forgave sinners and sought them out in order to forgive them. Jesus' ministry was the triumph of grace over law. Later on, within the early Christian movement, St. Paul taught theologically what Jesus had done in his life. Christianity's famous majoring on grace and compassion for sinners came naturally out of Jesus' closely observed and remembered way of living and welcoming.[64]

The continuity resides in the expression and interpretation of Jesus' words, attitudes, and acts but in a discontinuity with Judaism. The gospels express continuity in a theological expression of faith leading to understand how the first communities recognized in Jesus the Christ and the Son of God. The community gives testimony to faith making explicit Jesus' divinity. In doing that, they tried to resemble the faith of Jesus, now in a very new moment.

The Historical Jesus: Relevance for Latin American Christology

The process of historical Jesus study and its attempts to resolve the question of the life of Jesus moved scholars to vast new areas of research. The attempt to resolve the problem, especially by the influx of church authority and dogma, did not succeed during the first quest. The return to the question of Jesus of Nazareth to find unity with the Christ of faith is more significant for Christology in the 80s and 90s. The conciliation between the dogma and historical information about Jesus drove theologians in Latin America to considering the centuries of tragedy that contributed to marginalization and dependence in order to focus on the absurdity of the realities of suffering to verify the struggle for life and the incongruities of oppression. The method is defined by the poor of this world as place for Christology,[65] a social and theological place of God's revelation. Latin American Christology defines the historical Jesus as the methodological

---

64. Zahl, "The Historical Jesus," 25, 28–31.
65. Sobrino, *Jesucristo Liberador*, 47.

beginning of Christology.[66] In relation to Western, they don't face the challenge to "*demythologize* Christ"[67] but to recognize how human misery challenges the faith in Christ. Given the context of oppression and poverty, the historical Jesus becomes critical for Christology; it seeks to understand events and concepts informed by liberation.

Liberation Theology, Context of Latin American Christology

Considering the increasing poverty gap during the 1960s, Liberation Theologians linked their reflection to economic dependency and the contradictions it brings to the Christian continent. During the Second Vatican Council,[68] Latin American theologians introduced the concept of the poor considering the role of historical praxis[69] in a poor continent with little political influence. After the council, Latin American bishops and theologians met in Medellin[70] to address the difficult reality of the continent.[71] They confirmed the "excessive inequalities between social

---

66. Sobrino, *Jesucristo Liberador*, 60. The historical Jesus designates the life, mission, and destiny of Jesus of Nazareth.

67. Sobrino, *Jesucristo Liberador*, 75.

68. Actually, the Second Vatican Council (1962–1965) was initiated by the challenge of the reality of secularism in Western society. Even though the Council received three proposed themes—the modern world, the unity of the churches, and the world of the poor; the council only addressed the first two topics. The council was open to incorporate "the important secular and democratic values, in their broadest and most fundamental sense, into the reforms proposed by the Council for the Church itself." They also agreed to enter into an ecumenical dialogue with other Christian denominations. The third topic had a weak emphasis in the council but it was addressed by the Church in Latin America in response to two documents from the council, *Lumen Gentium* and *Ad Gentes* that carefully focused on poverty in the life of Christ. "They both refer to the evangelization of the poor, and *Lumen Gentium* bases a mandate on the fact that the image of the Lord is visible in them [the poor]" (Gutiérrez. *Density of the Present*, 65, 69).

69. Gutiérrez, *Theology of Liberation*, 8–10.

70. The Second General Conference of Latin American Bishops, CELAM, took place in Medellin in 1968, Colombia. Gutiérrez, *Density of the Present*, 67.

71. Gutiérrez points out "The 60s was a difficult period in Latin America. The Brazilian dictatorship was in its most aggressive period, the military regime in Argentina was harshly repressing popular movements, Mexico was experiencing the terrible massacre of Tlaltelolco, Peru was living the twilight of the Belaunde government, and the government in Chile held out little hope. Conflict was intensifying in Bolivia and Colombia. Oppressive and corrupt governments persisted in Haiti, Nicaragua, and

classes, especially in countries (where) few people have a lot (and) many people have little."[72]

Their concern focused on the growing frustration, marginalization, and inequalities in society. Bishops invited people to act with sensibility and justice with regard to the marginalized.[73] Poverty changed the Roman Catholic Church as it moved toward the poor, to defend their rights as a sign of commitment of solidarity.[74] The preferential option for the poor, following Christ's mission and the message of Luke 4: 18–21, was affirmed in Medellin and later ratified in Puebla[75] and challenged the "Church . . . to renounce the social privileges and to serve all, beginning with the poor and oppressed."[76]

The Poor and Poverty

The poor as "nonperson,"[77] representing the dehumanized majorities and their struggle to survive, was an invitation to a voluntary option for the poor.[78] Aware of the class confrontation, opting for the poor "is a theological option that means to take the side of the dispossessed, entering into their exploited world, and embracing their values and cultural categories. The option for the poor is to practice solidarity, to hold the interests and struggles"[79] in the perspective of justice. This option moves to be "artisans of peace,"[80] recognizing that in Latin America the struggles to confront structures of sin, which implies to love the sinners but to struggle against the structures. This invited theologians to act, preach, and develop a theology aware of their sufferings and struggles.

Paraguay. These situations aggravated the deep and perpetual poverty of the Latin American people" (Gutiérrez, *Density of the Present*, 84–85).

72. CELAM, *Medellín Conclusiones*, 48.

73. CELAM, *Medellín Conclusiones*, 49.

74. CELAM, *Medellín Conclusiones*, 149, 57.

75. "Los pobres merecen una atención preferencial . . . son los primeros destinatarios de la misión y su evangelización es por excelencia señal y prueba de la misión de Jesús" (CELAM III, *Conferencia General*, 237).

76. Gutiérrez, *Density of the Present*, 79.

77. Gutiérrez, *Power of the Poor*, 57.

78. "The option for the poor is a free decision that drives to be incarnated in the word of poor people to realistically and historically assume their causes and holistic liberation" (Lois, "Opción por los pobres," 9).

79. Gutiérrez, *Power of the Poor*, 45.

80. Gutiérrez, *Power of the Poor*, 48.

Hermeneutics: Relevant Lenses in Following Jesus

Medellin proposed to end the division between faith and life in order to understand reality as a whole in the light of Christ.[81] To comprehend the reality, theologians applied the method see-judge-act as a circular element in the praxis. According to Gutiérrez, to see refers to the analysis of the reality, to judge to the theological analysis, and to act to the pastoral action in response to the first two stages.[82] Theology nourishes its reflection in the intimate bond to the social situation[83] the context gives. The concreteness of reality originates a critical reflection nourishing theological reflection which becomes a "second step."[84] The critical reflection is a circular dialogue between the scriptures and events of the present. The interdisciplinary in liberation theology "open up the past (helping) to explain the present."[85]

This hermeneutic circle played an important role in interpretation as the exercise of suspicion which was applied to the ideological superstructure in general and to theology in particular. The theological analysis of reality allowed exegetical suspicion encouraging to a new interpretation of the scriptures.[86] It considers the power of interpretation[87] not helping to change oppressive interpretations. It requires rethinking the present in relation to the past and vice versa. It invites to re-interpret the message in a liberative[88] way harmonizing action and reflection. It allows awareness about one's own complicity in the dynamics of oppression and structural sin. Paulo Freire linked theory with praxis in pedagogy and influenced liberation theology. His "Pedagogy of the Oppressed" recognizes the alienation of the poor and emphasizes the process of "conscientization."[89] The poor are able to understand the false beliefs[90] that sustain oppression but

---

81. CELAM, *Medellín Conclusiones*, 34.

82. Gutiérrez, *Density of the Present*, 85.

83. Segundo, *Liberation of Theology*, 8.

84. Gutiérrez, *Theology of Liberation*, Cf. also Gutiérrez, "Spirituality and Theological Method," 4–7.

85. Segundo, *Liberation of Theology*, 8.

86. Segundo, *Liberation of Theology*, 14.

87. Segundo, *Liberation of Theology*, 16.

88. Segundo affirms that a theory that provides a methodology for ideological analysis would deserve to be called liberative and it will keep biblical interpretation moving back and forth between its sources and present day reality. Segundo, *Liberation of Theology*, 19.

89. Freire, *Pedagogía del Oprimido*, 24 and Gutiérrez, *Theology of Liberation*, 91.

90. Gutiérrez, *Theology of Liberation*, 95.

are not yet conscious and critically exercising active participation in the transformation of the world and their lives through creative thinking.

Being engaged in the transformation of the world, the poor embody discipleship[91] that "transforms the present . . . sinking roots where the pulse of history is beating at this moment and illuminating history with the Word of the Lord of history."[92] They serve in polarized contexts meaning "to seek out the historical magnitude of the gospel by starting with social praxis."[93] Liberation is not to build a new Empire and to defeat oppressors but to recover the meaning of love through the just option for the poor in light of faith and hope.

The *praxis of faith*[94] expresses conviction. Living in faith means practicing service which "illuminates the following of Jesus of Nazareth."[95] Service makes people more human and vulnerable, renewing their relation with the poor as person who has been "deprived of the most elemental human rights. (Justice is) authentic solidarity with the poor (that constitutes) the praxis of love."[96] Praxis is a response to the commission received from God. In it, servants "struggle against misery, injustice, and exploitation (aiming for) the *creation of a new man (and woman)*.[97]

Sin as Injustice—Justice as Liberation

Liberation theology understands sin as a personal and social fault against the neighbor and against God. Exploitation and injustice characterize the reality of sin[98] and urge a reconsideration of the causes of oppression. Sin is the egoist self not able to change his/her life and society, "sin is a personal and social intra-historical reality . . . it is . . . an

91. Segundo points out that service implies the strategy to make it succeed historically the cause of God and Christ. Segundo, *El Hombre de Hoy*, 773.

92. Gutiérrez, *Theology of Liberation*, 15.

93. Gutiérrez, *Theology of Liberation*, 85.

94. "Faith is the *formal* starting point or the 'determining hermeneutic principle' . . . and praxis is the *material* starting point, that is, the raw material. There is no contradiction here, but only an interrelationship of distinct 'instances' standing in reciprocal relation and duly ordered" (Boff, "Epistemology and Methodology," 59).

95. Dussel, "Theology of Liberation," 85.

96. Gutiérrez, *Power of the Poor*, 50.

97. Gutiérrez, *Theology of Liberation*, 146.

98. Poverty—the fruit of social injustice, whose deepest roots are sin, is taken up not in order to erect it into an ideal of life, but to bear testimony to the evil it represents. Gutiérrez, *Power of the Poor*, 55.

obstacle to life's reaching the fullness we call salvation."[99] People living under imposed economic and social structures suffer injustice as a consequence of international commerce and credits[100] determined by few persons. The conditions of dependence and servitude are expressions of structural sin. The "social transformation, no matter how radical it may be, does not automatically achieve the suppression of all evils;"[101] therefore, the situation urges humanization especially of those who determine the course of life in society.

Medellin addressed liberation in terms of justice.[102] Injustice exists because justice was neglected, as Gutiérrez affirms: "We are at the threshold of a new historical age on our continent, full of desire for total emancipation, for liberation from all servitude, for personal growth and collective integration."[103]

Liberation theology contextualizes God's action in Latin America and reinterprets the Bible to bring a rich, fresh, and refreshing message through active service. The emphasis in orthopraxis verifies belief as a "truly human attitude"[104] at the heart of the process of liberation. Juan Luis Segundo writes, "it is my feeling that the most progressive theology in Latin America is more interested in being *liberative* than in *talking about liberation*. In other words, liberation deals not so much with content as with the method used to theologize in the face of our real-life situation."[105] It confirms that theology has to connect with the *historical reality*[106] circularly for renewed reflection in each situation in history.

The church, in charge of preaching Christ the liberator, has remained in its sacred and comfortable space but is challenged to intensify the vertical communion between humans and God and the

---

99. Gutiérrez, *Theology of Liberation*, 152.

100. "Countries producing raw material . . . always remain poor, meanwhile industrialized countries get each time richer. The international credit system (does not) consider the needs and possibilities in our countries" (CELAM, *Medellín Conclusiones*, 50–51).

101. Gutiérrez, *Theology of Liberation*, 35.

102. "There are also responsible for injustice those who do not act in favor of justice with the means at their hands . . . Justice and peace are achieved through a dynamic action of awareness" (CELAM, *Medellín Conclusiones*, 55).

103. Gutiérrez, *Density of the Present*, 86.

104. Segundo, *Theology of Liberation*, 32.

105. Segundo, *Liberation of Theology*, 9.

106. Segundo, *Liberation of Theology*, 25.

horizontal communion among humans by embracing the power of Christ to transform the *human reality*.[107] Jesus' ministry, death, and resurrection integrated a process of new creation into history. That process implies today to practice justice in places where injustice still prevails. Salvation involves historical and political liberation, which during the 60s and 70s compelled the church to support the poor as the primary agent of social change.

The Poor: Center of Latin American Christology

Latin American Christology accepts Jesus as the Christ, truly human and truly divine. But because of the limits[108] of church dogma, it is necessary to know how Jesus is present in Latin America.[109] In relation to Christologies that assert faith in Christ -the post-paschal[110] expression of faith, Latin American Christology recognizes God indwelling and embodying human fragility. Christological study begins with the historical Jesus, his entire life and practice of service. Jesus' ministry is historic because his life has continuity until today, as it invites us to understand the scriptures in connection to the present.[111] The study of Jesus of Nazareth, as a methodological[112] beginning, focuses on Jesus' humanity, which reveals his divinity. The "access to the historical Jesus is the access to the Christ of faith"[113] who proclaimed liberation as essential component of the kingdom arriving in him. Liberation was essential to the good news of Jesus' kingdom that Latin American Christology[114] follows.

107. Segundo, *Liberation of Theology*, 151.

108. "In a context of death and oppression faith restores sense. The tension in life awakes us from spirit—body, private faith—public faith dualism. Latin American Christology promotes active faith in history while theorizing" (Sobrino, *The True Church and the Poor*, 37–38).

109. Sobrino, *Jesucristo Liberador*, 61.

110. "One of the criteria to understand the beginning of Jesus' ministry is to recognize that the post-paschal faith introduced into the pre-paschal event" (Segundo, *El Hombre de Hoy*, 72).

111. Sobrino, *Jesucristo Liberador*, 112–13.

112. "The resurrection of Christ as the starting point of Christology has the New Testament in its favor . . . The resurrection of Christ is not for faith, as formulas are, a pure concept but a real event . . . that is not known today but only form ta concrete perspective. The resurrection of Christ today becomes the object of knowledge, being at the same time an object of hope and praxis." Sobrino, *Jesucristo Liberador*, 60, 67.

113. Sobrino, *Jesucristo Liberador*, 116.

114. "One may wonder why *freedom* has been discovered in progressive

Jesus' incarnation is another central aspect to Christology. It demonstrates how God becomes one among humans in solidarity especially with the poor. "In Jesus' life one may find a partiality and a solidarity that are historically constitutive. Such a partiality . . . forms part of the "surprise" that the incarnation brings and that corresponds to a certain lack of knowledge on our part concerning humankind prior to the incarnation."[115] Contrary to the idea of an anointed king, God takes place in a newborn without a crown and power in the manner that people expected. Latin American Christology affirms the fragile and vulnerable expression of love and solidarity in the incarnated God. The surprise is that Jesus becomes human living in the most challenging conditions of poverty; a radical expression of love[116] that God demonstrates to the unprivileged reality of the poor.

Jesus among the fragile and vulnerable awakes hope. Jesus is real[117] and able to feel and know the suffering of his people, is able to experience anger and disappointment before injustice. In the gospels, Jesus is the God with us in "predilection for the poor."[118] The gospels are faithful and theological reflections about Jesus who reveals God. Jesus feels the circumstances and enters in the suffering people's struggles.

The Poor: Face of God, Place of Salvation

Acknowledging and affirming Jesus' humanity, Latin American Christology does not deny Jesus' divinity but wants "to translate (it through his) humanity"[119] considering the social context. As a common Jew,[120] Jesus lived and acted in a religious context he knew and respected. He

---

Christologies as essential to the gospel while those Christologies have not discovered *liberation*. And one can wonder why Latin American Christology has discovered the liberation that has been practically absent in Christologies for centuries." Sobrino, *Jesucristo Liberador*, 42.

115. Sobrino, *True Church and the Poor*, 150. Sobrino calls "lessening" to the decreasing of Christ.

116. Gutiérrez, *Teología de la Liberación*, 382.

117. In his discussion on the Chalcedon formula, Sobrino asserts the thesis that 'The human nature (of God) is possible because Jesus is real. Even though the emphasis of Jesus' humanity challenges the dogma, it is necessary because it is important to discover that Christ is not other than Jesus. Sobrino *La Fe en Jesucristo*, 447ff.

118. Sobrino, *Jesús en América Latina*, 34.

119. Sobrino, *Jesús en América Latina*, 58.

120. Segundo, *El Hombre de Hoy*, 31.

interpreted the scripture and acted within the religious, social, economic, and political context.[121] In time of tension, Jesus' ministry has political consequences. Opposed to the interests of the religious and to the administrative power, Jesus assumed the destiny[122] of the oppressed and in so doing uncovers the unexpected reign of God for the authorities.

What does it mean to live in poverty, in the ideal of living in austerity and indifference to material goods? In contexts of poverty where the relationship between neighbors is altered by the socio-economic system, the ideal of material and spiritual poverty distorts the message of the kingdoms in which power is different from the one God brings. Latin American Christology denounced poverty as scandalous[123] as consequence of indifference and exploitation. It challenged the sacramental notion of the Roman Catholic Church as institution while elevating the poor (non-person) to the level of "sacrament of God"[124] in which the encounter of faith is authenticly opened to God[125] committing them to solidarity with others.

The church is called to be in solidarity with the poor and their world.[126] Jesus' impoverishment,[127] sourced by *kenosis*, reveals God's solidarity with the "crucified reality in Latin America"[128] that is given as magisterium to the church. The concept of crucified people[129] refers to the poor and its negative and positive sides. The negative part opens the crude reality of crucifixion that unimaginable majorities live unjustly. The positive part points to the rich circularity between the servant of Yahweh in Isaiah and the savior in the gospels. It reforms the negativity of the suffering reality in Latin America because Jesus "suffered without having sinned: he was

121. Segundo, *El Hombre de Hoy*, 91.

122. Sobrino, *Jesús en América Latina*, 60.

123. Gutiérrez, *Teología de la Liberación*, 371.

124. Gutiérrez, *Teología de la Liberación*, 375. Sobrino emphasizes this notion of the poor through the oppressed and crucified people.

125. Gutiérrez, *Teología de la Liberación*, 382.

126. Sobrino, *Jesús en América Latina*, 60.

127. Sobrino, *Jesús en América Latina*, 233.

128. Sobrino, *Jesús en América Latina*, 106.

129. "The notion '*crucified people*' developed by Ignacio Ellacuría emphasizes the specific negativity of reality where great majorities suffer historical death in the active and historical deprivation of life. As injustice takes over the reality, Sobrino adds "that the crucified people are also denied a chance to speak and even to be called by name, which means they are denied their own existence" (Sobrino, *Fuera de los Pobres*, 20–21).

crushed for our iniquities . . . he will bring salvation to all, including his victimizers, because he has borne their iniquities."[130]

The equation between the crucified people and the suffering Yahweh happens when the reality of the poor is equated to the level of suffering servant of Yahweh[131] as a basis for understanding the crucified people as the place of salvation: "this crucified people is the historical continuation of Yahweh's servant, who the sin of the world continues to deprive of any human decency, and from whom the powerful of this world continue to rob everything, taking everything away, even life, especially life."[132] If Jesus reveals God, then the theology of the crucified people amplifies this notion by asserting that the poor reveal Jesus. In that sense, the poor is renewed in light of the suffering servant. The crucified people "includes not only the servant as victim . . . but also the servant's saving the history: historical soteriology . . . which is more alien to the theologies of other latitudes and difficult even to imagine if the reality is not seen."[133]

Salvation, the invitation to enter into the world of the poor, allows us to see what happens and distinguishes between the proper action and the process that reaches justice. "Salvation is dialectical, and at times it is dual. It takes place in opposition to other realities and processes, and even in conflict with them."[134] Salvation is then a conscious option against poverty, the recovering of humanity and the struggle for peace and freedom where death and oppression is present. It does not happen automatically in "the reality of the sin . . . not only from without, but also from within"[135] with hope in the face of the immense reality of suffering.

> We will do so by understanding salvation in relation to the poor and by seeing in the poor a locus and a potential for salvation. Although it may sound defiant, the formulation *extra paupers nulla salus* is indeed quite modest. Strictly speaking, we are not saying that without them there is no salvation—although we do presuppose that in the poor there is always "something" of salvation. What we aim to do, ultimately, is to offer hope, in spite of

---

130. Sobrino, *Fuera de los Pobres*, 22.
131. Sobrino, *Jesucristo Liberador*, 45.
132. Sobrino, *Principle of Mercy*, 51.
133. Sobrino, *Principle of Mercy*, 51.
134. Sobrino, *Fuera de los Pobres*, 84.
135. Taking on the reality of sin is the task to grasp the burden of things which includes an active exercise of promotion of life inside of the reality, living among the crucified people. Sobrino, *Fuera de los Pobres*, 18–19, 85.

everything. *From the world of the poor and the victims can come salvation for a gravely ill civilization.*[136]

The crucified people endure in hope, a hope that humanizes[137] the others to see salvation.[138] The crucified people are an access to change minds, affecting myths about the poor[139] and give the opportunity to turn back from arrogance. Salvation implies conversion[140] and, in the encounter with God in the poor, absolution takes place in terms of liberation. Forgiveness is a gift that formally brings the benefit of being conscious[141] to embrace the crucified people. It is the "historical essence of the Church of Jesus . . . a preferential option (that) re-creates the Church[142] into the road of grace and mercy.

For the crucified people, conversion is also a change of mentality that happens, like the disciples of Jesus, in the sense of "opening the eyes"[143] to resist the cruel and oppressive reality and to continue in the struggle with hope.

136. Sobrino, *Fuera de los Pobres*, 75.

137. "There will be no salvation or humanization if redemptive impulses to not emerge from that world of the poor . . . salvation and humanization will come only 'with' the poor. 'Without' the poor there will come not salvation that is humane" (Sobrino, *Fuera de los Pobres*, 101).

138. The crucified people also offer hope, foolish or absurd, it might be said; because it is the only thing they have left, others argue. But once again, it is there, and it must not be trivialized by other worlds. That it is hope against hope is obvious, but it is also active hope that has shown itself in work and liberation struggles. Sobrino, *Fuera de los Pobres*, 55.

139. The crucified people "challenge our understanding of social, environmental, and religious salvation in a world that does not belong to poor people but creates them; and they help to unmask the dogma that a poor people can only receive but not give—which is vitally important to keep the affluent societies from falling into arrogance and dehumanization" (Sobrino, *Fuera de los Pobres*, 23).

140. Sobrino, *The True Church*, 84. Sobrino's conversion to the reality of suffering in Latin America is described as an "awakening from the sleep of inhumanity" in the encounter with the truly poor, the "crucified people" who face daily death and the cross. The poor in Latin America have "hope . . . an active hope which unloosens creativity at all levels of human existence" calling to conversion. See, Sobrino, *The Principle of Mercy*, 4-7.

141. Sobrino, *The Principle of Mercy*, 92-93.

142. Sobrino, *Fuera de los Pobres*, 42-43.

143. "The disciples . . . need to *open their eyes* . . . to disembark their minds and resist the attacks of the mentality endowed with an alleged divine support and even deferred by its own victims . . . In order to penetrate the secret spaces of the kingdom of God, Jesus shares parables in two parts: fist, through the parables . . . you

The Kingdom of God and the Anti-Kingdom

Latin American Christology considers the relationship between the poor and the kingdom of God, but it also pays attention to the God of the kingdom.[144] The kingdom is the historical response of God to the concrete reality of Israel's suffering and its relevance is that Jesus gives continuity to the "tradition of hope for the oppressed."[145] The prophetic characteristic of the kingdom, recognized by the disciples in the resurrection, raised the confession of Jesus as "the Christ (the) mediator of God's word in history . . . who shows how to carry out the Father's will, but he does not himself exhaust the totality of mediation (because it) is the Spirit who sets history in motion and is the Lord and giver of life."[146] The Trinitarian action in the kingdom of God prevents the reduction of God in Jesus' activity. The kingdom is an inclusive reality where contact with "Christ's mediation (affirms) mediation of the Spirit."[147]

Jesus' prophetic ministry caused political tensions among dominant groups. The necessity to change the oppressors and the motivation to continue in their struggle in behalf of the oppressed depicts the dialectical presence of the kingdom. Conversion was "hope among the poor and radical change of conduct among the oppressors."[148] To the oppressed, Jesus preached hope and acted in love. To the religious and civil authorities, Jesus preached the urgency of change. The religious leaders were perplexed while confronted with the lack of solidarity. Jesus perceived the contradiction between the use of God's name and the inhuman conditions of the masses. Conscious of the socio-political tensions

---

will understand polemic orientations but revealing and accentuating conflict; second, consists in the explanation and interpretation of everything said parabolically, made in private to his disciples (See Mark 4,33–34)" (Segundo, *El Hombre de Hoy*, 207).

144. Segundo, *El Hombre de Hoy*, 95–96.

145. Sobrino, *Jesucristo Liberador*, 105. Continuity is revealed through God's love and through Jesus' palpable human actions of love. Jesus' actions based in love and compassion made unique his ministry and, at the same time, gave continuity to the hope of people.

146. Sobrino, *True Church and the Poor*, 42.

147. Sobrino, *True Church and the Poor*, 43.

148. That is the conception of *metanoia* and is related to the radical change that will propitiate change in the poor and in the oppressor. In that way, conversion is good news to the oppressed and to the oppressor because the last one hears the prophetical voice in relation to the poor inviting them to build peace and solidarity. See Sobrino, *Jesucristo Liberador*, 108–10.

and the absence of solidarity, Jesus confronted and disrupted that absurd indifference and apathy.

Religious authorities, accustomed to the practice of sanctification following the laws of purification, were urged to change their mentality and "to pass from the oppressive security of the letter to the liberating insecurity having to opt, even before God's word, for the poor."[149] Religious leaders refused to turn to the poor and refused to recognize the good news as good until they became Jesus' political adversaries.[150] They justified the oppression by using the law as God's mediation, and they allied themselves with powerful authorities in order to remove Jesus from the scene. Their association with the civil authorities[151] had the intention to develop a political- religious judgment to avoid being charged for Jesus' crucifixion. The political element in the religious machinery did not stop the kingdom of God; rather, it endured by demonstrating publicly Jesus' love for the poor until he was crucified.

The crucified was later recognized as the God of the kingdom which is for the Latin American Christology the center that gives "sense to (Jesus' ministry. Jesus) rests (in God but, at the same time, God) does not leave Jesus to rest"[152] because of the urgency of liberation. In the gospels, Jesus centers his life in the kingdom[153] by communicating the newness of liberation and opening its centrality in hope[154] as anticipation of life for the poor. But even though the kingdom renews hope, absence and neglect take place especially today in Latin America. Absence, the "anti-kingdom . . . the certainly not"[155] where structural and personal sin prevails becomes dialectic to the kingdom of God. But the logic of the

---

149. Segundo, *El Hombre de Hoy*, 196. "Solo la conversión (a la causa del pobre) podrá hacer lógicamente que la llegada del reino sea—mediante el cambio de valores- ocasión de alegría, evangelio. Dentro de este círculo . . . *reino, pobres* y *buena noticia*, se mueve lo que podríamos llamar el contenido profético de la predicación de Jesús . . . su mensaje y la clave de su actitud, de su ministerio y aún de su muerte" (129).

150. Segundo, *El Hombre de Hoy*, 131, 134.

151. Segundo, *El Hombre de Hoy*, 145. Sobrino accentuates that Jewish leader invoked other divinities—the civil authorities—to eliminate the mediator. Sobrino, *Jesús en América Latina*, 185, 190.

152. Sobrino, *Jesucristo Liberador*, 95.

153. "For Jesus Gpd is seen in a wider reality: 'the kingdom of God'" (Sobrino, *Jesucristo Liberador*, 97).

154. Sobrino, *Fuera de los Pobres*, 110.

155. Sobrino, *Fuera de los Pobres*, 113. Also Sobrino, *Jesucristo Liberador*, 165.

kingdom of God remains in its partiality and defense of the poor and therefore against the idols[156] of the anti-kingdom.

Latin American Christology recovers the important role of the historic Jesus and the kingdom of God. Jesus preached and lived love consciously so that love was opposed to the anti-kingdom. The danger of the cross and the resurrection did not change Jesus' partiality for the oppressed; rather, it has remained central to this conflictive history. The event of resurrection as liberation encourages oppressed people to experience life even where death establishes its conditions. Resurrection is a symbol of collective hope that people start to experience; resurrection of the cross is how God continues to liberate and move the kingdom today. The cross continues to be negative because it deprives people of the minimum of life and that reveals that God is not compatible with idolatry. Therefore, Latin American Christology works to demystify the reality of death by challenging people to affirm in which God they believe and in which they do not. For that reason, the demystification of the image of Christ[157] calls to the commitment to follow the God of life.

Reflections on the Tracks of Latin American Christology

Latin American Christology has its roots in the arrival of Christianity in the fifteenth century. This Christology proclaimed a celestial and monarchical Christ. At the end of the eighteenth century and the beginning of the nineteenth century, independent movements challenged the Church. Liberal leaders and elites had the courage to promote immigration. The intention was dual; first, to promote religious freedom and second, to reach development. Protestantism did not change the established Christology but preached Christ. Protestants who migrated from Europe remained for years serving their parishioners. Missionary movement in the nineteenth century preached to emphasize the spiritual Christ and call for moral change and life regeneration, which challenged Roman Catholic hegemony. Poverty continued to be a constant in Latin America especially among people located at the bottom of the social structure. In that context, Latin

---

156. Sobrino, *La Fe en Jesucristo*, 131. The idolatrous structure reveals a conflictive struggle between God, whose mediator is Jesus and its mediation the kingdom, and the idols of death, whose mediators are the oppressors and their mediation the anti-kingdom.

157. Latin American Christology accepts that the resurrected (Christ) is not other that the crucified (Jesus). Sobrino, *Jesús en América Latina*, 60.

American Christology had the merit to consider the poor as the place of God and to promote a Soteriological Christology.

The Methodological Rupture

Latin American Christology uses hermeneutical tools to interpret the historical presence and action of Christ, as eschatological event, making possible salvation in the reality of the poor. Christ in the Gospels is the profession of faith and theological interpretation[158] from the communities of faith. "Jesus of Nazareth arrives always already interpreted by people or groups interested in him."[159] Christology returns to Jesus of Nazareth to affirm that Christ is not other than Jesus. This first circularity brings a methodological point of departure where Jesus of Nazareth becomes a foundation. Without demystifying the person and the work of Christ, Latin American Christology understands that Jesus wants to de-pacify (despacificar) the reality of oppression by moving people to faithful actions of love.[160] Liberation theology does not question faith but puts emphasis on the way the good news are proclaimed. In doing so, liberation theology criticizes the nature of knowledge (epistemology) that is not in tune with people's suffering. This implies to know the implications of such suffering without the need to fix what was wrong but being aware of it implications to find new ways to act. It implies a knowledge conversion that brings consciousness in all dimensions that impact life.

Hermeneutics has also helped to reinterpret the notion of salvation. Salvation is not only developed towards a spiritual and future event; it is also an immediate reality happening in the world of the poor.[161] Latin American Christology insists that the specific context in which Christ was revealed helps to better understand his mission that now is contained in the scriptures. The actual context of the poor is, for Latin American Christology, theological. A second circularity in this Christology focuses in the actual reality which illuminates the understanding of the scriptures. It refreshes the scriptures making possible a contextual message. Then,

---

158. The evangelists read and interpreted Jesus' life in a religious perspective. Boff, *Pasión de Cristo*, 30.

159 Segundo, *El Hombre de Hoy*, 32.

160. Jesus trusted, thanked, and prayed the Father knowing the kindness which defined the ministry of love and service. Sobrino, *Jesucristo Liberador*, 186–88.

161. The poor helps to understand the scriptures and teaches to think. Solberg, *Compelling Knowledge*, 52–56

the reading of the scriptures will always be new given its continuity[162] with the ministry of Jesus creating and promoting hope, communion, and liberation; and its discontinuity while interpreting all these events anew from specific contexts.

Latin America Christology, considering the reality of suffering as the world where Jesus is incarnated, affirms that it is possible to know Jesus through the poor. The poor as the reality where God is incarnated is a scandalous presence[163] linking incarnation to the present reality. This movement sets actuality to the promise of the kingdom of God. Jesus brings salvation to the poor in concrete historical realities; the poor reveal Jesus and become the place of salvation especially for oppressors. The third circularity grounded in change is at the heart of the message of the kingdom of God. Jesus preached change knowing the exigencies of love of the God of the Kingdom. For Latin American Christology, the connection between the message of the kingdom of God and the God of the kingdom is the fourth circularity. It connects the proclaimed event of Jesus in history that increases the demand to choose among the God that has come closer or other idols; it intensifies the ministry of love and hope Jesus developed among and for the oppressed.

The goal of the methodological rupture of Latin American Christology is the liberation of the poor. In doing so, it takes a position against all images of Christ that has largely been used to oppress or alienate. Latin American Christology wants to de-idolize (desidolatrizar) Christ by identifying the idols hidden behind the name. The novelty, in relation to traditional Christologies, is that this Christology recovers Jesus of Nazareth to reinterpret the faith in Christ where Jesus has been absent propitiating oppression. Jesus' presence breaks the ideological character of Christ while moving to express that Christ is known through Jesus.

The Novelty of Liberation

Latin American Christology, articulated soteriologically, considers the oppression of the poor as the urgent reality calling for liberation. It reflects more deeply in Jesus' humanity in order to find sources for the historic liberation of the poor. The contextual reality of suffering in Latin America offers relevance to a Christology that aims to change that

---

162. Sobrino, *Jesús en América Latina*, 112–13.
163. Sobrino, *Jesús en América Latina*, 44.

reality. The return to Jesus and the connection between his ministry and the reality of suffering uncovers the use of the diverse images of Christ that justify oppression. The Christ from the Gospels is Jesus whose image liberates the oppressed of his time and today. Recovering the historical image of Christ means to meet a Christ that accomplishes salvation and liberates many in a historical way. Christ, the liberator, is revealed through Jesus' actions revealing the arrived kingdom. Calling Jesus the Christ means recognizing the power of love and kindness that changes social structures of his time, makes possible the kingdom of God announced, and lived in a prophetic manner. Jesus recovers the prophetic line, a messianic character emerging as liberator which gives sense to his death on the cross and to his resurrection.

The cross brings salvation[164] strengthening the profession of faith. Understanding the historical reasons of Jesus' death, as the highest expression of love that challenged a socio-religious structure of purity and law, the cross becomes a scandal. It is scandalous because ending Jesus' life is like putting an end to many others. It continues the repressive act against people today–history continues to produce crosses.[165] People hanging on the crosses today are the actual presence of Christ in history[166] but, in this actually history, resurrection makes it possible to verify salvation. Salvation is understood through the presence of Jesus in the history of the crucified people while verifying his resurrection through his following. The crucified people of today make present the body of Christ in history giving continuity to Jesus' passion for the world and bring the exigency of conversion. The crucified people are a theological place and the hopeful church[167] awakening from indifference and the

---

164. "We move here in two levels. At the deeper level of faith affirming that the cross brings salvation; and at the reflective/theological level to demonstrate how the cross offers salvation" (Sobrino, *Jesucristo Liberador*, 285).

165. Sobrino, *Jesucristo Liberador*, 298–99.

166. "Liberation Christology uses the language *crucified people* as factual. It does not only means poverty but death. As a historical-ethical fact, death is infringed by unjust structures. As a religious fact the cross reminds of faith, sin, grace, condemnation, or salvation" (Sobrino, *Jesucristo Liberador*, 322).

167. In the new configuration of the church in the poor, the historical Jesus is the methodological beginning and the poor becomes theological place. All these themes brought challenge to Sobrino before the Roman Catholic Church. After a process of dialogue, the Congregation for the Doctrine of Faith extended a notification in October 2006 expressing notable discrepancies with "Jesucristo Liberador, Lectura Histórico-Teológica de Jesús de Nazaret" and "Fe en Jesucristo: Ensayo desde las víctimas." In March 2007, Sobrino replied, through his superior, the notification giving reasons

scandalous of unjust deaths. The hope of the crucified people is the hope of God against injustices.

Liberation theology, too much engaged with the liberation of the poor, is criticized for its adapting in a more successful way reflections from Christian Western theology "the mechanisms of dependency are perpetuated in repetitive models . . . as sort of resurrection paradigm of the Western style of obsessive classification and moralization of ideas and behaviors."[168]

---

why the two books are not incompatible with the faith of the Church. Sobrino ratified his Christology affirms that there is "no salvation outside the poor," echoing his actual Christology. Congregation for the Doctrine of the Faith, *Notification on the Works of Father Jon Sobrino, SJ*.

168. Althaus-Reid, *From Feminist Theology*, 127.

3

Christologies from Latin American Women's/Feminists' Perspective

THE VALUES AND VIRTUES of the Latin American Christology are relevant to the reality of the continent. It is true that poverty is a growing reality where the poor are dehumanized, but the concept of poor has universalized and made it difficult to identify and see the ones who suffer the most among the poor. When establishing a hermeneutic circle for the liberation of the poor, to which poor does this possibility refer? When the crucified people assume the place of the church, what are the distinctions and the links between them and the institutional church? When Latin America is defined as victimized reality, where are the lines of presence and resistance produced by the popular religiosity within their own Roman Catholic Church?

Brief Review of Latin American Feminisms

Feminist movements developed during the seventies and eighties throughout Latin America. From Vargas' perspective, women addressed the particular and heterogeneous realities as they questioned traditional practices[1] through contact with feminists and popular urban movements of women. The particular view of women questioned the multiple subordinations experienced in their own contexts. Early in the struggle, two dynamics took place, the presence of feminists dedicated to academia and that of working women in contact with militant women involved in

---

1. Feminists questioned women's location in society and social and sexual practices inviting to change women's subordination and exclusion in the public and private spheres. The popular urban movement initiated its public activities conscious of the polarization of their roles, confronting and questioning the private. The side of women that joined more formal spaces of political participation questioned the autonomous organization within their political parties or unions. Vargas, "Los Feminismos Latinoamericanos," 1–2.

popular movements that nourished production and knowledge. The feminist movement made "visible the reality of subordination of women (and) produced epistemological breaks and the construction of new paradigms and new interpretative guidelines of the reality."[2]

In 1975, the United Nations declared the International Women's Year establishing "an important milestone for a cross-linking of women and an awareness of the explosiveness of the issue of women's rights also in Christian circles."[3] The seventies awaked women in church and society. Virginia Vargas, a Peruvian sociologist, feminist, and activist, affirms that feminists explored women's fragmented and constructed identity, questioning their roles in society. Feminists challenged the patriarchal capitalist system that, using diverse economic means, subjugated men and women, reinforcing a society based on economic power. In the capitalist system, women in the labor market faced collateral consequences: a) women's domestic unpaid work was assessed at its market value, reinforcing the myth of women as supplementary agent, and b) the capitalist system exploits men but the most to women who also suffered abuse, was less paid, and the first to be fired. The control of women's sexuality and their reproductive capacity was also neglected in the division of work.[4]

The religious-patriarchal system reinforced women's condition. Women's functions in the church faced religious subjugation. The use of the scriptures emphasized the notion of *deficient feminine nature* based on Jewish, Greek, and Patristic theology affirming submission. Women acquired their independence in reference to men.[5] The woman question, addressed by José Carlos Mariátegui and reflected later by the Communist party in Peru, delineates this religious submission and proposes an economic and social class struggle as the solution. The Communist Party of Peru, in its critical reflection of the Peruvian society during the sixties and seventies, asserted that in "the nascent Peruvian feminist movement . . . the woman question is part of the human question."[6] It is confirmed t that peasant women, the majority in the population, were destined to suffer social repression and exploitation under feudal roots of

2. Vargas, "Los Feminismos Latinoamericanos," 3.
3. Eckholt, "Creative on New Ways," 518.
4. Vargas, *Feminismo*, 7–8.
5. CCCP, *Marxism*, 3–4.
6. CCCP, *Marxism*, 19.

production and were confined to patriarchal traditions, having less access to education in the nineteenth century. It is also confirmed that women in cities were quite encouraged by the effects of modernization while participating in worker's unions, but they did not have tools to analyze exploitation and submission through the lenses of economic and politic realities. Seeing the absence of gender theories, the Communist Party proposed the political connection of worker women to the proletarian feminist organizations[7] mobilizing and organizing them in searching for their own political emancipation.

One has to take into account that the oppressed condition of women will not be overcome through political, economic emancipation or denouncing classist oppression. The economic aspect, attending social class struggles, will not solve women's oppression. The patriarchal component historically played a strong role in affirming power relations and determining women's condition. The social structure and economics were relevant components, but women needed to analyze, deconstruct, and critically reconstruct their identities from the sexual, structural, and racial matrixes. Economic emancipation was not enough; women faced a double oppression in the patriarchal ideology that controls "over two basic aspects of women, their sexuality –as capacity of reproduction and pleasure– and their labor force based in material property and the control of means of production."[8] The historical reasons denying equal and full participation of women in church and society were enough to perceive the inconsistency and danger of patriarchal capitalism. Feminist scholars predicted, during the period of military dictatorship, how democracy contributed to modernization by using political transactions including women's slavery. Women were recognized politically but did not receive any real benefit in decision making in the redistribution of power.[9]

The close relationship between patriarchalism and capitalism urgently moved women to re-define their status that was determined along class and race lines and by father or husband. Paradoxically, even women living the privileges of bourgeois reality did not have the privilege to choose. Economic autonomy had nothing to do with power over

---

7. The Communist Party of Peru distinguishes three tendencies of feminism: bourgeois feminism, the petty-bourgeois feminism, and proletariat feminism. The last one understands feminism as essentially revolutionary and adheres to efforts in the proletariat movement. CCCP, *Marxism*, 25, 26.

8. Vargas, *Feminismo*, 2.

9. Vargas, "Feminismos Latinoamericanos," 4.

their reproductive and labor capacity.[10] Feminists started using private spheres to attend to their personal relationships of power, sharing their life histories, and being more conscious of the power to decide over their own lives. Women explored political and economic policies that manipulated and used gender to perpetuate control, submission, and exploitation. The struggle of women in general and those of African and of Indigenous and aboriginal origin[11] in particular, opened doors to new analysis of machismo in specific contexts of women[12] through international, national, regional, and local networks. New topics like women's rights, reproductive health, and sexual reproductive rights became concerns of non-governmental organizations, universities, and governmental institutions. There were groups of women who remained autonomous[13] and used their insight to be critical of institutionalized practices. Women applied gender relations as a strategy to challenge the socioeconomic hegemonic patriarchal project. The dynamics of transformation slowly reflected adjustments and new periods reshaping agendas. Human rights, ecology, consumerism, globalization, racism, multiculturalism, gender justice, economic justice, and reproductive and sexual rights came to the table to democratize gender relations.[14] Gender experiences characterized by poverty, race, and classism continued to resist the patriarchal capitalist system.

The Walk of Latin American Feminist Theology

To navigate Latin American Christology from the women's perspective it is critical to consider some events in history. The sixties and seventies exploded with the presence of popular movements which shocked the political waters of countries living under military dictatorships.

10. Vargas, *Feminismo*, 9.

11. The racial component within Latin American feminist scholars arose in the late 80s and 90s with the influence of Black Women's liberation in Africa and in the USA as consequence of the civil rights movement in the 60s. Black women struggling against racism in the USA were suspicious of black male superiority and the intention to determine the policy of progress of black people without female participation in decision making and leadership. Murray, "The Liberation of Black Women," 232.

12. In the 90s, feminism was expressed by spaces of identity of black, lesbians, indigenous, and young women affirming their collective consciousness. Vargas, "Feminismos Latinoamericanos," 4.

13. Vargas, "Feminismos Latinoamericanos," 5.

14. Vargas, "Feminismos Latinoamericanos," 9–10.

Reformist plans addressed issues of land, education, health, and work in an effort to break the gap between social classes characterized by enormous economic disparities. Workers from the middle and poor classes organized local communities and some joined revolutionary movements, especially in Central America, in a common search for justice. Dictators repressed these movements violently. Liberation theology pointed out to injustice implicating the economic capitalist system, especially during the seventies.

Educational organizations linked to the Roman Catholic Church were also organized to promote dialogue, ecumenical interaction, and theological education. As example, the Centro Ecumênico de Evanelização e Capacitação e Asessoria founded in São Leopoldo, Brasil in 1973; the Instituto Bartolomé de las Casas founded in Lima, Peru in 1974; the Departamento Ecuménico de Investigaciones–DEI in Costa Rica created in 1976, and the Centro Ecuménico Diego de Medellín in Chile in 1982. These theological training centers developed education with emphasis on human dignity during dictatorship time in the continent.

Latin American feminist theology began to reflect on questions of justice specifically from the women's point of view. Using a hermeneutics of suspicion, women analyzed the specific sociological and economic reality of poor women, asserting that poverty and economic oppression were ideologically connected to patriarchy. They also recognized that poor as a concept hid and did not change the conditions of oppression of women in patriarchal societies. Suspicion played a key role in women's liberation by questioning theology, sociology, economy, education, and other key fields. Elsa Tamez urged women to accept their theological task to contribute as female agents who are "part of the broad collective subject (meaning men and women of the oppressed classes, races and cultures that) had not been adopted or systematized or put to use."[15]

The gender theory developed in Western countries was a critical tool to analyze women's conditions prompting dialogue between first-world and third-world feminist theologians thus nourishing Latin American Feminist Theology.[16] Latin American women theologians started to participate in international organizations like the Ecumenical Association of Third World Theologians (EATWOT), founded in 1976, which expressed concern for the lack of attention to gender issues in Third World

15. Tamez, "La Mujer como Sujeto Histórico," 63.
16. Aquino and Tamez, *Teología Feminista Latinoamericana*, 13.

theologies. But Third World women theologians developed their own way of doing theology which was respected by EATWOT leaders.[17]

> This proposal was accepted by the EATWOT leaders, and a four-stage process was planned: national, regional, and intercontinental meetings of Third World feminists. These took place in 1985 and 1986 . . . These were to be followed by a world consultation that would bring the Third World women theologians into a new stage of dialogue with First World feminist theologians. This was delayed as women in each region began to intensify their own regional organizing for meetings and publications. The world consultation finally took place in December 1994 in Costa Rica, bringing together forty-five women theologians from fourteen countries.[18]

Historical and Formative Encounters of Latin American Feminist/Women Theologians

Before the global consultation at the end of the 1970s, Latin American women theologians participated in encounters promoted by Third World Feminist theologians. After the Third General Conference of Latin American Bishops met in Puebla, Mexico in January 1979, women theologians gathered in October the same year in the significant event called "Mujer Latinoamericana, Iglesia y Teología."[19] This event, sponsored by the Mexican-based *Women for Dialogue*,[20] helped to discuss feminist theology and the traditional church structures. Women understood that traditional church structures failed to consider seriously the relevance of women's theological and pastoral action. The church continued to oppress and dominate women *"The church is a patriarchal structure dominated by men over women . . . Women do not participate at the decision-making level in the church. Furthermore, hierarchical, masculine church structures serve as a model for the oppressive male-female relationships found throughout Latin American society where men dictate, in terms binding of faith and conscience, what women should believe and practice."*[21]

17. Ruether, *Women and Redemption*, 242.
18. Ruether, *Women and Redemption*, 242–43.
19. Aquino and Tamez, *Teología Feminista Latinoamericana*, 46.
20. Ress, "Feminist Theologians Challenge Churches," 386.
21. Ress, "Feminist Theologians Challenge Churches." The author uses part of the final statement edited by *Mujeres para el Diálogo* in 1981, which is highlighted in italic.

The epistemological frame of suspicion added the praxis of liberation to denounce the omission of women's vision in liberation theology and invited a consideration of women's theological perspective.

Aware of their constitutive presence within liberation theology, women addressed the issue of women's subjugation challenging liberation theology to focus on women as specific subjects of the marginalized continent. In July 1983, the second Latin American Feminist Conference in Lima, Peru declared that

> while liberation theologians recognized that women are marginalized within society as *poor people*, they do not address patriarchal structures as such, either within society as a whole or within church structures. It is imperative that liberation theologians actively challenge the structure of patriarchy in both their own practice and their methodology, and make a specific option for women among the poor and oppressed.[22]

The option for the poor did not focus on gender oppression. Male liberation theologians resisted seeing women as singular subjects within the marginalized poor and the urgency of their emancipation and change of the patriarchal structures which resulted in the split between liberation theologians and feminist liberation theologians. The Latin American Conference on Theology from the Perspective of Women in Buenos Aires, Argentina from October 30 to November 3, 1985 reunited twenty-eight women from Latin America and the Caribbean. It was occasion to search women's treasure in doing theology from experiences, color, communities, and realities.[23] As a result, women's experiences became the method for theology. Women's daily life, faithfully interpreted, changed analytical tools used in a patriarchal manner giving "birth to something closer to life, something more densely packed with meaning (to topics like) the image of God, the incarnation, the experience of God, the Trinity, community, the body, suffering and joy, conflict and silence, the playful and the political, tenderness and beauty."[24] The decision to continue with the communitarian and relational legacy drove women to develop concrete and contextual theologies characterized by a spirituality of celebration and joy. Women's realities mutually enriched their theological reflections; their diverse experiences moved women to particular contexts where

---

22. Ress, "Feminist Theologians Challenge Churches," 387–88.
23. "Final Statement," 205.
24. "Final Statement," 207.

relationships were nourished in concrete realities where freedom was absent. Women also appreciated sense of humor as part of their spirituality and as a common gift that reoriented their view of history. Women left Buenos Aires carrying the invitation to share their drachma with other women and with members of the EATWOT.[25]

In December, 1986, theologians from Asia, Africa, and Latin America united in the Third World Women Doing Theology conference in Oaxtepec, Mexico, establishing common roots for doing theology in the Third World context. The diversity of the participants reaffirmed their renewed consciousness about their "own strength to modify the relations of domination in the church and society."[26] The topics focused on the reality of oppression of women, their spiritualties, their role in church, women and Bible, and Christology.

> The liberating process happened differently in the three continents. In Latin America, women organize themselves around survival strategies. In Africa, the rebirth of women takes place in their struggle to overthrow the oppressive elements in traditional African cultures and religions and the evils of colonialism. In Asia, the struggle is centered in discovering the pride of being woman, in building womanhood and humane communities, and in fighting against political, economic, and sexual injustices.[27]

A common sense in this developing spirituality was characterized by compassion and solidarity in the restoration of human dignity. The rejection of patriarchy gives space to highlight "those neglected elements that portray women as individuals in their own right as well as God's coworkers and agents of life."[28] The promotion of women's active participation in church and society addressed Christology

> By reflecting on the incarnation . . . we have come to realize the need to contextualize our Christology in the oppressed and painful realities of our continents . . . In Latin America, where poverty and oppression often give rise to a tendency to use religion to reinforce a passive and fatalistic attitude to life, Christology is necessarily connected with the preferential option for the

---

25. "Final Statement," 208.
26. Aquino and Tamez, *Teología Feminista Latinoamericana*, 48.
27. "Final Document," 185–86.
28. "Final Document," 187.

poor. In short, to Christoligize means to be committed to the struggle for a new society.[29]

The method of acting compassionately in order to re-discover new expressions in the Christian faith was the emphasis in 1993 women's formative encounter called "Espiritualidad para la vida: Mujeres contra la Violencia." Focused on women's attitudes against violence while theologians proposed ways to reflect, discuss, and practice life differently. Their own critical profile distanced them from liberation theology. Gender categories as ways to know brought theologians to marginal women's movements to pay attention to

> methodological categories like race, sex/gender, and social class, in the articulation of the specifics in theology like Black feminist theology or indigenous theology, in the continuing dialogue with feminist theologians from Asia, Africa and Black and Latina theologians from the United States, in developing intercultural and interreligious studies advancing the critical and feminist reconstruction of ethics, esthetics, hermeneutics and other related topics of systematic theology.[30]

Moving themselves from the point of seeking an identity as oppressed, poor and faithful women,[31] Latin American theologians recognized themselves as new subjects of action and spirituality with wisdom to nourish theology. As theology is a second step, it follows "contemplation and praxis"[32] in a very dialectic way. Women are aware of their social location as source of the problems to be examined and source of knowledge (epistemology) to act. This became a communal approach to reread the scriptures. It moved women's attention to interpret contextually women's liberation and turning the biblical feminist hermeneutics into a useful tool for doing theology in the context of women in Latin America.

---

29. "Final Document," 188.
30. Aquino and Tamez, *Teología Feminista Latinoamericana*, 49–50.
31. Tepedino, "Feminist Theology," 165.
32. Aquino, *Our Cry For Life*, 113.

Latin American Feminist Hermeneutics

The process of consciousness that feminist theologians and women leaders experienced for twenty-five years[33] was a process[34] of sharing and doing theology, rereading the Bible,[35] and interpreting it in the light of their experience in their socio-political realities in the seventies. Protestant communities encouraged the popular reading of the Bible while the ecclesial base communities promoted the reading of the Bible from the perspective of the poor.[36] The discrimination of women awakened them to be subjects of their own liberation and consequently of the theological production.[37] The promotion of women's personal and global liberation occurred by networking with feminists like *Mujeres para el Diálogo* in Mexico and *Talitha Kumi* in Peru. They were not aware of inclusive language and the contact with first-world feminists was minimal. For Christian women, it was difficult to identify as feminists given the negative religious stigma feminist couldn't trust theology and "women theologians rejected any feminist demand that did not articulate the economic global liberation of the society."[38]

Following the liberation theology link between the exodus and the historical Jesus, women theologians were able to reflect on equal gender relations and the economic relations[39] conscious of poor women's conditions. Rereading of the Bible had to offer a memory of the past[40] to validate the transformation of the present. During the revolutionary movements in the eighties in Central America, the Frente Sandinista triumphed in Nicaragua while the continent experienced the increase of the external debt. After the Congregation for the Doctrine of the Faith questioned Boff's militant ecclesiology, the hierarchy of the Roman Catholic Church punished him to a year of silence[41] in 1984. The

---

33. Tamez, "Hermenéutica Feminista," 43.

34. Tamez considers three milestones as determinant and coexisting experiences that consolidated the Latin America feminist hermeneutic: Mexico 1979, Argentina 1985, and Brazil 1993. Aquino and Tamez, *Teología Feminista Latinoamericana*, 81.

35. Aquino and Tamez, *Teología Feminista Latinoamericana*, 80.

36. Tamez, "Hermenéutica Feminista Latinoamericana," 47.

37. Tamez, "Hermenéutica Feminista Latinoamericana," 47–48.

38. Tamez, "Hermenéutica Feminista Latinoamericana," 48.

39. Tamez, "Hermenéutica Feminista Latinoamericana," 49.

40. Tepedino and Brandão, "Women and the Theology of Liberation," 222.

41. Tamez, "Hermenéutica Feminista Latinoamericana," 51.

Roman Catholic hierarchy systematically replaced Bishops in Brazil, Peru, and other countries dismantling the ecclesial base communities. Liberation theologians, recognizing the importance of women in the church, opened dialogue about women's reality, proposing that women's marginalization affected the entire society.[42] During this period of change, women theologians started using inclusive language, metaphors for God, validated women's daily experiences and compassion as part of doing theology. The "affection praxis"[43] brought sensitivity in praxis enabling women to be in compassionate solidarity with other men and women who are God's image.[44]

The selection of the sacred scriptures by women was a practice in the ecclesial base communities and local churches in search of the feminine presence of God. Consciously, women analyzed the male-centered structures in theology and rereading of the Bible "through women's eyes (made them) conscious of individuals who are cast aside because of their sex."[45] Grassroots and marginalized women unveiled the sacral-legislative nature of the scriptures understanding that justice and freedom are consequence of their liberation, naming the new meaning of being rebirth in "the Gospel, even when sometimes fidelity to the gospel forces the reader to distance her or himself from the text."[46] Women kept the spirit of liberation while analyzing the "feminization of poverty"[47] during the nineties. The intentional reconstruction of women's role and participation in church helped to affirm social and cultural aspects differing from patriarchal gender constructions. Theologies like "holistic ecofeminismo,"[48] black theology,[49] and Indigenous theologies made use of the impact of 500 years of imperialism. With

---

42. Tamez, "Hermenéutica Feminista Latinoamericana," 51.

43. Tamez, "Hermenéutica Feminista Latinoamericana," 52.

44. Tepedino and Brandão, "Women and the Theology of Liberation," 229.

45. Tamez, "Women's Rereading of the Bible," 179.

46. Tamez, "Women's Rereading of the Bible," 176.

47. This expression describes the composite image of poverty prevailing in North America. That image reflects far more serious situations surely, through the rest of the world. But even in the affluent society of the United States, the composite image of a poor person is female, black, without a high school diploma, unmarried, and with at least two children, one of them under six. See, Tepedino and Brandão, "Women and the Theology of Liberation," 228.

48. Aquino and Tamez, *Teología Feminista Latinoamericana*, 95.

49. Aquino and Tamez, *Teología Feminista Latinoamericana*, 97.

new analysis of the neoliberal economic policy in third-world countries, and the minimal government interference in the establishment of free markets, the growth of Pentecostal movements, the control of the Roman Catholic hierarchy over the ecclesial base communities, the sanctioning to silence of the Brazilian theologian Ivone Gebara in reaction to her critical pronouncement about reproductive rights,[50] the backwardness of Protestant and Catholic male leaders in failing to support feminist theology, the relegation of Protestant women in theological training, and the economic enslavement of the continent all occurred paradoxically, in a period when feminist theology became solid. Being nourished from gender theories, Latin American feminist hermeneutics promoted dialogue with the growing poor populations[51] and church that excluded women from ordained positions.

The rereading of the gospels focused on the liberating actions of Jesus considering his practice as epistemological criteria. Difficult texts[52] had to be liberated as Timothy and Titus. Their historical and cultural background studied to interpret the text instead of their literal meaning. The use of inclusive language also influenced male discourse and elevated the use of terms like infinite mercy, infinite grace, and mystery to God. Black hermeneutics contributed an emphasis on the ancestral spirituality and their vivid cultural elements. The body and the "cotidiano" became hermeneutical keys to develop a non-sacrificial rereading of the scriptures which raised women's bodies to the level of sacred texts[53] because in them, the divine continues to reveal in hope.

The growing of populations living under poverty and conditions of extreme-poverty moved feminist theologians to include reproductive rights in their agenda in response to the mass sterilization[54] of poor women, especially among Indigenous and African descendants. Sterilization promoted by government legal procedures, used the health system

50. See note 6 in Tamez, "Hermenéutica Feminista Latinoamericana," 56.

51. The Congress of Theology, in Bogotá 1999, addressed this issue through economy, gender, and theology. Tamez, "Hermenéutica Feminista Latinoamericana," 61.

52. Tamez, "Hermenéutica Feminista Latinoamericana" 60.

53. Tamez, "Women's Lives as Sacred Text," 62.

54. Smith, *Conquest, Sexual Violence*, 85. "In Peru the Health Ministry recently issued a public apology for sterilizing 220,000 indigenous people (primarily Quechua and Aymara) without consent during the presidency of Alberto Fujimori . . . During this period, the number of sterilizations increased each year to meet Fujimori's "family planning" targets. The rural villages that were targeted now face a shortage of young people that threatens their future."

to gain control of the population. The Peruvian government's plan suggested sterilization as a tool in the struggle against poverty, but ironically, the reason was the capitalist financial system control under the slogan of family planning.[55] None of the Indigenous women gave consent and were never consulted. The feminization of poverty needed to connect with just economies along with peace.

The plural context of liberation of women required rupture and continuity. Before realities of long years of militarism and internal war where poor and rural women were the most affected, rupture with such practices was an opportunity to bring emerging subjects in the struggle. It needed continuity in relation to justice based, for instance in ecofeminism which epistemology of the daily life opens paths to rebuild relationships of respect in a holistic way between women and nature.[56] The wisdom of reading the scriptures to analyze the culture from Black feminists had the purpose to strengthen relationships with ancestors who are present in each person in the community becoming place of God's presence.[57]

Theologians of African descent interpreted the Bible rejecting race subjugation and affirming their agency before the systematized exclusion.[58] They emphasized beauty, pleasure, and the recovery of the image of God in them.[59]

A particular gift to hermeneutics came from theologians challenging the universal in the concept of poor women. The hermeneutics of disruption, based in culturally determined sexual relationships, challenged the scenario of new and excluded beings. The disruptive and transgressive rereading of the Bible is done by persons with different sexual orientation, in a communitarian process,[60] leading to understanding the cross as the attempt of multiple killings and resurrections.[61] The careful rereading

---

55. In 1977, R. T. Revenholt of the U.S. Agency for International development (US-AID) announced the plan to sterilize a quarter of the world's women because (control was necessary) to maintain the normal operation of U.S. commercial interests around the world. Smith, *Conquest, Sexual Violence*, 80.

56. Gebara, *Intuiciones Ecofeministas*, 40, 42.

57. Silva, "Latin American Feminist Theology," 69.

58. Silva, "Por Caminos y Senderos," 16.

59. Silva, "Por Caminos y Senderos," 17.

60. Althaus-Reid, *From Feminist Theology*, 46.

61. Althaus-Reid, *From Feminist Theology*, 174–76.

of oppressive texts[62] has two moments. First, take distance from the text, in order to second, concentrate on the word that must be impregnated[63] by the experience of the person involved in interpretation.

The intentional selection of texts that liberate is a way to find new meaning in the scriptures. Feminist theologians recognized the *"logos loaned"*[64] that over the centuries did not change power relations; an evangelization that used economy[65] to present the Imperial logos and divine commerce.[66] Its redemption excluded the profane idolatry manipulating the Biblical logos to which, feminist theologians respond as *hermanas*[67] and friends through relations of solidarity and strengthening their daily resurrection.

Christologies from Latin American Women/Feminist Perspective

The Greek system[68] influenced anthropology to continually dislocate gender relationships or to relocate them through one-sided decisions by those who acted as citizens, governed, owned the means of production, determined participation in public and private, and decided who would make decisions. Patriarchalism, infused in all structures of society, was used to determine power dynamics where the elites used strategies of freedom and

---

62. "(Latin American) feminist hermeneutics consolidates more and more. It is a feminist hermeneutics that confronts the Bible as a patriarchal text and disavows interpretations that harm women . . . This feminist hermeneutics Latina American and Caribbean aligns with other feminist exegetes from other continents, share methods, but without neglecting the situation of the great absence which questions and judges for the life of all people" (Tamez, *Bajo Un Cielo sin Estrellas*, 24).

63. Tepedino and Brandão, "Women and the Theology of Liberation," 228.

64. Tamez, *Bajo Un Cielo sin Estrellas*, 23.

65. Grau, "Divine Commerce," 176–77.

66. Grau, "Divine Commerce," 183. Divine commerce refers to redemptive forms of agency not merely understood through Christ's incarnation, death, and resurrection. It extends to the thoughts and acts of those who would imitate such acts of redemption in their own lives.

67. Tamez, *Las Mujeres en el Movimiento de Jesús*, 121.

68. Democracy, according to the Greek understanding, proposes social and political common good in society and supports a structure of masculine aristocracy. Participation is unequal based in the lordship structure that subordinates slaves, barbarians, or women. "The patriarchal Greek democracy is constituted by the exclusion of the 'others', who do not participate in the land but whose work sustains the society" (Schüssler Fiorenza, *Pero Ella Dijo*, 158).

liberty to maintain sophisticated slavery practices and to increase aggressive economic divisions, taxation, and exclusion. The impoverished middle class and the poor class sustained with taxes that structure. Poor women, especially Indigenous and African descendants, did not participate in decision making and its implementation. They have been represented by whites, particularly men or educated women. The represented raised their voices as strategy to be present especially in the religious power systems. Challenge to the patriarchal Greek mentality implied challenge to the notion of God, Christ, salvation, and the church.

Rebuilding Anthropology

Christologies done from a Latin American feminist perspective consider the nature of women within the constructed patriarchal biblical hierarchy and pay attention to ecclesiastic traditions. The scriptures, the source of normative patterns, helped to affirm the subjected women's condition in church and society. The emphasis on women's submission to men (1 Corinthians 11:3) based on the hierarchical structure that woman was made for man (1 Corinthians 11:7b–8) determines that Eve, being created second (echoing Genesis 2:21–23), was the first to transgress. (1 Timothy 2:13–14) This emphasis relocates women to the position of sinners and consequently condemns them to submission and silence (1 Timothy 2:11). Because of Eve's failure, women were not permitted to teach or to have power over men (1 Timothy 2:12); rather, they were taught to reach salvation through conception and motherhood (1 Timothy 2:15).

All these arguments were reinforced along the centuries by Church fathers and theologians who argued subordination of women under male authority. Tertullian (116–225 BC) asserted that Eve was responsible for the sin in the world and consequently for Jesus' death.[69] Origen (185–254 BC) stressed that women are physically, mentally, and morally weak.[70] Augustine (354–430 BC) considered "the image of God in her rational soul, but not in her feminine sexual body (for which women were subordinated to men who) symbolize the excellence of the divine image."[71] Aristotle (384–322 BC) emphasized feminine inferiority and the ideology

---

69. Deifelt, "The Recovery of the Body," 28.
70. Deifelt, "The Recovery of the Body," 29.
71. Bingemer, "La Trinidad," 137.

that women were defective and misbegotten, existing only to function as the receptacle for male seed. [72]

This construction of the condition of women urged anthropological review especially of the narrative of creation. Women demonstrated that creation and the existence of humankind was proof that women's identity is in the image of God. The biological does not define the social roles and functions.[73] The scriptures propose for men and women dual roles, two beings with different and specific characteristics, and inclusive anthropology that distinguishes the being from the acting. The order of creation does not affect the image of God in the female or male person;[74] rather, it affirms that women have "the function to testify God's presence exercising the priesthood of creation"[75] in equal participation of the divine mystery and of being inhabited by the Spirit of grace and life.

As images of God, women, especially poor and marginalized, are sacred spaces where God continues to move and act. Deconstructing the Western Christian tradition that determined sacred in opposition to the profane, salvation takes place in women; what is considered as profane in women is honored by virtue of God's presence. The sinful condition of women by reason of being women just degraded what was precious in God's eyes. María Teresa Porcile, elevating the feminine space[76] to sacred, argues that Eve's body worked as a space of salvation, as a space inhabited by God, opening the place for life in the context of death and exile from paradise.[77] Eve's body is place of grace to which salvation connects to liberate. This is today, the search for continuity of life. In bearing children, the hope and delight expression of existence mobilizes life that triumphs above immobilizing death. Women's bodies are a space for life, participation, and incarnation, where the divine dwells.

---

72. Deifelt, "The Recovery of the Body," 31.

73. See Porcile Santiso, *La Mujer, Espacio de Salvación*, 259–60.

74. "The central point is that both are the image of God; that difference in the way of incarnating the image does not affect the human vocations itself: the mandate is given by God in the same way to male and female; it means that the difference is in the way of being incarnated as an image; that is to say: the difference is in the modality and not in the function, mission or task" (Porcile Santiso, *La Mujer, Espacio de Salvación*, 261).

75. Porcile Santiso, *La Mujer, Espacio de Salvación*, 264.

76. Porcile Santiso, *La Mujer, Espacio de Salvación*, 371.

77. Porcile Santiso, *La Mujer, Espacio de Salvación*, 370.

Why did the subordination of women to men become pervasive using race, gender, social class, and sexuality too? The paradox of anthropology of imposition and exclusion disfigured women's image and determined women's condition as inferior. Conceiving of women as the image of God carefully lights the perception of God revealed through relations of justice and compassion evidenced in Jesus' ministry. The feminine image of God is depicted with metaphors like the wind and the womb engaging the female side of God. Once it is accepted that women have been created in God's image, it opens the way for women to participate more actively in religious life. The feminine images of God[78] is reflected in Jesus' actions toward women helping to explore the relationship of God and poor and marginalized women.

The Womb of Life, Motherly God

The socio-cultural influx in the translation and interpretation of the scriptures moved the approach to God toward an anthropomorphic and religious language determined by the masculine. The engendered image of a warrior and jealous God who governs from heaven moved to a search for the feminine dimension employing a vocabulary to help to theologize God's actions rather than concede sexual attributes. The Trinitarian theology from women's experience and reinterpretation of the Bible moved to find metaphors and concrete figures to express God's maternal and paternal dimensions based on merciful, kindhearted, and compassionate actions. For instance, the figure of God conceiving life comes from the hebrew *rachamim* (the root *rechem* refers to womb) which describes "a woman's body where a child is conceived, nourished, protected, grown and later is given birth."[79] The mysterious intimacy that God develops with the entire creation, the profound connection and caring that the image of conception and nourishment reflect are elements to expand the understanding of justice and salvation. Justice, expressed through

---

78. The feminine and the masculine aspects of God are not simply a product of imagination. They have their roots in Christian imagination, the access to emphasize the masculine or feminine reality of God. In the case of feminist Trinitarian theology, there is an intentional searching for terms and images that transform the patriarchal notion of God, integrating the feminine and the masculine, and inviting to the use of metaphors and images that make possible the creation of a language that helps to portray the divine. See Bingemer, "La Trinidad," 141–42 and 162–63.

79. Bingemer, "La Trinidad," 61.

protection and attentive care, happens through the continued presence and constant fidelity of a God who also bears children.

This figure which enhances God's tenderness giving place to the Spirit of life, the feminine figure of conception, brings an understanding of God feeding the beloved. The picture of a divine "motherly heart"[80] allows us to see and feel a more intimate God, who knows the sufferings of her daughters whose bodies provide what is necessary to sustain life and whose soft arms embrace and protect. An emphasis on merciful motherly-father image, familiar to human beings, highlights life and the strength to sustain it even in the midst of struggles. Faith in the merciful God is a gift because God's presence reminds us of the intimate moments when we were gestated and where we grow and rest. This image helps us see a God present in our entire life and community and helps us to reunite with those who are part of the family. The image offers theological elements in order to reconcile as if encountering with one who is part of our community. Reengaging in a familiar relationship allows us to experience concrete acts of love; we need to trust our experience of God's motherly-fatherly love.

Incarnation—Embodiment

The transcendent, omniscient, and omnipotent attributes of God become real through the incarnated and redemptive Christ that triumphs over sin. The vertical logic that emphasizes relationships characterized by sanctity centers more on the ethics of the law. God's indwelling within creation opens paths for contextualization of Christology. The motivation to address feminine expressions of God intentionally works to change the patriarchal understanding that theologically lacks accessible elements to understand Trinitarian questions. Reconnection of the masculine and feminine drives to identify in the Paraclete, John 14:15, the motherly-fatherly variable missing in the undeniable presence of God when abandonment takes place. The splendorous movement of the Spirit of life, like a gentle breeze or strong wind, refreshes memory teaching her daughters and sons "to murmur the names of the Abba-Father,"[81] a dimension of a warm and affectionate God known and named by Jesus.

---

80. Bingemer, "La Trinidad," 62.
81. Bingemer, "La Trinidad," 74.

God's mystery becomes familiar just because it is in relationship, the presence in the notion of incarnation, of an affectionate and relational God moving people to experience and follow tenderness and solidarity. The concreteness of companionship[82] does not take place by charity alone; rather, it is moved by deep affection that exhorts and invites trust, "there exists a feminine principle in the divinity which makes it possible to believe, worship, and love God not only as the strong Father who creates us and liberates us with his powerful arm, but also as a Mother, full of tenderness, grace, beauty, and receptivity, who accepts the seed of life and feeds it in her womb, so it may become a full being in the light of day."[83]

Jesus' ministry embodied love, and for that Jesus was incarnated. God came to us impregnated with mercy, care, nourishment, tenderness, and empathy for those in suffering. Salvation took on life in a context of oppression and subjugation, and love approached, offering alternatives to suffering. Jesus proclaimed the mystery of God, a proclamation in tension with the expectations of the Messiah who should defeat the oppressor. In order to express God's mystery, Jesus rested in God's hands, developing a close and loving relationship to the point of recognizing God as Abba. The "predominant emphasis on the vertical and an anthropology (that) portrays God as masculine (has) little relationship between this God and Jesus' Abba."[84] Jesus' cultural background did not change the foundation of love which guided Jesus to act differently toward seen as impure. Culturally, women's presence challenged this relational love but women received worthy treatment from Jesus which, in Christology is essential to ministry.

Who Do You Say I Am?

The messianic question (Mark 8:29) and its answer in the Latin American context are, according to Nelly Ritchie, influenced by the situation of dehumanization and victimization of women in Latin American.[85] The question and the answer are accepted in Latin America but the women condition calls for an engagement of liberation from their multiple instances of oppression. The biblical statement of faith that declares that

---

82. Porcile Santiso, *La Mujer, Espacio de Salvación*, 384.
83. Bingemer, "La Trinidad," 67.
84. Porcile Santiso, *La Mujer, Espacio de Salvación*, 139.
85. Ritchie, "Mujer y Cristología," 119.

Jesus is the Christ is a truth to be discovered.[86] Therefore, Christology became a more contextual subject, more related to the specific reality of people who are hopefully and actively searching "for a new form of cooperation, solidarity, and life (in their) cosmic vision."[87]

Women discover Christ in their active walk and practice of grace. Addressing the messianic question and answer, Wanda Deifelt asserts that traditional Christology has less to do with confession of faith and more with hierarchical power. The church credited and made relevant Peter's answer[88] which determined privileges in ministry and influenced "power and hierarchy."[89] Contrary to this practice, Jesus developed a ministry based in service, inclusion, and mercy. *You are the Christ, the Son of the living God* (Matthew 16-:13–20) is a confession similar to Martha's, but Peter receives "the privilege to be the rock of the church and to hold the power of the keys."[90] Peter's answer prevailed and shaped the Church as institution differently from the intention that the incarnated one developed. Martha's confession (John 11:27) expresses the same conviction of faith as Peter's, but Jesus' answer is different. Perhaps it was intentionally not written and consequently had a different effect in the ecclesiastical tradition.

> Martha's statement of faith was relegated to oblivion, while Peter's was commended. Apparently Christological statements are not simply a matter of confessing the faith correctly or living it out with sincerity . . . but essentially on who does it so that the ecclesial tradition gives him/her the adequate credit.[91]

The prioritization of one confession over another is problematic. The body of Christ is shaped by prejudice or a "correct" answer locating women's experience of faith in the periphery. The question back to Christology resides in the why and the reasons that moves Peter and Martha to confess Jesus as the Christ. It is not a matter of determining the correct

---

86. Ritchie, "Mujer y Cristología," 120.

87. Ritchie, "Mujer y Cristología," 120–21.

88. Peter's confession says: "You are the Christ, the Son of the Living God" (Matthew 16:16) while Martha's confession expresses belief: Yes, Lord, I believe that you are the Messiah, the Son of God, and the one coming into the world" (John 11:27).

89. Deifelt, "The Recovery of the Body," 26.

90. Deifelt, "The Recovery of the Body," 25.

91. Deifelt, "The Recovery of the Body," 25.

answer but in expressing faith in different manners. This emphasis turns Christology back to Jesus' liberative and welcoming ministry.

Christology must work from different perspectives engaging in service which revealing Christ reshapes the church's task and ecclesiology at the same time. Jesus' ministry invited many to confess their faith. This gave rise to a Christology distinguishing inclusion and relatedness[92] as main roots. Despite their different answers, both Martha and Peter's confessions are the result of a liberative experience lived in their encounter with Jesus. This liberative ministry is at the center of Christology done by women. Women are in an active "caminata"[93] with Jesus present initiating dialogue rather than finding a normative reply. The question is "a transformative question and as such is a challenge to Christology,"[94] it does not lead to standardized answers creating division and affirming patriarchal structures.

Christology needs to consider specific challenges and sufferings which rest heavily on a contextual reflection where people are able to account for personal experiences and are moved to affirm that Jesus is the Christ. In Latin America, Jesus portrayed as close friend splits from the normal "traditional depictions of Jesus"[95] as almighty. This disobedient act comes from the need of people to live outside the "nostalgia for the utopian kingdom (and outside the church) as an agent of social change."[96] It is disobedient but sacred that makes faith genuine as expression of deep engagement of God the Christ.

Jesus' Attitude toward Women and Women's Attitude toward Jesus

In the face of the Christology of imposition, Latin American feminist theologians became aware of images of dominion. In this specific Christological area, they did not continue to apply circumstantial Christological titles that distance Jesus from them. The alternative to capture God's revelation through the process of critical re-reading and dialogue with

92. Deifelt, "The Recovery of the Body," 32.
93. Women became aware of themselves as valuable in ministry by Jesus' solidarity. See Tamez, "The Power of Nudity," 188.
94. Althaus-Reid, *From Feminist Theology*, 59.
95. Deifelt, "The Recovery of the Body," 24.
96. Althaus-Reid, *From Feminist Theology*, 61, 62.

the scriptures posited new questions to God who is revealed as liberator in Jesus.[97] These new questions connect to the conditions of the life of women in contexts of patriarchal oppression. The itinerant movement initiated by Jesus initiates liberation shocking people in his culture. Jesus, addressing the Jewish laws of purity and impurity that relegated women to the constant condition of being polluted, welcomed women considered impure to be part in the followers' community. While interacting with women in different circumstances, Jesus challenges the religious and social atmosphere. His intentional contact or response to women in need reveals a ministry where women are welcomed. Invited to be part of Jesus' movement, women are religious, social, and financially active. In a society with little value for women, their social status is restored. Jesus' invitation integrates women in ministry which relationship intensifies mutually until the point Jesus has to learn that even the dogs eat the children's crumbs, meaning the outcasts can receive God's favor. This ministry renewal resides in the concrete manifestation of the promise of the kingdom, a new time sustained by Jesus' actions of love and forgiveness, strengthening and liberating burdened woman.[98] Jesus' specific attitudes toward women continue to be significant for Latin American feminist theologians. Women know that they are not limited to salvation through their biological and reproductive function but a movement motivating them to put in practice their talents. Jesus Christ becomes a close companion that recovers women's dignity.

> Jesus wanted to free those who were disinherited, rejected, sinners, pagans, marginalized in any way, including women and children who were not considered very important by Jewish society. Jesus gave these people privileged places in his kingdom . . . Jesus' liberating practice in regard to women tore down and destroyed . . . the body-soul dualism by accepting women as they were, including their bodies . . . Jesus announced and integrated an anthropology that valued the human being, composed of both body and soul.[99]

This gracious attitude toward women radically transgresses the law. Allowing the woman who had bled for many years to touch him, Jesus overcomes cultural practices that reduces the body to an immobile

---

97. Deifelt, "The Recovery of the Body," 122.
98. Ritchie, "Mujer y Cristología," 126, 128.
99. Bingemer, "La Trinidad," 155.

and unclean being "during the menstrual cycle, which can be translated, first, into sexual codes of purity and, second, into a way of structuring relationships of production in our society."[100] By stopping the women's bleeding, Jesus succeeds in allowing the woman to recover her humanity. Unfortunately, Jesus did not change the oppressive law but puts new sense to what is considered impure.[101] Christology requires attention to the core life, including women's bodies, to reinterpret laws that determine the ability of the body to be in the bigger body of Christ.

Women who work in Christology balance the liberating action of Jesus toward women and focus on the strength those women had to transgress imposed cultural laws and roles. Christology must pay attention to the attitudes of women toward Jesus, daring to make decisions, to "argue, to discuss theology, transgress, sit at Jesus' feet, touch him, confess their faith and recognize him as the Messiah."[102] There were women disciples, missionaries, leaders, and women who disobeyed. For instance, the woman who suffered hemorrhages is an example of courage. She misbehaves according to the rules of her time and before her community. For many years she spent time and money searching for a cure. Bravely, she stole a miracle from Jesus, overstepping the rules; she finds access to healing demonstrating her profound desire to overcome the duality of purity and impurity. Her tenacity allowed her to enter into a community of respect and where the women's bodies[103] are never underestimated. Another example is found in the foreign and gentile Syrophoenician woman who argued in favor of life, rejected exclusivism, and surprisingly revealed to Jesus her genuine faith, courage, and compassion with non-Jewish populations.[104] The social outcast woman who anointed Jesus "challenges the patriarchal and economic norms of her community becoming someone who was not afraid to let others know how she felt, who loved unconditionally, who offered what she

100. Althaus-Reid, *From Feminist Theology*, 50.

101. A popular messiah with deeper insights into the structures of discrimination and oppression could have established a dialogue with the woman and with the community surrounding them concerning the theme of menstruation and women's oppression . . . the only salvific gesture recorded in the Gospel is the suppression of the menstrual flow [and there is a way of accepting that] in the menstrual blood is the occasion requiring laws of oppression and discrimination. Althaus-Reid, *From Feminist Theology*, 51

102. Deifelt, "The Recovery of the Body," 35.

103. Tamez, *Las Mujeres en el Movimiento de Jesús*, 79.

104. Tamez, *Las Mujeres en el Movimiento de Jesús*, 87.

had, and who anointed him with her life. She had already been admitted . . . into the presence of grace."[105]

These interactions inform a Christology centering on women in search of support and care. Women's contextual Christologies consider the limits of a messianic action that disobeys laws bringing awareness to reshape church and provides arguments for their ministry. Jesus the Christ did not impose his maleness but used his authority to reveal God who receives men and women equally. Christology, considering the different contextual women's experiences, continues to be meaningful through the Jesus of Nazareth,[106] not reducing his ministry to his maleness[107] but focusing concretely in his actions.

The basic Christology exists in Jesus' life and ministry that is intentionally soteriological. In that intention liberation happens through care and compassion expanding God's passion for all. Jesus' relocation on the periphery allowed him to feel and engage people's need and to plant the seeds of the kingdom of God at hand. Nevertheless, Jesus' lack of consciousness of the political and patriarchal structures of his time[108] did not help him to encourage dialogue and to completely change laws that produce oppression. The political and patriarchal structure of power is the same that drove Jesus to the cross. Today the daily survival of women from different cultural and racial backgrounds is the re-imagination of

105. Ritchie, "Mujer y Cristología," 126.

106. The emphasis on the Historical Jesus widely used in Latin America encourages the discussion of Jesus' life and ministry to recover the meaning of Christ as liberator. Deifelt, "The Recovery of the Body," 32.

107. "The two natures' formula offer a challenge to the argument presented by theologians that Jesus' incarnation as man implied a greater proximity between men and God, placing women in a peripheral position. The Calcedonian formula affirms that the same Christ . . . exists without confusion . . . If, therefore, we attribute the masculine aspect of his humanity to divinity, we create confusion between the two natures, attributing characteristics from one to the other. The fact that Jesus was a man does not imply in God's greater proximity to the masculine gender, and even less that God is a man. Of importance is that God chose to become incarnate as human in order to be in solidarity with and to uphold the suffering human race" (Deifelt, "The Recovery of the Body," 37–38).

108. Althaus-Reid pays attention to the generosity, pardon, reconciliation, justice and peace in Jesus that but also to what remain oppressive and colonial. She intentionally calls the reader to examine the Christ-community model where Jesus' words and deeds were celebrated, opening a place for dialogue and going beyond the individual messiah. Continued dialogue is required because women continue challenging Christology with their sufferings that require a critical analysis in order to act in relation to what is producing that suffering. See Althaus-Reid, *From Feminist Theology*, 52–53.

resurrection. Incarnation is meaningful because the ones who die every day by force of poverty and indifference have the opportunity to worship and reaffirm their faith while experiencing signs of the resurrection through solidarity. Poor women arrive at the table conscious of their place and role in life. Women who survive the catastrophes of life become new protagonists who reshape the community of faith and Christology.

Women's Bodies: Sacred Texts

The study of the nature, character, and actions of Jesus Christ center the Christian dogma on Jesus' divine and human natures. Jesus' origin, begotten from the Father, Jesus as God of God, mediator of salvation, the one who will come at the end of times, and other topics that form part of Christology are not woman-friendly subjects, at least not in Latin America. Given their context of suffering, women recognize Jesus as compassionate God but find it difficult to deal with a Christology that locates them on the perimeter of patriarchal anthropology. Traditional Christology, as well as systematic theology, makes women homeless. The lack of female gender images of God sets up barriers moving women to question Christology. Women did find some benefit in affirming Christological dogmas but they faced the task of analyzing patriarchal elements in Christology.

Feminist theologians in Latin America, conscious of the influence of male epistemology, rejected dualistic and hierarchical patterns of thought. Women are conscious of their task in Christology in breaking the continuum of the colonial legacy. Women are concerned in their objectification based in ideology of being objects. "The exploitation of women in history is the invisible basic source upon which the high sexual content of theology and liberation theology is developed, that is, the sexual and gender roles which determine relationships."[109]

The presence of the incarnated is as important as contextualizing it by women. It pays attention to their bodies allowing rediscovery of the divine revelation already written on their own skins. Women's bodies are sacred texts[110] and engage in prophetic dialogue as their own bod-

---

109. Althaus-Reid, *From Feminist Theology*, 76.

110. Women's bodies are elevated to divine revelation because women claim that the Spirit of God speaks to us and evangelizes us from the specific situations in which women suffer, struggle, and overcome. See, Tamez, "Women's Lives as Sacred Text," 57.

ies already denounce suffering.[111] The prophetic motif leads women to find their presence in the narratives of their communities by correcting the shame patriarchal society[112] uses to set up terror. Women's suffering reflects how the Bible texts are desecrated. A prophetic-Christly-community denounces such misery by affirming change and hope as "prophecy and deeply subversive Christology (that) takes us beyond a 'banking' Christology and makes us assume our responsibility as a Christian community to be part of a process of Christological development."[113] The sacrality of women's bodies is proclaimed by the presence of God in their daily resurrection done by the strength of the Spirit.

The relationship between women-living texts and written-sacred texts develops an *intratextual* connection creating space for epiphanies. "These women's life stories also bring the insensitivities of the salvation history written in sacred texts and codified by tradition into the open."[114] In their struggle to survive, women's bodies bring rich experiences that sacred texts do not deal with; therefore, women's lives are epiphanic and reveal the mystery of sacrality.[115] Women's stories implicate both crucifixion and resurrection, crucifixion in the category of the agonies in life, resurrection in the recovery of dignity, pleasure, and life in the midst of marginalization.

Women who cross boundaries to recover their humanity discover that their own bodies[116] carry out meaningful and real revelations. The rereading of the sacred-texts enlightened by the living-texts[117] generates

---

111. Nancy Cardoso identifies the poor, basically women and children, as those who prophesy with the denunciation of their suffering, not through words but through their own bodies. In Althaus-Reid, *From Feminist Theology*, 56.

112. By recreating the story of women in the Bible the sacred text has come back to life in the actions, attitudes, and dreams of many women today. Tamez, "Women's Lives as Sacred Text," 60, 61.

113. Althaus-Reid, *From Feminist Theology*, 56.

114. Tamez, "Women's Lives as Sacred Text," 59.

115. The living text metaphor can be applied to the life stories of black, indigenous, and other people. The only difference is that women's lives run through all societies and cultures; oppression of women is found in all the various cultures, as is their struggle against it. Tamez, "Women's Lives as Sacred Text," 63.

116. Women are part of the *imago Christ*, it is in the whole ministry of Jesus Christ present in the world that reveals the wisdom made flesh and permits to participation in a body that is not male centered but coherent with the liberating actions developed by Jesus of Nazareth. See, Deifelt, "The Recovery of the Body," 37.

117. Elsa Tamez, "Women's Rereading of the Bible," 179.

liberative actions and attitudes[118] which promote a process of rediscovery of women's own dignity. Marginalized women identify with and follow the persistent and audacious attitude of women who transgress the patriarchal structures of power. Marginalized women read the sacred texts in an intentional search for ways that do not generate domination by using the lenses of their own experience. The intentional selection of texts is a hermeneutical key to re-signify the sacred texts[119] in the light of their own experiences. The reactivation and re-signification of the scriptures provokes a hopeful interpretation of active communities that inspire healing in the face of sickness.

The Slaughtered and Resurrected Body: Queer Christology

Christology from the Queer perspective uses indecency as its main hermeneutical motif. Through indecent lenses, Queer Christology interprets religious concepts and theories related to sexuality. This hermeneutic develops Christology from an impolite, subversive and pleasurable sexual category that appears when asking, *what does women's sexuality tells us about Christ?* Althaus-Reid considers prostitution and sexual option as essentials to theological studies differentiating sexual pleasure from affectivity and focusing on the flesh of the ones who suffer as result of sexual preference or because of the economic use of sex. The construction of Christology critically addresses the given categories of indecency as a posture in opposition to a "decent woman." [120]

Indecency, that brings to the surface the hidden sexual preference, is also connected with sexual exploitation. Disarticulating a Christology that serves to make uniform, Queer Christology proposes one of diversity and difference[121] that unmasks the neutralized sexuality or the sexuality that culturally or religiously becomes decent. A critical reflection on who Christ is in a context of sexual suffering leads to a reverse Christology about what is indecent. The subversion behind the descent notion rejoins the pieces of broken bodies, which includes the entire understanding of

---

118. Tamez, "Women's Lives as Sacred Text," 63.

119. Tamez, "Women's Lives as Sacred Text," 60

120. Indecentist categories denounce prohibition, repression and at the same time announce sexual desire through images of transgression. Althaus-Reid, *From Feminist Theology*, 89.

121. Althaus-Reid, *From Feminist Theology*, 85.

the self. Indecent Christological consciousness affirms that in the body of a queer person, Christ suffers the marks of the cross.

The indecent category works to increase consciousness that the sacred is constant, incarnated and manifested in life experiences. Women and men who are sexually excluded or abused realize that "Christ has become Christ-the-decent-woman, making of our concept of God a permanently dualistic shortcoming."[122] People who perform indecency challenge dualisms that condemn the enjoyment of their bodies and the traditional approach to the scriptures. Excluded people read the sacred texts from the memory of their bodies since they have the marks of suffering written on their bodies. The practice of reading from memory challenges essentialism because indecency celebrates difference and diversity.

Indecency contributes to destabilize authoritative standards in relation to sexuality by engaging and, at the same time, paying attention to the excluded. Traditional Christology is asked to rethink love and salvation. Love, as the fundamental matter in Christology, searches for radical and concrete expressions of care and affect "challeng(ing) patterns of relationship and affection coming from the excluded (and) contributing to a significant spiritual dimension (by practices like) rejunte."[123] *Rejunte* is resilience that expresses the spirituality of survival, and detaches people from projects which want to normalize life. *Rejunte* critically contributes to the understanding of people's alienation from religious institutions. *Rejunte* is not interested in marriage[124] but, given people's capacity to rebound/recycle and to be resilient, they

---

122. Althaus-Reid, *From Feminist Theology*, 90.

123. *Rejunte* brings the notion of the nomadic movement of persons, and sometimes members of families, who having terminated a relationship or facing the terrible situation of being dislocated or in the streets, search the support, help, and love of friends or past partners who receive them for an uncertain period of time. The notion of repetition that the word "rejunte" (re-joining) brings already expresses the struggle of the ones experience an again, or a coming again to past relationships or the return to people who are part of an earlier time in their personal history. Althaus-Reid, *From Feminist Theology*, 150.

124. The church's instinct has always been to re-order family structures by encouraging or coercing people to marry (to baptize their children), as if the idealized family structures promoted by the church were independent of the socio-economic conditions which support them. For instance, it is expected that the life of the individual or family group will include habitats which encourage privacy, homes supplied with electricity, a 'progressive' conception of time including, for example, a concluding period of retirement. Althaus-Reid, *From Feminist Theology*, 152.

build up new and singular ways of coping, creating new family systems and subverting the usual family order.

> *Rejunte* Theology unveils the diglottic dialectic of the life of the excluded, exposed to an ecclesial theology and a state discourse which are untranslatable into their lives. The division between the public and private discourses of national identity is then relocated. The public worship of Jesus in the Christian churches is transformed into a bodily, private and hidden worship.[125]

The endeavor for survival in the re-encounter with another slaughtered body develops a Christology of reciprocity between the ones who worship God in the sphere of the new relationship. The practices of giving and receiving go beyond duties or charities and unveil the sacred notion of the self. God/Christ, identified in solidarity, is one more among the excluded that impolitely appropriate the redemptive notion through the stubborn practice of sharing, re-building, and propitiating life within the community of destitute people.

Jesus Christ does not represent male sexual categories for Queer Christology. Gender issues, as well as a category of the poor, are present in Queer Christology but the need to address deviant sexualities helps to deconstruct, in a positive way, what is considered normally masculine or feminine that still delimits prevailing sexual expressions. "Indecent theology is produced by that element of sexual dissidence, rooted in class analysis and the reality of the life of the poor in an urban mega-city such as Buenos Aires, mixed with the complexities of issues of race, sexuality, economic exclusion and elaborated gender rituals. However, sexual dissidence among the poor became the catalyst element of the process."[126] Indecency, as a vehicle, exercises the ex-centric that enters "from outside the sensuous field of theological experience [a circle of] orthopraxis"[127] that hermeneutics in liberation theology proposes but works in indecent theology in an unconventional manner, from the exile, and focuses on the struggle of the poor in the specifics of the economics of sexuality.

If liberation theologies reflected in politics and economy, Queer Christology pushes to address women's and men's sexuality which is tied to economics and politics. Sexuality has been an element absent from the study of the historical Jesus and from contextual Christologies. "The

---

125. Althaus-Reid, *From Feminist Theology*, 162.
126. Althaus-Reid, *From Feminist Theology*, 63.
127. Althaus-Reid, *From Feminist Theology*, 72.

historical Jesus had a limited historical consciousness; he was not outside the context of his time, language and culture. He might have been advanced for *his* time, but not necessarily for ours."[128] Contextual Christologies reread the scriptures and Jesus' ministry in a transgressive way. This method is connected to the meaning of resurrection that contravenes death. The circularity between resurrection and death experiences that poor dissident men and women in Latin America experience is relevant. Queer Christology points to the 'purification' societal concept in the paranoia of killing homosexuals in Argentina. The rereading of the scriptures from a transgressive stance helps to discover that "the category of resurrection appears every time that Jesus is made redundant . . . God is declared so redundant that forgetting himself Jesus cries to God from the oblivion of the cross. In reality, the cross is the attempt to kill once and for all the multiple resurrections of a Queer Jesus, to fix him once and forever on a stable cross so that no Queer God would do what Queer Gods do, that is, to exceed the border limits of a fatigued heterosexual foundational epistemology which has reduced religious experience and human love . . . The resurrection of the Queer God is . . . already a possibility . . . exceeding the narrow confines of sexual and political ideologies."[129]

But cruci-fiction is real among sexual dissidents. The parallel that Althaus-Reid builds between the death of a transvestite and Mark 15 exposes a crude experience of ostracism, abandonment, and denial. The search for identity happens through multiple deaths facing processes of purification or normalization that makes agony and execution redundant. "They are a kind of reasoned killing, which becomes part of a discourse of 'expected deaths', since death is portrayed as the consequence of a sexually transgressive lifestyle . . . sexual dissidents are portrayed as ones who seek their own death . . . Jesus knew what was coming. He could have avoided going up to Jerusalem."[130] The life story of the sexual dissidents who experienced deaths becomes a Christic act[131] because people's stories recount the reality of life destabilizing the patriarchal to develop Christology. Althaus-Reid's works challenge platonic metaphysics, and enhance the power of incarnation. Christ takes place in the life of a poor

---

128. Althaus-Reid, *From Feminist Theology*, 80.
129. Althaus-Reid, *From Feminist Theology*, 175, 176.
130. Althaus-Reid, *From Feminist Theology*, 174.
131. Althaus-Reid and Isherwood, *Controversies*, 95.

young prostitute or in the transvestite's story whose life is full of rejections, humiliation and resistance.

The Christ Images

Latin American Christologies from women's perspective address the communal nature of Christ manifested in the specific contexts of suffering where relationality plays a key role. Some positions prefer to maintain a metaphysical link or to detach from it. The context of suffering in Latin America influences the question as well as the answer that Jesus elicits from Peter and Martha. Ritchie states that the incarnated is the Messiah, savior, and lord who engages in dialogue with women in suffering. Women recognize Jesus as the gracious and liberative Word, who renews the meaning of the kingdom coming to the encounter of exploited women and empowering their humanity to be active actors of their own lives.[132] The nature of the one incarnated, according Bingemer, is addressed in the Trinitarian perspective. God's nature of Maternal Father or Paternal Mother "opens the door to the formation of a community of men and women that in the communion of the Holy Spirit is able to overcome the privileges and domination of every king."[133] In Jesus' attitude toward women is discovered the presence of the Maternal Father and the love of the Holy Spirit. Christology is built up going to the hypostatical essence of the incarnated. The Word, embodied in a man whose "masculine mode of being . . . integrated the feminine dimension"[134] of the Trinity, promotes his essence in a community of tenderness, compassion and infinite mercy; therefore, Christology needs to recover the metaphors of the feminine in Jesus. Jesus is Sophia and his attributes connect believers to living water[135] that springs especially through Jesus' actions toward women.

A posture that challenges Christological metaphysics pays attention to women's everyday life and the embodiment of Christ. Deifelt recovers Jesus' humanity by connecting his ministry to the daily life of women. Women embody the divine dimension and therefore are able to contravene the prevailing and historical dichotomies that devalue their bodies.

---

132. Ritchie, "Mujer y Cristología," 128–32.
133. Bingemer, "La Trinidad," 161.
134. Bingemer, "La Trinidad," 156.
135. Porcile Santiso, *La Mujer, Espacio de Salvación*, 392–93.

The divine continues to be revealed in the flesh of women who painfully suffer. Women are the *locus* of revelation, the concrete passion that makes possible resurrection. Overcoming the objectification of women's bodies, based in the Greek-platonic-stoic notion, women's bodies are the home of God, never inferior to their soul or to male gender.[136] Women embody suffering and violence without resignation and their struggle, enlightened by the cross, represents dignity and daily resurrection.

Contextual Christologies that assert the rereading of the scriptures from daily experiences consider women's bodies as a hermeneutical category. Cardoso Pereira, approaching the dichotomy of soul-body as the locus of oppression and appropriation of women, finds relevant the restoration of the physical body considering that their sufferings and pleasures are present in Jesus' passion and resurrection. "The lacerated bodies in Latin America . . . require us to contemplate the raped bodies of men and women, boys and girls, and to feel the urgent need for resurrection of these bodies now."[137] Women's liberated bodies know the social constructions and asymmetries already imposed on the tissue of their skins. Suffering bodies are elevated to the level of sacred and discourage patriarchal dualisms. Women's bodies' accounts of suffering embody God's revelation and make Christology an open topic. Christology continues to be enlightened by new images and experiences that give sense to people's lives by destabilizing monolithic images and paying attention to Christic actions that embody practices of tenderness and companionship in the suffering of women and men.[138]

Incarnation does not remain particular to poor women and men in their suffering. Incarnation, in breaking from Greek metaphysics, is built in the context where sexual transgression takes place. The Queer Christ breaks the traditional postures of incarnation because of diversity. Moving away from the obsession of Christ in the patriarchal discourse, Christ embodies and becomes present in significant sexual stories of real people in suffering; "these moments are the breaking through of the challenge to embody the Christ we proclaim we believe in."[139] The stories of prostitute children, transvestites, or gays are courageous and transgressive and place the image of Christ even beyond

---

136. Deifelt, "The Recovery of the Body," 39–44.
137. Cardoso Pereira, "The Body as Hermeneutical Category," 2.
138. Tamez, "The Power of Nudity," 184, 187.
139. Althaus-Reid and Isherwood, *Controversies*, 97.

the female image that crushes patriarchy. The potential of incarnation manifested in this posture contributes to a non-metaphysical Christ which is an invitation "to enter our human-divine natures more fully and in so doing makes countercultural living a reality by embodying the kingdom of earth."[140] As these postures delineate, Christology is a topic that discloses the significance and importance of Jesus from different contexts and in different moments in life.

These rich Christological perspectives from Latin American women theologians and get into the specific Peruvian context and drives one to consider how evangelization and Christianization happened for people whose religious world started considering specific Christian concepts such as resurrection, cross, and trinity.

---

140. Althaus-Reid and Isherwood, *Controversies*, 97.

4

Christ in Peruvian Evangelization

THE PERUVIAN REALITY IS one of multiple contexts where the ancestral divinities reverberated in the encounter with the Christian world. The amalgam from that fusion, the combination of the two world views, remains in the Indigenous' spirituality today. The adoption of the cross and Christ is depicted through the context of evangelization that integrated the Quechua language. In order to make a connection between the historical process of evangelization in Latin America and the Peruvian reality, it will be useful to consider important elements that the evangelizers used to instruct the Indigenous.

The texts for evangelization and the doctrine for the instruction of the Indigenous were primarily written in Spanish and later translated into Quechua. The main purpose of these texts was to use religious elements from the Indigenous religious realm in order to introduce their main Christian concepts. The evangelizers succeeded in this work because "the Catholic worship was superimposed over the Indigenous rituals,"[1] but, even in the case of the imposition of the reverence to God, "the Incas' gods that reigned over a multitude of inferior divinities, present before the Inca's empire and rooted in the land and soul of the Indigenous as instinctive elements of a primitive religiosity, were destined to survive."[2] This dynamic will be studied in light of the process of evangelization and the religious elements present and employed in such a process.

Peruvian Christianity in the Context of Evangelization

To till the land of the multiple Peruvian contexts, it is necessary to revisit the process of the fracturing of the Peruvian panorama in order to understand the drama of disarticulation and re-articulation. Peru inherited

---

1. Mariátegui, *Siete Ensayos*, 128.
2. Mariátegui, *Siete Ensayos*, 131.

various vivid expressions of Indigenous' spirituality from the Inca Empire. The Spanish conquest was not a new experience; the Incas subjugated pre-Incan cultures and populations by governing vast territories in a very hierarchical imposition. The Incan caste had privileges in almost the entire territory of Peru.[3] But the Indigenous' inter-relationality, their connection with nature, and their reciprocity were elements that allowed them to survive in the midst of conquest. The Andean population, mystic by nature, in their encounter with the Western Christian culture, absorbed the new religion in a natural way. In the end, some characteristics of their spirituality survived and others were mixed with the imposed official Christian religion coming from Spain.

The Evangelization in Quechua

An account of the evangelization in the Quechua language is found in the *Plática para todos los indios* written in 1560 by Domingo de Santo Tomás.[4] It calls on the Indigenous to live by keeping God's commandment of faith. The document describes the Indigenous as beings constituted by body and heart/spirit and moves to the understanding that the spirit is rewarded with the heavens after death. In Quechuan thinking, when somebody dies, the body dies but not the heart or *songo* because it is the essence and place where the emotive capacity is concentrated. The spirit or *camaque* (from the Quechua *camac*) is the internal source that transmits the vital force to humans or things. In the Platica, Domingo de Santo Tomás uses *camac* to name the creator[5] because the heart and spirit live eternally in the heavens.[6] The document also introduces baptism as a reward for being a good believer. On the contrary, the document confirms that those who do not accept God's commandments will go to hell or to the house of demons.[7] Through the use of known Quechuan elements and animals, Domingo de Santo Tomás explains creation to affirm that life originates

---

3. See Burga, "¿Cuándo se jodió el Perú?," 41.

4. Taylor, *El sol, la luna y las estrellas no son Dios*, 19. Domingo de Santo Tomás was a Spanish Dominican and grammarian who used Quechua in the process of evangelization.

5. Taylor, *El sol, la luna y las estrellas no son Dios*, 23–24.

6. Taylor, *El sol, la luna y las estrellas no son Dios*, The Quechan word for heaven is "hanaqpacha" meaning the space above the earth, a superior stratum that has its inferior stratum called "kaypacha." See Estermann, *Filosofía Andina*, 156.

7. Estermann, *Filosofía Andina*, 30.

from God. Domingo uses the word *yachachi*[8] instead of *camac* because the equivalent of *yachachi* indicates the redoing or doing again from someone who transmits knowledge or some other capacity. The origin of all races is linked to Adam and Eve who also are connected to the fall as a result of the demons' temptation. In this topic, the document ends confirming that the demons continue to tempt today, moving the Indigenous to "praise the *huacas*, the stones, the sun, the moon, the earth"[9] instead of God. Repentance from such a sin is the path to restoring the Indigenous' behavior and being accepted by God.

The *Plática*'s aim is to advise and to convert the Indigenous. Conversion is the reformation of Indigenous behavior by stopping them from worshiping their gods, to be authentic Christians[10] who only worship God. Because the *Plática* was translated from Spanish to Quechua, the Conquerors used concepts already present in the Indigenous realm to make it easier to understand Christian concepts. Quechua helped Domingo de Santo Tomás discredit vital elements of the divine Indigenous' pantheon like the huaca, sun, moon, stones, and Mother Earth herself.

The words God, Adam, Eve, angels, Christian, and horse are completely new to the Indigenous. The word devil, for instance, was known in Quechua as *supay* but its meaning indicated bad, something of an awful aspect. *Supay* did not have a negative connotation[11] but the *supay* had an awful appearance. For that reason, Domingo de Santo Tomás used the Spanish *diablo* to introduce a new notion to depict the tempters' presence and opposition to angels. In the new figure, *Diablo*, Domingo wanted to impute confusion to the Indigenous. According to Tomás, out of that confusion the Indigenous' worshiped stones or idols rather than God, recommending the Indigenous not confuse God with the *huaca* or any other gods. The particularity of the Christian God was linked to belief in Jesus Christ. The Trinity was more complicated for the Indigenous to understand, since that concept was developed through centuries and councils. Even though these notions would fascinate the Indigenous, at the same time, they would be disorienting. Christ was accepted as one more God in the Indigenous'

---

8. This word also includes the capacity to promote what already existed. Estermann, *Filosofía Andina*, 22–23.

9. Estermann, *Filosofía Andina*, 37. Huacas were immense honored rocks or mountains which constituted sacred locations. They were also places of residence of mummies of the Inca dynasty.

10. Estermann, *Filosofía Andina*, 37.

11. Estermann, *Filosofía Andina*, 24–25.

pantheon but the evangelizers, using Quechuan concepts, tried to establish the new religion and tried to explain theological elements that were different from the spiritual worldview of native Indigenous Andeans.

The Christian Doctrine for the Instruction of the Indians

The second document created to instruct the Indigenous in Christian doctrine was written in 1584 in *Castellano*.[12] The document entitled *The Christian Doctrine for the Instruction of the Indians*,[13] was translated to Quechua and Aymara. This document was the result of the Third Council of Lima. It invites the Indigenous to know how to be saved. An innovation appears in the use of the Spanish term *Dios* for God, with a capital letter, and the word *dios* in small to name Indigenous' gods. The contrast between *Dios* the creator and the gods like the *huaca*[14] reinforces the notion of a powerful creator[15] who created all that exists for the benefit of humans.

> The ambiguity that results from the use of Spanish, *Dios*, constantly writing with a capital letter, used to emphasize the supremacy and uniqueness of the person identified with this name, but also utilized to refer to a category of supernatural and powerful beings that would have been called *huacas*, if this term had not been reserved to define the "Idols," the false gods par excellence, create a problem of transcription for the normal version.[16]

12. Castellano is a dialect from Castilla. Spaniards who arrived in South America came from that area.

13. Taylor, *El sol, la luna y las estrellas no son Dios*, 47.

14. The term *huaca* was used by Indigenous Quechuas to refer to powerful and supernatural beings. Lamentably, evangelists used the term to define the idols. Taylor, *El sol, la luna y las estrellas no son Dios*, 58.

15. The root *camac* in Indigenous' mentality refers to the vital force but authors forced its meaning to creation ex-nihilo. The confusion increased with the support of the root *pacarichi* (to give origin) that contradicted the evangelization because it was a common word for the mythical origins of their communities in the *pacarinas* or hills. See, Taylor, *El sol, la luna y las estrellas no son Dios*, 51.

16. "Ambiguity that results from the use of Hispanicism God, written constantly with a capital letter in the sense of the supreme and unique being designated by this name. But it also was used to refer to a category of powerful supernatural being called *huacas* if this term would not have been reverse to refer to idols creating a transcription problem in the standardized version" (Taylor, *El sol, la luna y las estrellas no son Dios*, 52).

To emphasize the idea of salvation, the text contrasts the bad men with the good men. The bad ones, who do not follow God's commandments, will be expelled to hell for eternal suffering. The good men who believe in God will go to heaven, a place of eternal and happy life. New life is explained using the word ánima[17] or soul, introducing, at the same time, the platonic duality soul-body.[18] It is complicated to explain that notion because ánima refers to the inner part of humans and the Quechua word *ukunchikkunawanchu*, from the root *ucu*, refers to body in the inner, the interior sense. Aycha is the Quechua for flesh and *tullu* for bones. *Tullu* is absent in the document, which demonstrates that the colonizers used the dualist-Greek-philosophical term based on the perception of the being with soul and body,[19] which contradicted the Indigenous' holistic notion in relation to the body.

The text is a pioneer in bringing the Trinitarian concept: "*Dios* Yaya, *Dios* Churi, *Dios* Espíritu Santo are not three gods even though they are three persons."[20] The argument follows the Greek notion of three persons which uses the *Castellano* word *persona* to emphasize the Trinitarian concept. The contrast between God and god works perfectly in the written text, but for the Indigenous, accustomed to the oral message the differences were not relevant. Besides, the *huacas* were mysterious for native people. They welcomed the new three persons into the world of their *huacas*/gods based on the relational and non-exclusivist notion. The written text often accentuates the *huacas* as false and evil beings but God.[21]

The Christological explanation addresses the nature and work of the Son, affirming, "The son of the almighty God is *Jesucristo* who became man in the womb of the *virgen Santa María* and was born (did not originate) from her."[22] Jesus Christ and the Virgin Mary play

17. The Spanish word ánima does not have an equivalent in Quechua because *supay* refers to shadow and was already used for devil, the world *samay* indicates breath-spirit, and the world *camac* as the fountain that animates but relates to the *huaca* that was one of Indigenous divinities; therefore, it was associated with transgression creating the word *camazapa* for sinner and *camallicuni* for the action of sin. Taylor, *El sol, la luna y las estrellas no son Dios*, 52.

18. Taylor, *El sol, la luna y las estrellas no son Dios*, 56–57.
19. Taylor, *El sol, la luna y las estrellas no son Dios*, 51.
20. Taylor, *El sol, la luna y las estrellas no son Dios*, 58.
21. Taylor, *El sol, la luna y las estrellas no son Dios*, 59.
22. Taylor, *El sol, la luna y las estrellas no son Dios*, 58.

a key role in the origin of Christ. For the Indigenous, accustomed to mythological narratives to explain that their divinities and Incas proceeded from powerful entities, the story of Jesus Christ, the son of God, would be naturally understood. The presence of God and Mary was also natural because of the dual, not dualistic, understanding of the world. Jesus Christ originates from God, who is in heaven, and Mary will be understood not following the Greek notion of his divinity and humanity but by the dual complementarity between male and female. The difficult element to understand will be the virgin presence. She is Jesus' mother; she is a virgin but is not divine. There is not a Quechuan word for virgin; therefore, the evangelists used the Spanish word *virgen* to introduce a new and particular concept without explaining its meaning. They mainly emphasized Jesus Christ's eschatological task and his role as judge, rewarding the faithful or punishing the infidels.

In the context of the effects of the Ecumenical Council of Trent (1545–1547), especially because of the Protestant Reformation in Europe, which condemned the principles and doctrines of Protestantism and affirmed the doctrines of the Catholic Church, emphasizing the sacraments as highly relevant because the true propitiatory sacrifice of Christ is offered through the consecration of the wine and bread in the Eucharistic ritual. The term *transubstantiation* took on a special accent using the Aristotelian–Scholastic explanation that Christ is "really, truly, substantially present" in the consecrated elements. That true presence of Christ in the consecrated elements reaffirmed the ministerial and ecclesiological understanding of the sacerdotal power conferred on ordained ministers. Above them, Christ also conferred power on the Pope, who became the supreme arbiter to maintain the rules of the Christian faith and who was so venerated that the Indigenous continued being confused when it was required to respect the only God. Justification, linked to the accomplishment of God's commandments, also promoted the following of Jesus Christ and of the cross as a sacrificial-salvific act.

The text used the Spanish word *cruz* because the Indigenous did not have the notion of a place where Jesus Christ died in their vocabulary. Colonizers mixed and used the word *cruz*pi chacatasca[23] ("being crucified on the bridge") for the meaning of the crucifixion. Jesus Christ was crucified by his own will to save and to guide humans to heaven.[24] But to

23. Taylor, *El sol, la luna y las estrellas no son Dios*, 51.
24. Taylor, *El sol, la luna y las estrellas no son Dios*, 58, 60.

be Christian, baptism[25] was required as way of changing their aboriginal names to Spanish ones. Evangelization was a way to impose imperial dominion and changing nomenclature was a strategy to increase control. The specific topic of Christology played a key role in this process. Christology imposed upon, abused and changed the divine Indigenous notions while promoting theological concepts completely new and that followed the Greek-platonic influence. The Indigenous were thus moved to embrace Jesus Christ as the increase of their suffering was connected to his suffering on the cross.

The Passion and Triumph of Christ

If the emphasis in the period of evangelization was to believe in Jesus Christ as God and to fulfill God's commandments, years later, the focus became Jesus Christ's passion and triumph. The passion motif was represented in art work, literature, homilies, and poems. One exponent who contributed through poetry was Pedro de Peralta Barnuevo,[26] who in October 1687, as a result of the devastating earthquake in Lima, wrote the poem *Delante de una Imagen de Christo*[27] *Crucificado*. The poem asserts that Christ after death redeemed the future sins of humankind which turned relevant in an atmosphere of fear and devotion.[28] Peralta's work *Pasión y Triunfo de Christo*, written in 1738, contains ten prayers: The Prayer in Gethsemane, the Arrest and the Judges, Pilate, Herod, and Flagellation, The Coronation of Thorns, The Carrying of the Cross, The Crucifixion, The Triumphant Cross, The Grave and the Limbo, The

---

25. It is well known that baptism was used politically during the conquest and evangelization. On one hand, it was a massive and official practice used for entry into the Catholic Church, and on the other hand, its use was abused because Indigenous were not taught its meaning because masses were done in Latin. But behind these practices was the affirmation of Spanish imperial sovereignty that used the ecclesiastical branch to subjugate the Indigenous politically, even changing their names and identity. See, Rivera, *A Violent Evangelism*, 230–33.

26. Pedro de Peralta is an eighteenth century Peruvian writer who belonged to the elite. Peralta was born in Lima in 1663 and died in 1743. His major works are *La Galería de la Omnipotencia* (around 1729), *Lima Fundada* (1732), and *Pasión y Triunfo de Christo* (1738). Peralta's literary work enriched Peruvian literature and showed a deep religious life, offering an understanding of Christ and his work. Slade and Williams, *Bajo el Cielo Peruano*, 13.

27. The word *Christo* is used exclusively by Peralta which comes from Latin influence. Slade and Williams, *Bajo el Cielo Peruano*, 21.

28. Slade and Williams, *Bajo el Cielo Peruano*, 97–98.

Resurrection, and The Ascension. The prayers are an account of the suffering, anguish, and pain of Jesus Christ the Lord, Glorious King, Redeemer, Son of God, Lord of Anguish, King of Pains, Savior, Eternal Verb, Omnipotent Author, King of the Universe, Patient God, Eternal Isaac, Painful God, Savior of the World, etc. The emphasis on Jesus Christ's suffering is remarkable. In Jesus' passion God's love is expressed in an antithetical way because the more suffering Jesus experienced, the more exalted he became:

> The highest Divine Majesty saw Jesus from the celestial heaven; then, the more he yielded, the more exalted he was. The more weakly he walked to the scaffold; the faster he was driven to the Throne. The Divinity sustained and left him. Love held and pressed him. The angels gave him the greater assistance in not helping him. The angels served as his family and not as aid. [29]

The method to describe Jesus' triumph over death insists on suffering. The document is rich because it does not deny suffering but overemphasizes it. The acceptance of torment and suffering are key elements for submission and conquest. It is no surprise that Peralta would be a good exponent of the use of the cross as metaphor for suffering. The same cross that will remove Peralta from his cross or sufferings emphasizes the idea that suffering, to carry the cross, [30] is a necessary aspect of a faithful life. The glorification of suffering and the glorification of the cross is a sign of a faith that elevates the suffering of the Redeemer animated by Love.[31] Love, in this way, makes sense of the incarnation and the task of opening the doors of heaven[32] expresses justice and mercy. Love is the expression of Jesus Christ's silence and the expression of his voice in favor of those who injured him. In this manner, Jesus is an example of forgiveness. He forgives those who offended, wounded, and crucified him[33] shining in mercy and grace.[34] Dolorous trust and imploration are expressed through the Man, but the divine God makes present the promise of eternal life.[35] The prayer endorsed and mirrored divine suffering and motivated the reader

---

29. Slade and Williams, *Bajo el Cielo Peruano*, 255.
30. Slade and Williams, *Bajo el Cielo Peruano*, 259.
31. Slade and Williams, *Bajo el Cielo Peruano*, 265.
32. Slade and Williams, *Bajo el Cielo Peruano*, 266, 268.
33. Slade and Williams, *Bajo el Cielo Peruano*, 176.
34. Slade and Williams, *Bajo el Cielo Peruano*, 277.
35. Slade and Williams, *Bajo el Cielo Peruano*, 278.

to accept suffering that was already carried out by Christ. Even the Man suffered death yet God triumphed over it.[36]

The glorification of Christ's suffering goes hand in hand with the glorification of the cross. The cross is the sacred wood,[37] not a place that causes death. The cross resembles triumph in war because it is like "the banner of the empire of Jesus, the ancestry of the nobility and place of the lineage of Glory."[38] The cross is the expression of the divine strength[39] where Jesus, in the silence of his pains, made it a sacred wood. The cross was consecrated by the contact with his patient Redeemer and animated by his divine love.[40] The cross is the expression of a major lament; it is the cry converted into joy, the major Sacrifice of what had been an instrument of punishment, it had been the throne of Glory of what was torment.[41] The triumphant cross advances the gospel's message of conversion,[42] and it reflects the image of the eternal triumph;[43] therefore, in the cross resides the essence of greatness.

Resurrection then explains the victorious side, emphasizing the triumph of God over fault and death.[44] Pedro de Peralta uses power and glory to stress the immortality of the Lord, accentuating the strength of his Divine Mother. It is not the first time that Mary was conceived as a celestial being. Mary was also divinized and glorified along with Jesus' passion, Mary was the "dolorosa" but superior to any other women who was with Jesus after his resurrection.[45] The resurrection was required to complete Jesus' glory and the ascension was necessary in order for Christ to occupy the place that was prepared for him since eternity to enjoy his monarchy and his throne.[46] The triumphal ascension echoes the monarchical triumph of the Christian empire over Jew[47] and idolaters.

36. Slade and Williams, *Bajo el Cielo Peruano*, 284.
37. Slade and Williams, *Bajo el Cielo Peruano*, 268.
38. Slade and Williams, *Bajo el Cielo Peruano*, 290.
39. Slade and Williams, *Bajo el Cielo Peruano*, 274.
40. Slade and Williams, *Bajo el Cielo Peruano*, 265.
41. Slade and Williams, *Bajo el Cielo Peruano*, 287.
42. Slade and Williams, *Bajo el Cielo Peruano*, 288.
43. Slade and Williams, *Bajo el Cielo Peruano*, 297.
44. Slade and Williams, *Bajo el Cielo Peruano*, 311.
45. Slade and Williams, *Bajo el Cielo Peruano*, 317.
46. Slade and Williams, *Bajo el Cielo Peruano*, 345.
47. Slade and Williams, *Bajo el Cielo Peruano*, 172, 229, 282, 290.

The *Pasión y Triunfo de Christo* expresses the continuum of a triumphant evangelization. The language in this prayer is highly elaborated to glorify suffering, the cross as divine wood, Mary's suffering and Calvary itself. It is an example of devotion that carefully uses the mystery of the incarnated who suffers and triumphs over the cross. Even though Peralta is conscious of Jesus Christ's divinity and humanity, his work was censored by the inquisition. Peralta argued that his prayer's metaphors and hyperbe were divinely inspired.[48] If Peralta's creativity was criticized by the inquisition, the prayers are an example of the introduction and spread of the tenets of glorification and triumphalism during the eighteenth century in Peru. His Christology follows the suffering, triumphant, and glorious idea of Christ. Peralta was a layman whose talent was criticized for not having "knowledge of the complex histories that documented and interpreted the life of Christ."[49] Peralta's prayer depicts the passion as expressed in the iconography and art that Roman Catholic churches and cathedrals have. Peralta developed a spiritual exercise that helped him to externalize his faith.

Blend of Indigenous Spirituality and Sacred Christian Beliefs

Peruvian society became even more complex with the presence of African slaves brought, during the sixteenth century, to replace the Indigenous in the mines and on farms. Social strata arouse out of these diverse people determined by economics and race. The social structures were highly determined by economics but race played an important role in that structure. The Indigenous and African people worked the land for the Spanish crown. Spaniards distributed and administered the lands in order to secure tributes. The administrative and juridical reorganization of towns and cities were in the conquerors' hands, and they changed names or founded new towns. The local and national administration accentuated existing Incan Andean organization based on hierarchy that placed conquerors at the top of the structure.

> The interracial mix resulted in new racial and ethnic categories that exist today, for example, "mestizo" (the mix of white and Indian), "cholo" (the mix of mestizo and Indian), "criollo" (the

---

48. Slade and Williams, *Bajo el Cielo Peruano*, 107.
49. Slade and Williams, *Bajo el Cielo Peruano*, 119.

descendant of white Iberians born in the Americas), "white" (the white Iberians born in Europe), "zambo" (the mix of Indian and African), "mulato" (the mix of white and African).[50]

Conquest re-configured the social organization and accentuated a structural pyramid based on economic and racial privileges. The presence of white Europeans first and Africans later reinforced the pyramid which supported economics and racial differences. Spaniards and Portuguese transplanted their lordship mentality and their Christian crown structure. Indigenous and African descendants under the rule of Europeans were mixed and located at the bottom of the structure, ranked according to patterns of most dark-skin or black-skin color. The colonial society named the other members of society. Some were considered mestizo, chollo, criollo, etc. not only to determine the racial mixture but to denigrate those who were mixed. A sense of purity and impurity became defining. To be called mestizo, for instance, indicated mixture and devaluation for being a product of an illegitimate union, either by rape or consensual, but illegal partnering. The term cholo was used to describe the dark-skinned Peruvian, Ecuadorian, and Bolivian people who had emigrated from the Andean towns to the big cities where the criollo population resided.[51] The distinction between darker from whiter-skinned people determined their socio-economic status and consequently their access to education, work, and other social privileges. Therefore, it was easier for a mestizo to be educated than a cholo or an Indigenous person.

These breakdowns characterized Peru's history when the dream of an Andean renaissance in the nineteenth century failed its utopian vision to rebuild a multi-ethnic and more equal society. The struggle during the period of Independence was remarkably influenced by the socially organized mestizo and criollo oligarchies, which highlighted the already marginalized condition of Indigenous people and people of African descent. The privileges shared between the white dominant classes and mestizos and criollos strengthened the feudal system whereas independence had been inspired by freedom, equality, and fraternity, ideals that in 1821 benefited the oligarchy but not the majority of the population, composed of mulatos, cholos, native Indigenous, and African descendants. The new criollo and mestizo oligarchy desecrated the lands that remained in hands

---

50. Quispe-Agnoli, *Geopolitics*.
51. Quispe-Agnoli, *Geopolitics*.

of the Indigenous population[52] and ignored Afro-Peruvian populations. During the Independence the term mestizo was used to accentuate the racial differences of the population; therefore, to be mestizo signified to have certain privileges and an elevated social standing. To complicate this structure, the economic power of people in different social strata allowed them to be placed in a higher level of the structure, further confirming the relevance of economics-power in power relations that influenced the hierarchy. The movement of dark-skinned people to a higher social level created a new layer within the structure, again based on skin-color labels and economic power.

The Latin American Christian context did not remain pure. The beliefs and gods of Aztecs, Mapuche, Tupí-Guaraní, Incas, among others, and the introduction of the African spirits, moved the context of evangelization to productive fusions. In Latin America, a productive land in which singular rituals, expressions of faith, and theologies flourish is revealed a cultural-racial-religious blend where cracks are still evident in the belief system that help us to understand how this amalgam came together and became imposed on the dominant belief. These mixtures have reinforced the spiritual and sacred while renewing and revitalizing the manifestation of Christ.

Quechuan Spiritual Components and Fusions

To survive the political and spiritual conquest, the Latin American inhabitants both accepted and resisted the new religious order. Survival was a painful transformation. The violent incorporation of the *"historia salvationis* . . . substantially transformed and diminished the identification of their inhabitants . . . the basic dilemma was that missionaries could not understand, because of their Iberian-Catholic formation, that the destruction of (native) ideology did not involve an automatic acceptance of a new one that destroyed the former."[53] The imposition of the history of salvation assaulted native Indigenous' spirituality and beliefs. The Indigenous accepted the new faith by mixing their truths with the new truth. The Western claim of the possession of the absolute truth put in

---

52. After the approval of the Constitution of 1928, the Indigenous have the right to elect and to vote and to be elected, to buy and sell, and to mortgage their lands. As a consequence, Indians lost more than half of their lands and became servants of landowners. See, Delgado "¿Cuándo se jodió el Perú?," 30, 55.

53. Dressendörfer, "Acercándose a una realidad opaca," 25.

the hands of the conquerors the power of determining the human condition and existence. Natives struggled to be considered humans, but they soon realized that they were considered as objects or slaves in the accomplishment of the conquerors' cause. The Western truth was at the service of the empire. The empire exercised the religious monopoly, enforcing a system of conquest while using the Christian truth to secure power for the Spanish crown. The strategy of evangelization was to oppose any other truth and this was one of the characteristics of the colonial mission. But the mission to abolish idols did not kill pagan beliefs because historically rooted native spirituality was reconfigured, renamed, enriched, and embodied.

Informed by the Quechuan society, the Indigenous embraced subcultures who interacted with them in their relationship with the Pachamama or Mother Earth. The Pacha and Apus[54] were relational and consecrated spaces because they constituted for the Indigenous the habitat and source of life. The Quechua's sacred rituals and celebrations were connected to the earth for communal benefits even though they had a hierarchical organization where the Incan cast was privileged. But the notions of inclusiveness, relatedness, reciprocity and complementariness were practiced in community. The Quechuas were economically based in agricultural and cattle raising activities and prioritized contact with the earth, runas,[55] and living beings. Reciprocity played a central role in these relationships. There were no unilateral actions but actions determined in community. Communal relationship was the basis for the social organization, an organization that embraced differences and diverse truths without needing a universal one. The dual criterion was important because social life was conceived in balance resulting in complementation.[56] Quechua was the means of communication and even though it was considered the noble language, other dialects and languages like the Aymara, Wanka, etc. were allowed. Relatedness with mother earth and all created beings and the dual criteria have religious bases. Quechuas, collectively and symbolically, integrated rituals, myths, ethical norms, and organization in their

---

54. The word Pacha refers to the cosmos and includes the notion of space and time in the Quechua world view. Apu refers to mountains or hills.

55. Runa is the Quechua word that designates human beings in general. After conquest, the word was used to refer to the Andean people who spoke Quechua or its dialects. The Runas lived closely linked to the Earth because they believed that humanity came from Earth.

56. Marzal, "La Religión Quechua Sur Andina Peruana," 199.

relationship with the Pachamama, the Apus, the Inti or the Viracocha or Pachacamac gods.[57] The Quechuas' rituals celebrated life giving, thanks for the propitiation and sustenance of life.

A circular relationship with the Pachamama included the community, the cosmos and divinities. The Pachamama herself develops life in a cyclical movement, affirming renovation and recreation. Since Pachamama is life itself, she invites living and wisdom. In this sacred reality, the Runas learned to worship her by offering, in reciprocal manner, recognition and returning to the earth what belongs to and comes from her.[58] Respect and recognition allowed an understanding that their belief was earth/cosmos-centric rather than human-centric. Humans were important but did not play a determinant role in the cosmos.[59] The centrality of this relationship was their rituals of recognition and thankfulness, elements that became Christianized later.

For instance, the period of drought initiated the notion that the earth dies. It was re-symbolized to refer to the death of Christ to which were added new elements like the cross and Good Friday. The Quechuas did not qualify the earth as virgin. The earth was sacred but the virginal notion was introduced by the Spanish. The term virgin earth was used by Spaniards instead of Pachamama even though virginity had no value in Quechua. Today, peasants consider Pacha as a virgin as long as it has not being cultivated. In order to work it, an act of defilement, peasants must ask for her permission[60] and provide an offering. There is no doubt that the presence of the Virgin Mary influenced and, in a certain manner, replaced the sacred relationship of the Quechuas with the earth.

The duality of the Quechuan world view consists of opposites and complementariness. The word panaka refers to the masculine and feminine that generates life. For instance, the hanaqpacha or the world from above and the qaypacha or the experience in the world are two antagonistic and interrelated dimensions. The word ukinchi refers to the presence of the spirit but also to the body. The body is not only the material element, it also considers the inner the spirit. The body and the spirit are

57. Viracocha and Pachacamac are the name for the creator. Viracocha was used at the north side of the Inca's empire and Pachacamac at the south. See, Intipampa Alinga, "Lo divino en la concepción andina," 59.

58. Tancara Chambe, "Tuve una Importante Revelación," 40.

59. Tancara Chambe, "Tuve una Importante Revelación," 42.

60. Licenciaykiwan is a mixed word made up of the Spanish meaning license and kiwan which means to allow or to grant.

one; therefore, the spiritual world is composed of spirits who are considered persons. The spirits cannot be represented through idols or images with physical appearances. The spirit is a helper or comforter that changes its characteristics according to the needs and situations of the moment.[61] There are superior, ancestral, and immortal spirits residing in the huge mountains, and there are inferior spirits living in the wakas.[62] Even though their role is to help present generations, the spirits give continuity to life, the basis for the myth of the manifestation of life, because life happens in a geographical space and in cyclical time. The myth of the first Inca occurs at Lake Titicaca at the beginning of human existence, and it flourished until the arrival of the conquerors.

The integration of the natural and supernatural builds interdependence between the divine, the community, and nature. This integration is essential to understanding the Runa's dual notion of natural-supernatural, material-spiritual, and human-divine[63] in the Quechua and Aymara world view. During life, the Runa (men or women) interact in the community dimension; when he or she dies, the spirit goes to the natural dimension, to sacred places in the mountains or hills. When the spirits address the sacred state, their task is to protect the community. The same occurs with the condor, the jaguar, the snake, plants and other living species.[64] The Quechuas conceive these abstract notions as concrete elements. The sun and the moon are deities considered father and mother. Other natural phenomena develop functions and manifest specific divine elements according to the context. These deities are masculine and feminine beings manifested in the context of the community or Ayllu.[65] The ayllu is a place of encounter, reencounter, interaction, realization, complementation, relation, solidarity, self-realization, historical events, identity, and participation, and a place where the divine is present.

---

61. Miranda Luizaga and Del Carpio Natcheff, "Fundamentos de las espiritualidades," 26.

62. The word waka indicates a place where the ancestral sacred resides.

63. Intipampa Alinga, "Lo divino en la concepción andina," 51.

64. Intipampa Alinga, "Lo divino en la concepción andina," 52.

65. Intipampa Alinga, "Lo divino en la concepción andina," 55, 56. Ayllu is the nucleus where the Runa (human being) cultivated the land in a cyclical and rotary manner. The earth is not transferable because it is a place where communities were living for generations. There can be areas that are individually cultivated but as soon as the product is harvested, the earth returns to the community. Intipampa Alinga, "Lo divino en la concepción andina" (72).

The Chakana[66] is a symbol of relationality that plays a critical role in the encounter between the Runas and the divinities. The Chakana-bridge makes complementation possible. It works horizontally between the masculine and feminine and vertically between the hanaqpacha and the kaypacha. The hanaqpacha is the cosmic order of superior status but not the heavens. Kaypacha refers to the time-space reality here and now. For instance, relationality happens in the encounter between the sun, the reality from above, and the earth, while illuminating the reality of here- kaypacha. The correspondence between the up above and the down below is based on the complementarity of the feminine and masculine that is present in the entire cosmos. For Quechuas, death and birth are not antagonists but complementary realities that work perfectly, as when the end of the year just brings the beginning of another period. The notion of relation highlights what is almost arriving rather than the end of a period. The Chakana-bridge allows for the phenomenon of the horizontal/complementary and vertical/relational. It was an always present mediation in the disequilibrium of the cosmos. The Runa participates to celebrate this cosmic balance through rituals that express gratitude for the benefits.[67]

The arrival of conquerors changed this notion because the evangelizer used the root chaka for crucifixion. Cruzpi chakatasqa or crucifixion uses the concept of the Chakana, adding to it the Christian meaning of the death of Christ. The evangelizers knew that the Chakana played a crucial role in the Quechuas' relationship with the earth/cosmos. The Chakana, a square cross, corresponded to the Southern Cross formed by stars that helped the Quechua culture to develop its understanding of the world and divinities.[68] The cross, during the conquest, continued to develop the relational role because it was placed at the top of hills. Inserting the Christian element of salvation into the sacred (pacha and apus) spaces promoted the connection between the ancestral living spirits and

66. Chakana means "cosmic bridge" and indicates the point of transition in the notion of relationality. Estermann, *Filosofía Andina*, 155.

67. Estermann, *Filosofía Andina*, 155, 198.

68. "Cuando los españoles entraron al (templo) Coricancha, en el pared que podría coincidir con el altar mayor de un templo cristiano . . . se encontraba . . . la cruz cuadrada que adoraban los Incas [que] correspondía a la representación de la mítica Cruz del Sur, que sólo puede verse en el hemisferio sur . . . debajo de la cruz había una hornacina donde se ponía la momia del inca; al este, ya a la misma altura se encontraba la representación del Sol, correspondiente al lado izquierdo de la hornacina; y al lado derecho . . . al oeste, la representación de la Luna" (Pini "La Cruz precristiana," 25–26).

the cross. Christian Quechuas, by virtue of relationality and reciprocity, received the cross as a new sacred symbol.

Faces of the Peruvian Christ

Evangelization emphasized Christ as savior and the cross substituted for Indigenous' sacred places. The evangelizers moved Christ to the center, placing the cross where the Indigenous had praised their gods. Altars and images were destroyed and sacred houses were used to celebrate mass.[69] This substitution strategy aimed to destroy the Indigenous' religion and identity but determined their condition without success. "The evangelization, the catechesis was never consummated in its deep sense . . . the missionaries did not impose the Gospel; they imposed their cult and worship, adapting them in a sacred manner to the Indigenous customs. The aboriginal paganism subsisted beneath the Catholic worship."[70]

The Indigenous resisted the new teaching but after realizing the danger in resisting, they moved to a sort of quietism as a facade to dissimulate. The conquerors hated this dynamic because they knew that the Indigenous' acceptance of the Christian faith would not stop them from practicing their own rituals and convictions.[71] The fusion of the Indigenous' spirituality and Christianity caused the cross to become the main symbol for the Christian Andean religion.[72]

The Concilio Limense or Third Council of Lima (1582–1583) established pastoral guidelines, because of the political power of viceroy Toledo to stop idolatry and syncretism.[73] The Jesuit José de Acosta played a central role in the Council because of his interest in evangelizing a society characterized by idolatry. Acosta recognized the Viracocha and the Indigenous' relation to their creator, and the Quechua helped Acosta preserve Indigenous customs and traditions that did not contradict the new faith.[74] Andean religious elements came to be found in Peruvian Catholicism. By the seventeenth century, the Indigenous population of the Coastal and Andean areas believed in God, the saints, the devil and practiced rituals

---

69. Marzal, *Tierra Encantada*, 269.
70. Mariátegui, *Siete Ensayos*, 136.
71. Dressendörfer, "Acercándose a una realidad," 29.
72. Pini, "La Cruz precristiana," 27.
73. Urbano, "Rituales andinos," 138–39.
74. Marzal, *Tierra Encantada*, 269–70.

like baptism, marriage, burial of the dead, and organized festivities to the saints. The local holidays, celebrated annually, were linked to the cross or certain saints. Despite all this, the aim of evangelization to reinforce the presence of the Roman Catholic Church did not succeed.

> The passivity with which the Indigenous allowed themselves to be catechized, not even understanding the catechism, made Catholicism in Peru spiritually thin. The missionary did not have to pay attention to the purity of the dogma; his mission was reduced to be a moral guide, to be an ecclesiastical pastor of a rustic and simple community that was not spiritually motivated.[75]

Christology particularly in Peru is reflected through aspects of the official church connected to Rome, the unofficial/Quechua church connected to popular Catholicism,[76] and African elements like the presence of the spirits that came from Africa.[77] The official Church stands on the teaching of the incarnation of Christ, in the authority of the sacred scriptures, and in promoting the following and imitation of Christ as part of its spirituality. Christ interceded for salvation until the point of death on the cross. To follow Jesus means to accept his way to the cross and to imitate such a sacrifice. Christ is really present during the Eucharist, bringing hope and healing based on the theory of satisfaction.[78] To follow God obediently means to accept Christ and to believe in his future return.

Christology in the popular/Quechua church developed through images because the experience of Christ was symbol centered. Believers knew, even though they did not have access to the scriptures because most of them were illiterate, that Christ is the Lord, that he was born from the Virgin Mary, that he did miracles, died on the cross, was resurrected, and would come again. In order to praise Christ the Lord, the Indigenous built their own images of Christ in their own towns and contexts, like the Lord of the Huaca, the Lord of Temblores, the Lord of Ayabaca, the Lord of Qoylur Rit'i, the Lord of Achajrapi, and others.

---

75. "La pasividad con que los indios se dejaron catequizar, sin comprender el catecismo, enflaqueció espiritualmente al catolicismo en el Perú. El misionero no tuvo que velar por la pureza del dogma; su misión se redujo al servir de guía moral, de pastor eclesiástico a una grey rustica y sencilla, sin inquietud espiritual ninguna" (Mariátegui, *Siete Ensayos*, 137).

76. Further explanations of the official Christology and the popular are found in Marzal, "La Religión Quechua Surandina," 252–54.

77. Mariátegui, *Siete Ensayos*, 138.

78. Migliore, *Faith Seeking Understanding*, 183, 184.

The images of Christ generated devotion because, according to believers, they heard their sorrows, consoled them, and did miracles. Christ is a concrete intercessor in the images. Christ does divine favors to preserve and renew the faith of his people. Miracles are the way Christ gets into relationship with people because they are concrete responses to difficulty. When a miracle did not occur, people believed that God was punishing them for their lack of faith. Local celebrations served to praise Christ[79] publicly and to carry out their promises to Christ made in exchange for the received material miracle. The Eucharist is not a central element in the local festivities; Christ is present in the sacred and profane elements, in their prayers and dances. Celebration is central to their spirituality because people are conscious of their daily crosses and struggles. Even though the centrality of Christ was carefully imposed, the Indigenous attachment to the Virgin was connected to the veneration to the earth and the Lake Titicaca. "Worship to the Virgin was centered in Lake Titicaca from –where the Incas theocracy seemed to arise—its most famous sanctuary."[80]

The "Pachacamilla Christ" or "Señor de los Milagros," is a black Christ symbolizing the racial composition of Peru. Animist African beliefs were joined combined with devotion to the image of Christ when the Angolan population formed the Pachacamilla brotherhood when the Jesuits evangelized them in 1620. The promotion of brotherhoods was a strategy for evangelization. The participants themselves invited families to celebrate religious rituals, to pray, and to sing. Their songs evoked freedom.[81] In the Pachacamilla brotherhood, a slave painted the image of the crucified on a rustic wall. That painting was later improved by the painter José de la Parra. During the earthquake of 1655, the wall on which it was painted did not suffer damage. Because the cross miraculously remained intact through constant earthquakes, the population started walking on the wall to the Cathedral of Lima. Since that time, the image was called

---

79. The religious festivities have the social function to integrate the population. They are organized by a yearly rotation assumed by "mayordomos," a traditional practice where a person or family assumes the organization and payment of certain economic expenses that the celebration will require. The celebrations accomplish the religious dimension because for people they are ways to offer gratitude to the Lord for the favors and miracles given to his people.

80. "El culto de la Virgen encontró en el lago Titicaca—de donde parecía nacer la teocracia incaica—su más famoso santuario" (Mariátegui, *Siete Ensayos*, 135).

81. Benito, "Historia del Señor de los Milagros," 150.

"The Lord of Miracles."[82] The growth of devotion and the annual processions were influenced by captain Sebastián Antuñano who in 1688 made a copy of the image and promoted the procession of the image accompanied by prayers and songs, and stopping at some corners and squares.[83] In 1671 the images of the Virgin Mary, Maria Magdalena, Saint John, the Father and the Holy Spirit were added to the image of Christ.[84]

The crucified Christ's image has, since the conquest, been the foundation for Christian faith. Crosses were placed in visible places like civil and religious houses. But the image of the crucified predominated over his resurrection. The devotion to the crucified Christ projected the believers' suffering on the crucified one,[85] and the crosses and Christ's images were given new dimensions to illuminate the higher level of devotion.[86] Believers searched for protection and salvation in Christ because he responded with individual and communal miracles.

This combination worked as the epistemological basis to recognize the transcendental[87] and to affirm the popular as truly and deeply religious. This Peruvian Christology is paradoxically the major expression of faith among the population,[88] a "valid mediation to live the Christian faith,"[89] but not really Christ-centric.[90] Marzal asserts that the popular Christology is the devotion to the variety of "Saints Christs"[91] that express the multi-ethnic character of Latin American faith. Christ, reduced to images, can be one more divinity in the divine pantheon of Andean

---

82. Benito, "Historia del Señor de los Milagros," 134. The image survived the tsunami of 1687 and an earthquake on October 28, 1746 in Lima. Since the last natural phenomenon, processions have been performed each year on the same date.

83. Benito, "Historia del Señor de los Milagros," 153.

84. Benito, "Historia del Señor de los Milagros," 163.

85. There are many characteristics of the cross. Some have the crucified with marks of his passion like the rooster, the crown of thorns, the hammer, the sword, the stairs, the cartel INRI, etc. Benito, "Historia del Señor de los Milagros," 76.

86. Marzal, *Tierra Encantada*, 323.

87. Marzal, *Tierra Encantada*, 315.

88. Manuel Marzal asserts that in Latin America it is well known that the popular Catholicism/religiosity is everywhere, therefore, (Marzal qualifies it) as omnipresent because it is the most popular sector of the church. Marzal, *Tierra Encantada*, 334.

89. Marzal, *Tierra Encantada*, 384.

90. Marzal, *Tierra Encantada*, 322–25.

91. "The Holy Christos." In Peru the diffusion of the Cross and the Crucified is deeply rooted in the suffering Christ that comes from the time of colonization. Pini, "La Devoción a la Cruz," 76.

people because the Trinity does not speak to them. The Father and the Holy Spirit are present but the one who was crucified was Christ, a tangible element of their own sufferings that paradoxically both console and renew their faith.

This panoramic view of the Peruvian Christology encourages the study to address a specific experience. For that specific case, the research will consider literature. Three novels from Clorinda Matto de Turner will help us to dive and swim in the perspective of a writer. From Matto's novels some Christological elements will illuminate a further reflection.

Suffering and Salvation in the Novels of Clorinda Matto de Turner

HAVING EXAMINED THE REALITY of the Peruvian context and observed the process of evangelization and its inroads it will be pertinent to turn our attention to the reality of life presented in fiction. Novels are like mirrors. Through beauty and fascination, literature reflects concrete situations. The fluid recounting of past and present dilemmas and events engages readers in the author's concerns. When a novel's message reverberates or resonates with reality, the reader is inspired by its vivid meaning to connect to contemporary challenges. Novels place before the reader significant perceptions in the imaginary realm. They include beliefs, feelings, frustrations, and dreams, and they develop chains of relationships and organization. Novels powerfully and artistically clarify and reveal notions and experiences. Ultimately they function as vigilant eyes and critical reflections ripe with theological gifts and insights.

The Inspiration for Clorinda Matto de Turner's Novel

The work of Peruvian writer, Clorinda Matto de Turner (1853–1909), offers the possibility to contemplate past generations' lives and struggles. In her novel *Aves sin nido*, Matto reveals that "the novel has to be a photograph that stereotypes the vices and the virtues of a town with the consequent corrective moral for [past generations] and the homage of admiration for (the new ones)"[1] The corrective intention points to moral issues within the concrete Peruvian Indigenous' traditions. What does *Mita* mean to the Indigenous Peruvian, for example? How has this communal labor practice changed and a new meaning come to be defended by the political, religious, and civil authorities? How are women used in this communal concept? Matto, an active and heartfelt observer, develops

---

1. Matto de Turner, *Aves sin nido*, vii.

a careful scrutiny of ecclesial, political, and civil authorities. Traditions and practices were subverted by the authorities and Matto highlights this dangerous subversion.

Matto's vivid language brings the reader to a comprehension of new realities. Matto, a Spanish speaker, understood the value that the Indigenous culture offers; therefore, she entered into the world view of the Indigenous to find visible places where Jesus incarnates. Matto's deep commitment and solidarity with the Indigenous population invites one to approach her literary production from the theological and Christological angle. Matto's insights make full sense. The raw material contained in Matto's novels makes possible a dialogue that will enrich theology and Christology. The narrative reflections nourish the theological exercise;[2] they are like fresh land, the fruits of which speak from a determined moment and circumstance. To "pay attention to human dilemmas [and enigmas] that literature reflects"[3] is a duty because a theologian enriches her/his perception precisely while embodying human dilemmas.

In Latin America, mythic-religiosity is vital. It is essential to understand these expressions of "the real marvelous [to perceive] the extraordinary things behind the superficial epidermis of the ordinary things."[4] By attending carefully to the ordinary, the "mythic-religious reverse[s our idea of supernatural focused on the power of men and women, seeking] refuge in gods and myths to [move up] hope against all hope."[5] By reading Matto, we read into the reality of marginalized men and women. This reality leads from bodily defect to the body of Christ.

To work with the three important novels of Clorinda Matto de Turner, *Aves sin nido*, *Índole*, and *Herencia*, moves us also to be in touch with the author herself. Matto, who translated into Quechua the Gospel of Luke and the book of Acts, reveals her deep love towards and solidarity with Indigenous people. The novels challenge the Christology of her time, which was comprised of a mixture between the atonement theory of satisfaction and the Christ the Victor theory. The emphasis in the suffering of the vicarious Christ is used to impose suffering on Indians as part of their destiny, and the notion of Christ the Victor is used to emphasize the triumph of Christ over evil and pagan (Indians' gods) forces and powers.

---

2. Rivera, *Teología y Cultura*, 62.
3. Rivera, *Mito, Exilio y Demonios*, 8.
4. Rivera, *Mito, Exilio y Demonios*, 28–29.
5. Rivera, *Mito, Exilio y Demonios*, 31, 37.

Matto offers relevant topics for Christology: the condition of women in a very patriarchal and racial-economically structured society, the solidarity between women who are able to overcome their racial and economic disparities, the notion of abjection that reveals social systems where people of Indigenous and African descent are treated cruelly, the ethics of the ordained ministry that connects directly to Jesus' ministry, and the notion of salvation that is, in a certain way, informed by the notion of progress.

Suffering and Salvation in Clorinda Matto de Turner

Since the cross plays a central role in the Christological Peruvian context, it will be considered in the theological reflection that the novels offer. Clorinda Matto de Turner presents three rich novels, *Aves sin nido*, *Índole*, and *Herencia* in which she reveals a deep love for the Indigenous. The novels seek to identify a Christology of suffering, impregnated by the mixture of the atonement theory of satisfaction. Although Christ is not present *Aves sin nido*, the idea of satisfaction is present through the demands of justice that the Yupanqui family needs to pay, and in consequence, the Marin family pays the financial debt. Reading *Aves sin nido* from the Marin's perspective, it will be easy to see the Marins as saviors because they stand up to the rural authorities who oppress and abuse the Indigenous. But the Marin's defense of the Indigenous results in the death of the Yupanquis' parents. The girls' parents are the ones who pay with their own lives. In order to confirm this notion of salvation or not, the present research will engage in a theological reading of Matto's novels.

Consciousness, Engagement, and Fragmentation

Clorinda Matto is an insightful reader of reality, one who can contemplate past generations' lives and struggles and translate these events into a meaningful portrayal of the Andean population's suffering. In her novel *Aves sin nido*, Matto observes that "the novel has to be a photograph that stereotypes the vices and the virtues of a town with the consequent corrective moral from (past generations) and the homage of admiration for (the new ones)."[6] Morality encompasses Matto's novels because the ethical element becomes necessary in order to untie the complex knot between

---

6. Matto de Turner, *Aves sin nido*, vii.

the religious, political and civil authorities. Matto tends to be prescriptive about how individuals should act. Her novels have a clear moral focus. Matto's reading of the social context allows her to identify the relationship between the civil, political, and religious authorities, characterized by corruption and greed, as a source of the exploitation of the Indigenous. Matto's corrective intention employs morality to raise consciousness about the authorities. In *Aves sin nido*, Matto depicts how the authorities use their power to adapt colonial practices while alluding to ancestral traditions. Matto deplores the use of the Indigenous' traditions, inviting us instead to rethink the notion of the *reparto* or *mita*[7] and its distortion to continue the exploitation of the Indigenous populations.

Clorinda Matto, a privileged daughter of her time, came from a Spanish speaking family and had the opportunity to learn Quechua in her childhood. She was well educated, having the opportunity to study under different tutors including Trinidad María Enríquez, "the pugnacious provocateur that promoted intellect and liberation of women"[8] who influenced Matto's understanding of Indigenous populations and especially Indigenous women. Being sympathetic, Matto points out in *Aves sin nido* and *Índole* the injustices and abuse that some priests practiced against women. First, *Aves sin nido* narrates the hidden suffering of two women, Petronila, the mother of Manuel and Marcela, the mother of Margarita. Manuel and Margarita are the son and daughter of the priest Claros, who is the former priest of the town.[9] Second, *Índole* details the tortuous and sensual personality of the Priest Isidoro Peñas

---

7. Mita was a communitarian labor system. Mita was often used interchangeably with *repartimiento* and *encomienda* that not only refers to forced labor but to the colonial practice where repartimiento was connected to the mita to sustain forced labor in mining and agricultural tasks. Matto's novel narrates and highlights the use of this practice while distorting and transposing it in favor of the local authorities. Matto de Turner, *Aves sin nido*, 5.

8. Tauro, *Clorinda Matto de Turner y la Novela*, 9.

9. Matto challenges the notion of Priest's celibacy by demonstrating the clergy abuse of women in *Aves sin nido*. On one hand, the Indigenous Marcela, before dying as the result of a shot, reveals a secret to Lucía and to the Priest Pascual Vargas that her daughter was not the daughter of Juan Yupanqui, her husband, but the daughter of bishop Claro, a former Priest of Killac. Matto de Turner, *Aves sin nido*, 71, 183. On the other hand, Manuel believes that he is the illegitimate son of Don Sebastián, who is actually the husband of his mother Petronila and the governor of Killac, but he discovers that his love for Margarita is impossible because he also is the son of the former priest of Killac, Pedro Miranda y Claro. Matto de Turner, *Aves sin nido*, 60, 182.

who eagerly requests the love of a married woman paying no respect to her honesty and marriage.[10]

Matto also exposes the suffering of the Indigenous by connecting it to the *mita* tradition used by the local authorities to abuse and exploit the Indigenous. Servitude was imposed by forcing Indigenous families to receive an advance payment in exchange for the wool production for the year. The local authorities knew that the imposed payment would cause the Indigenous to spend what they needed for their daily life. Consequently, the local authorities increased the taxes and made the Indigenous' economic condition even more difficult. In *Aves sin nido*, Matto develops a plot of subjection by identifying the local social system of power. She treats the reality of misery and suffering and proposes the education of the Indigenous as a necessary solution. Education is, for Matto, a way to make progress toward the greater goal of national integration. Education, crucial for progress, is promoted for Indigenous and women. Matto practiced what she preached, so to speak, when she founded the paper *La Equitativa* in 1889 and employed only women to work for it.[11]

What Matto seems to propose in her novels *Aves sin nido* and *Herencia* is that national integration occurs by evening out differences, which in the case of the Andean people means that their customs must be suppressed by their assimilation into the modern reality of Lima influenced by Western development. Instead of the preservation of the Indigenous condition and traditions, Matto proposes transformation. In the dramas of *Aves sin nido* and *Herencia*, the two orphans that the Marin family adopts are moved to the capital city where they enter into a new reality, a new language, a new worldview. The author affirms the value of the modernization of the capital city. Again, modernization and progress are intended to cancel the traditional values and principles of life in Killac by emphasizing the advantages that the capital city offers.[12] On the one hand, Matto is captivated by the simplicity of the Andean population, by the beauty of their women, and the splendor of nature, but on the other hand, Matto dilutes these positive distinctions by promoting the ideal of national integration that is not possible in the Andean reality.

---

10. In *Índole*, the Priest Isidoro Peñas recognizes his pathetic behavior as weakness rather than a crime, and later he declares his love to Eulalia claiming that his feelings are spiritual affection, requesting the same spiritual love in return. See Matto de Turner, *Índole*, 98, 77.

11. Tauro, *Clorinda Matto de Turner y la Novela*, 1–17.

12. Cornejo Polar, *Clorinda Matto de Turner*, 36.

The overemphasis on the simplicity of the Andean population prevents the author from finding the richness of the Indigenous agency and their capacity to overcome their reality.

Matto touches on the conflicts of Killac and points to the group of corrupted authorities who subjugate the population. Matto is clear in her attack against the subjugation of the Indigenous. Nevertheless, in her aim to propose a global solution, Matto promotes a suitable integration of the two Indigenous girls into the larger reality of the capital city. That reality is also characterized by chaos, disorder, and confusion. The proposal to adopt the girls and move them from the Andean area to the capital city is an easy solution because it does not and does not need to resolve the dilemma of the ones who remained there.

Even given this situation, the educational proposal is pertinent. But as the girls' adoption happens, Matto sees education as integration. The Marin family is Matto's paradigm; therefore, Lucía acts as a mirror for Indigenous women. She is white and her face is identified with the face of the Virgin[13] by Marcela, the birth mother of the two adopted girls. Margarita, the daughter of an Indigenous women and a priest, inherits from Lucía, her adoptive mother, education which allows her to succeed in the life of modern Lima.[14] The education that Margarita will receive, according to *Herencia*, from her adoptive mother will be the distinctive mark that will determine who the person is.

Education is linked to national integration and its achievement seems to happen in Lima and not in Killac. Matto suggests integration through fragmentation. The breakup and separation of the girls from their small community, traditions, and biological relatives enrich their experience and enable them to succeed in metropolitan Lima, while looking toward the horizon of Europe. Matto is open to the description of different realities but life is in Lima. Lima, according to Matto, is the bridge where the encounter between the modern and the conventional takes place. Lima is also a place where corruption and chaos exist. Although

---

13. First, Marcela talking to Lucía says, "you have the face of the Virgin to whom we pray and worship and therefore I come to ask to save my husband . . ." Second, When Marcela shares her conversation with Lucía, Marcela confirms to her husband Juan, "I have seen the same face of the Virgin in the face of Mrs. Lucía." See Matto de Turner, *Aves sin nido*, 5, 16.

14. Education as a component of modernity leads Margarita and Rosalía, the two orphans adopted by the Marin family to be educated in Lima and to mirror the ideal women. The social sphere gives, especially to Margarita, the opportunity to exercise the inheritance bequeathed her adoptive mother. Matto de Turner, *Herencia*, 176.

this is a fact, it is also a key to note that Matto is a pioneer in feeling and exposing the unavoidable in-between of mixed races and faiths of the Andean population. She is also pioneering in sensing that the movement of the rural population to the capital city is unavoidable. Matto's proposal to move the Indigenous to the capital city and to educate them according to family values has the patronage idea that avoids the promotion of the Indigenous' own subjectivity and capacities.

Exposure of the Human Condition

Matto, an active and heartfelt observant of reality, portrays a careful scrutiny of the role of the ecclesial, the political, and the civil authorities in Killac. She unmasks the misuse of the mita tradition whose original intent before the Spaniards' arrival was to pay a collective tribute to the Incas. During the Incan empire, the mita served on agricultural function that sustained Indigenous life. Matto observes the distortion of the mita by the local authorities in Killac. They use the mita to promote servitude and to punish those who do not accomplish their interests. The Indigenous who were unable to pay the church services or who failed to produce raw materials were requested to serve, especially women, in the monastic house and church.[15] Marcela, for instance, desperately seeks help from Lucía, asking her for money to pay the family debt of ten pesos that the authorities advanced them for wool production. Her family also borrows money from the church because of the burial services for Marcela's mother in law's funeral.[16] Marcela knows the sacrifice of the mita; she recognizes that women who serve the mita in the church go home looking at the ground;[17] therefore, Marcela implores Lucía to help.

In *Aves sin nido* published in 1885, *Índole* published in 1892, and *Herencia* published in 1895 the *abjection* motif is radically developed. In *Aves sin nido*, the author relates abjection to the excessively humble

15. Matto de Turner, *Aves sin nido*, 11, 31.

16. If the Indigenous neglected to produce the wool for the ten pesos pay in advance, they were charged 120 pesos. If the family was not able to pay this amount, the authorities took one of their daughters or sons to sell them in pay of their debt. Matto de Turner, *Aves sin nido*, 3, 24–25.

17. The mita in the novel implies not only someone to wash dishes and clothes in the church but also to supply sexual favors; for that reason the Indigenous Marcela conceived Margarita, the daughter of the priest Claros. Matto de Turner, *Aves sin nido*, 11, 31–32.

attitude mixed with passivity manifested by Indigenous people. The Indigenous were considered wicked because they were humble before a structure of oppression imposed by the local authorities. According to Matto, the Indigenous are modest and she admires that, but this attitude makes their miserable condition even more difficult. Exactly because of their modesty they are exploited and abused. The Indigenous naturally accept suffering. This absurd element is for Matto contradictory because it leads the Indigenous to a vile state.[18]

Marcela, for instance, always expresses an extreme respect for the authorities and the Marin family. She trembles before the priest and does not make eye contact with Lucía and Fernando because of her great respect. The same happens with other Indigenous like the priest's servant or pongo who meets all the needs of the priest.[19] The abject and miserable always apologize. It is a characteristic that the author brilliantly highlights but her emphasis of the Indigenous' simplicity does not allow us to see other strengths and qualities like their feelings, customs, and traditions to deal with difficult situations. Instead of elevating their weakness and natural kindness, which make them dependent on the foreigners, Matto needs to explore a bit more the qualities of the Indigenous.

But the virtue of the novel resides in stressing the Indigenous' abjection as a consequence of exploitation and submission. Matto sees the Indigenous' potential and the local authorities' cruelty. She observes how the authorities use the Indigenous' docility to promote passiveness and obedience. Matto denounces the use of passivity to impose absolute submission which increases the Indigenous' disgrace and the deterioration of their human condition. The Indigenous' misery and humbleness is for the authorities a gift disrupted by the presence of foreigners[20] who are open to helping and to reversing that situation.

In *Índole*, Matto expands on the theme of abjection. The recognition of the Indigenous' miserable condition happens because of their misery and poverty. The Indigenous survive by holding on to their dejected situation and by accepting servitude. Matto criticizes this abject misery as a

---

18. Matto de Turner, *Aves sin nido*, viii, 69.

19. Matto de Turner, *Aves sin nido*, 37.

20. Conscious of the threat that the Marin family implies for the priest and the governor, the local authorities conspire against the Marin family, "the foreigners who arrived to impose laws modifying our customs that subsisted since our ancestors." The local authorities affirm their unity in order not to change the "repartos." Matto de Turner, *Aves sin nido*, 20–21.

result of being sentenced to life in poverty. Poverty is not a coincidence but a result of the oppression that this race has been subjected to.[21] In an effort to unmask the reality of abjection, Matto points to historical reasons for the disjunction between object and subject that generates the state of Indigenous' marginalization. Matto sees that even the mestizo, in the condition of servant, is objectified by their lord in order to accomplish the lord's will.[22] Matto is exceptional in revealing this condition, but she does not return to the past in order to address the historical roots of poverty and oppression. Matto links submission to obedience, but in *Índole* a dissonant element occurs when Idelfonso betrays his lord's desire by staying at his girlfriend Ziska's place before accomplishing the mandate to follow Mr. Valentín.[23] Idelfonso dreams of marrying and he accomplishes his will, but he does not change his servile state. The central element in *Índole* is to portray Eulalia as a model for women to follow because she resists the priest's intentions.[24] Matto focuses on abuse and submission while unmasking the authorities' motto to sustain exploitation based on local traditions. In both imaginary communities, Kíllac and Rosalina, Matto details the corrupt environment. In Killac, the authorities used traditional customs to sustain immorality and to leave the Indigenous in servitude.[25] Exploitation is a subtly present practice intended to degrade and to maintain Indigenous people in misery.

In *Herencia*, Matto also touches on the abjection motif by focusing on the condition of the poor. The abject poor are skillfully depicted through the suffering and survival of Espíritu Cadenas, a single and abandoned mother of African descent. Espíritu lives in a small and dense corridor in a barrio of Lima.[26] In order to survive and to nourish her two daughters, Espíritu takes out a loan and trades objects for money.[27] *Herencia*

21. Matto de Turner, *Índole*, 2.

22. Idelfonso is a mestizo who serves and accomplishes even the requirement of Mrs. Asunción to follow and spy on her husband Mr. Valentín. Matto de Turner, *Índole*, 12.

23. Matto de Turner, *Índole*, 23–25.

24. Matto de Turner, *Índole*, 94–95.

25. The civil, religious and political authorities conspire against the foreign couple Lucía and Fernando because their influence intends, according the authorities, to change their customs that subsisted and received from their ancestors. Matto de Turner, *Aves sin nido*, 21.

26. Matto de Turner, *Herencia*, 27–29.

27. Matto de Turner, *Herencia*, 39–40.

sets out different patterns inherited by women of diverse social classes. Espíritu reveals her traditional practices but her struggle for survival and the necessity for her to make compromises[28] is clearly depicted. Espíritu's miserable financial condition is mixed with abuse. Espíritu's body is marked by the lines of suffering, shame, frustration, bankruptcy, as well as the mercy she receives from her neighbors, and the enjoyment of occasional relationships and celebrations. Even though Espíritu is a secondary character, her presence makes real the class structure and the abject state of her being miserable, poor, a woman, and black.

Conversion and Salvation in *Aves sin nido*, *Índole*, and *Herencia*

Matto depicts the Indigenous and the women of African descent as abjected beings. Abjection related to humbleness and misery places the Indigenous in front of a structure that oppresses, but paradoxically the abjected accept almost naturally these circumstances. In the face of this absurd and cruel reality of suffering, resistance does not take place;[29] rather, Matto proposes a notion of salvation promoted and developed by the Marins. In the case of *Herencia*, Espíritu is a great character but she disappears in the narration because the main argument of the novel is to demonstrate how successful the Marins were in educating, raising, and imbuing Margarita with the virtues of a good family.

In *Aves sin nido*, the author establishes the Marin family as a paradigm who evoke the notion of salvation. The author develops events and circumstances where the foreign family receives honor and recognition. In *Aves sin nido*, Marcela identifies Lucía's face with the face of the Virgin but also Fernando Marin is called Viracocha by Juan and Marcela Yupanqui[30] that, according to the novel's clarification, the author uses as a synonym for lord. Even given that explanation, the concept still identifies the foreign as the son of the sun god. In the case of Espíritu Cadenas, in *Herencia*, the savior motif does not take place because the author's aim is to describe Espíritu's life and to affirm that she inherited nothing good from her ancestors. This clearly points to a lack of consciousness about the historical struggle of African slave

---

28. Matto de Turner, *Herencia*, 41.
29. Matto de Turner, *Aves sin nido*, 69.
30. Matto de Turner, *Aves sin nido*, 25.

descendants and the subjugation that they lived. Inheritance in the experience of Espiritu needs to be read through different lenses than the ones that Matto is uses to read Margarita's heritage.

In *Aves sin nido*, Matto uses the abjection motif, the radical conditions of Indigenous' exclusion, in order to introduce the rescuers who, in the novel, act as saviors. The Marin family plays the savior role which is connected to the idea of patronage, even though there is not a relationship of patron–servant between the two families. The economic support that Yupanqui receives to rescue their second daughter and the money to pay the priest for the funeral services that also rescued Marcela from the mita service were provided by the Marins. Without them, the Yupanquis would not have saved their daughter and themselves. The Marins are not only recognized as an excellent family, they have the economic power to confront the corrupt authorities of Kíllac.

Salvation and purification occur in *Aves sin nido* and *Herencia*. Salvation is an economic condition because the Marins provide what the Yupanquis lack, money, to solve the abuse suffered by the Yupanquis at the hands of the religious, political, and civil authorities. There is no other way to get the authorities to see the reality of suffering of their neighbors. First, the authorities are called to conversion; Lucía makes the effort to persuade the priest, in the name of the Christian religion, to change his behavior and attitude against the Yupanqui family.[31] In her intercession, Lucía makes the priest reflect on the reward of heaven if he exempts the poor family from their debt. Fernando, on his side, pays the Yupanquis' debt to the governor to rescue Rosalía, the Yupanquis' second daughter, who was taken as hostage for the debt.[32] The purification theme is solved by the author when the Marins adopt Margarita and Rosalía as daughters and drive them to Lima in order to decontaminate them from the vices of Kíllac. Both girls are decontaminated from immorality and depravation; both girls are educated and saved from ignorance; both girls will live the promises of a better world where progress is the means to succeed as a person, community and nation.

It is important to note the idea of victory in the triumph of the Marins (Christ) over the power of the local authorities of Kíllac (the evil and pagan forces). It makes it possible to understand a Christology based on benefactors and patronage. The Marin family act as the redeemers for

31. Matto de Turner, *Aves sin nido* 10.
32. Matto de Turner, *Aves sin nido* 12, 28–29.

the Yupanqui and, especially, for the orphans Margarita and Rosalía. The virtue of the novel resides in building solidarity between women but that solidarity happens by change and loss; the orphans will have new opportunities and new influences in the future, but they will lose their culture, identity, and past. Matto discusses the moral values of the ordained ministry. Her contention is that priests would serve better being married,[33] but in criticizing celibacy, Matto connects ministry and salvation to the notion of progress. Progress means development; therefore, according to Matto's vision, the task to overcome archaic Christian practices to advance towards a higher standard is needed in the Peruvian society at the beginning of the nineteenth century.

Matto's method of purifying the abject is to remove them from their real environment. There is no conversion of the Marins to the reality of Kíllac because that conversion will signify struggling against the corrupted structure and its authorities. This breakdown is avoided because progress will be difficult to achieve in the reality of Kíllac, and in this way, Matto depicts a hopeless future for those who remain in the small town of Kíllac and for those who continue to suffer from abuse and exploitation. The challenge to re-conceptualize the presence of the body of Christ, also present in places like Kíllac and not only in the so-called progressive Lima, and its resurrection goes beyond progress. Matto invites a review of progress, one that will challenge the extraordinary focus on material development and technology. There is the need to identify a way to see the extra-ordinary in the Indigenous and the impact they can have on progress through their own condition.

Matto believed in progress as a national project, just as the colonizers did in Christianity. The Indigenous express their faith in concrete elements and, in the case of Matto's novels, they do believe in the foreigner. The Indigenous demonstrated their ability to expand their spirituality, their capacity to create space for new gods, especially when survival was at play. The sophisticated ways of both accepting and resisting new elements that challenged their beliefs also created a means to resist complete submission. Matto perceived the submissive state of the Indigenous and tries to rescue them from that state. The evangelizers emphasized the passion and triumph of Christ in order to maintain faith, while Matto proposed progress, almost a new religion where the glorification of development and the market was to come. The Indigenous accepted with

---

33. Cornejo Polar, *Clorinda Matto de Turner*, 49.

fervor both proposals because the process of evangelization would never be the inverse, would never come from the Indigenous' side. In that sense, Matto's novels contain an element of hope but this hope is limited by the foreigners' actions that help to change the Indigenous' condition.

An Attempt to Read Clorinda Matto's Novels from a Different Historical Period

Clorinda Matto de Turner captures the cultural and religious notions of a small population of the Andean Indigenous. Matto reads the context of suffering and offers ways to understand Jesus Christ's solidarity with the Indigenous' suffering. A theological reading that tries to review a literary production not considering the time and challenges that the writer faced has the chance to develop a chronological mistake in its analysis. Matto is moved toward the suffering of the Indigenous and even her proposal for change is influenced by progress;[34] she offers unavoidable elements to Christology. Solidarity is one of the topics that arises. In the context of the devastating Pacific War with Chile,[35] there was the need to propose a solution because the Indigenous suffered most the consequences of the war. Matto analyses the roots of injustice based in that reality, but she is able to feel the experiences of the Andean context. The fact that the Indigenous' tragedy lived for centuries is again connected to the war. Reading Matto within her time and within the parameters of the novel, it is helpful to consider that her proposal to promote justice is linked to the sociopolitical, religious, and racial matrices. Matto lifts up the abject reality of

---

34. It is correct to affirm that "the problem of the Indigenous is not a problem of education" considering that pedagogy needs to take into account the social and economic factors. See Mariátegui, *Siete Ensayos*, 33. But Clorinda Matto was in the vanguard of her time. Even though her proposal of education is linked to development, she does consider the economic and social factors without necessarily making a punctual analysis of them as Mariátegui requires. Matto is a writer who offers elements that illustrate the need to be educated as an access to employment, to recognition, to have an academic title. In a country where more than half of the population was illiterate, education was needed.

35. The Pacific War took place from 1879 to 1884 and "the Indigenous men were forced into the front lines of the battle and critics of Peru's entry into the war claimed that the indigenous populations lacked the patriotic fervor necessary to win the war. For these critics it was not that the indigenous soldiers were innately unpatriotic, but rather it was the state's purposeful exclusion of indigenous peoples [who were illiterate] from the benefits of citizenship that had contributed to their weak sense of national solidarity during the war period" (Castillo, *Indigenous*, 6).

the Indigenous because she is conscious that among the rural authorities there is a prevailing practice of injustice both supported and employed by certain religious authorities. Matto understands that injustice is not the nature and the way human relations should be developed. In her insistence, she is able to name injustice from different angles. Social injustice is created through the social strata or structure that divides the authorities and the indigenous populations. Matto makes us aware of religious injustice. Matto eloquently invites a review of celibacy, a dense drama within the Roman Catholic Church presently. Matto approaches the juridical injustice because her novel invites us to understand that the legal system, instead of moving its power in favor of needy people, becomes part of the corrupted system. And although Matto does not develop an analysis of the impact of the economic system based on the private ownership of the means of production and distribution of goods, she is able to realize that when abuse takes place the appropriation of the means of productions is part of the abuse that the Indigenous unjustly experience.

The Consciousness of Clorinda Matto de Turner

Clorinda Matto was a conscious woman. She illuminates a critical understanding of the Andean reality. She embraces the hopeless by proposing hope. *Aves sin nido* was controversial because it opens the wounds that uncover oppression and challenges even the religious realm.[36] Matto believed and dreamed of a more human church. She envisioned a church where their ministers would be able to touch their humanity and to accept the need of marriage. Matto challenges the religious vow, affirming that it does not work for all. Matto, being conscious about the celibate state, tries to open a difficult but real dilemma of being human given the disposition to serve as an ordained minister.

Matto strongly continued to deal with the ethical dilemma. In *Índole*, Matto points out the contradictory behavior of the authorities, their procreation of unrecognized children,[37] and the alteration of marriage, arguing that "simple compassion for the simple and incommensurable

---

36. In 1890, the bishop from Arequipa extended an ecclesiastical interdiction against *Aves sin nido*. For around five years, Matto tried to overcome this situation and continued publishing *Índole* and *Herencia*. After years of hard work the exile was unavoidable. Matto left Peru and established herself in Argentina. See Tauro, *Clorinda Matto de Turner y la Novela*, 16–23.

37. Matto de Turner, *Aves sin nido*, 183.

affect" by the priest.[38] Matto uses the moral element to show the problematic nature of celibacy and to address the ethical problems behind corrupted authorities. She virtuously protests the abuses and injustices while helping us to perceive the complexity of the Andean world[39] and in doing so, she does not neglect to point out the suffering and unjustified misery of the Indigenous experience.

Matto is a woman with serious commitments. Her kind reading of the reality of suffering of particular women inspires me to approach a gender reading. Even though gender was not Matto's first concern, she is in tune with the suffering of women of Indigenous and African descent. Matto proposes solidarity in her effort to build a different nation. In *Herencia*, she argues for the potential of unity and cohesion in the introduction to the different class realities of Lima through of the adopted daughters of the Marin family. The story in *Aves sin nido* ends with the orphan Margarita being adopted by Lucia and Manuel Marin. In *Herencia*, the new family settles in Lima only to deal with social and class issues. Even Matto demonstrated that Lima is not so different from the Andean reality. She introduces new characters like a woman of African descent and "investigates the factor and characteristics that define the parameters of social class, of social mobility, and the tactics of surviving in the new environment of aggressive capitalist competency."[40]

Matto can be criticized because in *Aves sin nido* she engages too much in a romantic reading of the Indigenous reality or because she is too caught up in the celibacy motif. But the virtue of the novel is that Matto touches important elements like injustice, corruption, abjection, abuse, and celibacy. I criticize *Herencia* because it determines the condition of a person and the proposal to change to the side of the Marins and not to that of the Indigenous. I admit that *Herencia* offers great potential when approaching Espiritu, a women of African descent woman who lamentably disappears in the novel.

In that sense, Matto's aim to accomplish the national assimilation motif is depicted through Margarita's story. This young Indigenous is able to learn and to be part of a society that welcomes, challenges, and invites her to assume a new life. Margarita, ironically, inherits new and vital elements for her life. Her adoptive mother receives all the merits and in

---

38. Matto de Turner, *Índole*, 98.
39. Cornejo Polar, *Clorinda Matto de Turner*, 63.
40. Mary Berg, "Prologue," in Matto de Turner, *Índole*, viii.

there the concept of change presents theological challenges. The novel does not deal with reconciliation and although its purpose was never the theological task, it brings concepts to engage in theology.

Theological Challenges: A Theological Approach to Clorinda Matto de Turner

After reading Matto's novels, especially *Aves sin nido*, the Christology of patronage seems to be present. The reason for this affirmation remains in Matto's proposal of salvation. If the novel has the virtue to denounce the injustices and corruption, it also moves to the tragic death of the Yupanqui. Matto does not leave a place for reconciliation. In *Aves sin nido* the Indigenous recognize Fernando as the god Viracocha and Lucía as the Virgin. These connections alert us to the period of colonization where, in tune with the author, a white family with a good socio-economic position wants to change the Indigenous culture. For that reason, the Marins are a model proposal to save the Peruvian nation.

The novel appears to propose salvation as the liberation of the Indigenous suffering through the process of correction and morality imposed on the corrupted authorities. Even though this proposal seems valid for the author, she does not develop this topic. The authorities were opposed to the Marins and they respond attacking them until the point that Juan and Marcela lost their lives. Salvation is wrongly expressed when it remains in economic terms; that is when the Marins pay the Yupanquis' debt to recover their daughter and their land. By being benevolent benefactors, the Marins drive the Yupanquis to the cross. At this point, the Yupanquis pay for the conflict with their own lives.

The idea of salvation is narrow in *Aves sin nido*. Salvation remains at the Marins' side and is economic. Perhaps because that proposal collapses, they have the moral duty to adopt the two orphans. The transactions reveal suffering and the reality of the orphans' loss. In this sense, the novel does not explore the dimension of loss, orphanage, and adoption. Apparently, the Marins liberate the Indigenous from the tortuous hostility and avarice of the local authorities. But what really happens is a consequence of the Marins' position, the Yupanquis and the entire town suffer the consequences of the loss: loss of trust, loss of the Yupanquis' parents, loss of energy, and loss of the opportunity to get in dialogue. It is relevant to notice that restoration seems pertinent here but it does not take place in *Aves sin nido*.

Reconciliation and restoration are needed. Salvation in Christological terms leads to the actions of Jesus that in the first place will invite some to the commitment of solidarity and others to consciousness. What *Aves sin nido* lacks is a time to sit down to engage in dialogue. Through dialogue it is possible to touch the wounded being and to unwind what has been hurt. Instead, Matto sustains a kind of white messianism that has economic power. Salvation in the novel follows the ransom atonement motif that enhances patronage and dependence. Dealing with the death of the Yupanquis, the novel proposes a new salvation in the adoption motif. The problem with this concept is that the Marins want to possess and to duplicate, as *Herencia* points out, who they are in two orphans. Their success will indicate the kind of person Margarita is. The concept of adoption in the novel is narrow. It does not allow relationships to be built based on freedom and in the recognition of the person, her customs, legacy, and history. It also does not promote autonomy that will inspire the Marins themselves to change because change happens mutually.

Redemption of the Marins' type is confusing because payment of the Indigenous debt does not solve their problems. They became the benefactors and protectors of the two orphans; they wanted the others to change but they were not open to change. In the case of the orphans the proposal has its high moment. Only Margarita succeeds, or at least she is the only one who inherited the Marins' way of being. Wishing that the orphans do not suffer their parents' suffering is a good desire but more than avoiding that suffering they needed to grow equipped with tools to face the changes and difficulties of life. They needed to be conscious of their roots and to learn strategies to survive and succeed in a very aggressive but at the same time, hopeful reality.

Matto finds Lima to be the Promised Land. This eschatological reality leads us to see the capital city like the last reality where people dream of being. Therefore, the movement from the town side to the capital has an escapist notion. The Andean town is not hell. As any other place, in the small towns people can find corruption-injustice and love-justice. Moving the orphans from their Andean town, Matto makes a break. In her proposal, this break is critical because education and progress only occur out of the Andean context, in the promised Lima.

Metaphorically, the division between earth and heaven takes place in Matto's novels. According to *Aves sin nido,* Killac and the corrupt authorities represent the earthly sinner reality while Lima and the Marins symbolize the heavenly reality. The two antagonistic realities remain separated without a proposal for conciliation and reconciliation. The author offers an artistic proposal to relocate the Indigenous at the center, in Lima. Ironically in this proposal, the Andean context remains corrupted. Heaven seems to be located in the capital city, a reality outside of the Indigenous reality. Even more ironic is that *Herencia* reveals that the heavenly Lima is illusory. In this sense, Matto's insistence to see the capital and later Europe as promised places comes with the mystery of progress.

Despite these problematic elements from the theological side, Matto should be thanked for her consciousness about the inhuman condition of the Indigenous. She bravely denounces the view of the Indigenous as abject. Perhaps her dream was to move the authorities to progress, but since this movement was absent, Matto's proposal for change is specific to the orphans. But change is created and directed towards the Roman Catholic Church. In this sense, Matto succeeds because she uncovers a motif that was negated and avoided for centuries. According to Matto, celibacy is an archaic practice that inhibits some priests from living their humanity fully. Eagerly, Matto proposes the marriage of priests, recognizing that bad priests use their power to fulfill their human instincts and leave unacknowledged sons and daughters. The local authorities are part of this corrupted system. They continue the insane circle that blinds them to see and feel the suffering of their people. Matto identifies with that suffering, sees the victims, denounces injustice, and identifies the perpetrators. From that, she proposes the marriage of priests but does not open a dialogue among the community, authorities and population, to bring fresh and deep insights about celibacy. This is a task that, step by step with consciousness, this research finds pertinent for today.

6

Who Do You Say that I Am?
A Relational Christology

THE PERU OF TODAY, rooted in a multifaceted cultural and religious history, can be recognized as the Peru of *Todas las Sangres*,[1] of diverse cultural and religious experiences where the struggle to build up identity and change walk hand in hand. Peru, a country with much diversity, cannot avoid the social hierarchy set up in the colonial period determined by economic power and race. The imposed Western Christology failed to be contextualized. Conquerors and the evangelizers were unable to consider the sacred religions present there.

Jesus Christ in the Diverse Peruvian Context

Jesus Christ arrived in the southern areas of the Americas through the expansion of the Iberian Spanish Christian Empire mainly disregarding the Indigenous' world views. Judged as inferior, the Indigenous faith was discredited–including their culture and history. And that history and culture were disrupted by believers in Christ.

Forced conversion to the Christian faith was an excuse the conquerors used to support the image of an earthly king through the process of celestial transference of power to the ones who ruled the empire. Their intention was also to maintain oppression justified through the fraudulent use of the monarchical image of Christ. The conquerors continuously reinforced and manipulated the death of Jesus Christ, and his passivity on the cross, for political and religious purposes. Jesus' death image

---

1. In an attempt to reconstruct the changes in Peruvian society, Arguedas analyses and depicts colonial capitalism, forced emigration from Andean to coastal areas, and the landowner system. To reconstruct change, Arguedas depicts the tension dynamics that impeded transformation. *Todas las Sangres* was written in 1964.

came from the Iberian Peninsula, specifically from southern Spain and reflected the experience of common people under Arabian and Muslim domination. This Jesus suffered for the people but was defenseless, impotent, and defeated. The image of the dead Christ was carried in processions and venerated in churches. The people identified with the suffering of Christ and his spilled blood; they were not mobilized to transform their situation of suffering.[2]

Cross–Insertion–Fructification

The cross and Christ are two relevant Christian symbols imposed in the Indigenous' sphere. The conquerors initiated an evangelization strategy in Quechua. The use of the Indigenous' language was a vehicle to convey the Greek dualism of the two natures of Christ and the division of the soul and body. For the Indigenous, the body and soul were intrinsically united. They believed that life continued after death because the essence of each human being continued to live in their communities. Relationality thinking affirmed that after dying, Indigenous were living in the great mountains (Apus) and their task was to care for them. The Western soul-body dualism focused on incarnation, even though it was fundamental Christologically, as a personification from another sphere. With the spiritual emphasizes on salvation, the soul was more appreciated than the entire being. Therefore, Indigenous were not considered fully humans.

The cross, inserted into sacred hills, and the resurrection of Jesus were to the Indigenous complex elements. On the one hand, the Indigenous hardly understood Jesus' crucifixion and death. Death, an experience caused by sickness or by enemies[3] drove Atahualpa to question Jesus' death on the cross. The sacrificial notion was not part of the Peruvian Indigenous religion and spirituality. The Indigenous sacrificed animals on occasion to please the Inca but never sacrificed humans to please their gods. On the other hand, Jesus' resurrection complicated their relational understanding. The reality of heaven, a metaphysical concept that connects to the beyond, was absent in the Indigenous minds. The Andean Peruvians had moral codes but not a church structured like the Roman Catholic. The state ruled and organized their

---

2. Altmann, *Luther and Liberation*, 14.
3. Garcilaso de la Vega, *Comentarios Reales*, 332.

faith. The political authorities were their same spiritual authorities.[4] Heaven, a reality where Jesus went after being resurrected, became then a separate reality from the communal reality implying division between the reality from up above (hananqpacha) and the reality from down below (kaypacha). The person who mediated the two realities was then Jesus Christ rather than the relationships among them and all that surrounded their communities.

Resurrection and ascension also challenged the relational and communal understanding. The Western epistemology emphasizing the division between heaven and earth invalidated the relational and communal aspects. Heaven was then far away from their hills. The distressing act of inserting crosses into the hills reinforced suffering making Indigenous to identify with the suffering Christ and venerate the crucified Christ. The cross' solidarity was neglected because suffering easily convinced Indigenous in their "defenseless, impotent, and defeated"[5] realities. Strategically, faith kept the Indigenous in a place of oblivion. Nevertheless, in their suffering, Indigenous were able to reverse their situation. They found strength in the crucifixion. In fact, it came to be venerated because it gave them the strength to resist in silence, "In the most literal sense, it was passive resistance. The exhausted Jesus, the dead Jesus is the victim of the evil and injustice, not its legitimator."[6]

Submissive Resistance and Consciousness

Submissive resistance has its central element in life. The intimate message of Jesus Christ was present in the passive resistance seeking to survive. Scorza develops, using parody and humor, concepts of resistance and survival to demonstrate how the Indigenous living in crisis of cultural identity after losing their lands at the hands of landlords and the state are able to resist and to transgress the limits of realism through the imaginary of being invisible. The novel, based on a real

4. Mariátegui, *Siete Ensayos*, 128.

5. In relation to the figure of a dead Jesus, Altman affirms, the image came reflecting "the experience of the common people under Arabian and Muslim domination. This Jesus suffered for the people but was defenseless, impotent, and defeated . . . The people identified with the suffering of Christ and his spilled blood; they were not mobilized to transform their situation of suffering" (Altman, *Luther and Liberation*, 14, 15).

6. Altman, *Luther and Liberation*, 15.

history,[7] reveals the struggles of the Yanahuanca community, located in the central Andes of Peru. They suffered a massacre while defending their communal land. Fermín Espinoza, Garabombo, was invisible and transparent[8] because of the authorities' threat against the ones holding communal meetings except for religious or public purposes.[9] Garabombo, whose soul was supposed to be captive and submissive, knew that his communal land abusively expropriated could be recovered. He moved people to be aware of their power to overcome captivity. Knowing that the community needed to believe in freedom, Garabombo dared to walk toward the house of Juan Lovatón, the president of the community that is monitored day and night. After rescuing the documents that validated the communal property, he empowers his people. They risk to act of being invisible[10] established a different parameter and meaning to action. Without revealing his fragility; his invisibility demonstrates the power to venture when the authorities ignore him. Dissimulation is a source that "protects the subject as well as the result of violence, violence that makes the subject ineffable."[11]

The myth of invisibility makes sense in a context impregnated with communal sensibility. Through the myth of resistance, Scorza tries "to put into consideration an exercise of interpretation about the cultural phenomena and how collective and personal imaginations . . . succeed in conceiving new stories and myths (that) give a new meaning to the historical movements in Andean America, from an absolute consciousness of history."[12] The myth of invisibility demonstrates the capacity to challenge impossible situations. The myth evokes consciousness. The turning point of this experience is that even with imposition and subjugation, human beings can see beyond the symbols to undermine paralyzing situations.

Christologically, suffering is portrayed in *Tayta Cristo*, a small narration of Good Friday, written by Eleodoro Vargas Vicuña.[13] It beautifully

7. Scorza, *Garabombo*, 154.

8. Scorza, *Garabombo*, 11.

9. Scorza, *Garabombo*, 166.

10. Scorza, *Garabombo*, 74–80. Garabombo discovers he is invisible knowing that Ponciano ignores him. Garabombo uses this strength to walk in forbidden places and the authorities are unable to capture him.

11. Westhelle, *Voces de Protesta*, 49.

12. Ramírez, "La presencia y significado del mito," 1–2.

13. *Tayta Cristo* is a small collection of stories published in 1953 that combines the real and magic of the Andean reality.

captures the suffering of the poor before the crucifixion. The persons who are really poor are unable to notice that they are the real crucified walking on the way to Golgotha day by day. The narration relates the community's suffering while witnessing Alejandro's death after carrying the cross to overcome the shame caused by his son. Everyone in the town sees Alejandro's suffering, everyone cries at each step, everyone is shocked with his death, but no one realizes their own suffering.

At the beginning of the narration, the author offers the perspective of two persons in relationship to the crucified Christ: Aurelia Ramos and Jacinto Navarro in the temple contemplating the figure of the crucified. While Jacinto praises the excellent art work, Aurelia, feeling the suffering of the poor guy hanging on the cross, suffers with him. Aurelia voices Christ's feeling with the word "pobrecito." Jacinto, capturing the irony of Good Friday in Aurelia's attitude, consciously sees his people suffering much each day. Jacinto sees the broader picture revealing, "a poor person saying poor."[14] He identifies the commonality between the suffering of Aurelia and his people and the tension: the capacity of the poor to be moved by those who suffer. Jacinto ironically discerns his people's daily struggle understanding at the same time their stage of defeat of the crucified–an image remaining in suffering that does not allow people the discovery of transformation.

Suffering continued to be present for centuries. The Indigenous accepted Jesus Christ even though it was difficult to understand theological concepts like the trinity, two natures, etc. Jesus Christ was welcomed as one more among the other gods. For instance, in *Todas las Sangres*, the people of San Pedro see Christ as somebody living in the Apus and Wamanis.[15] The hills and mountains are places dead people inhabit.[16] The Wamani is the second god after the Pachamama.[17] After becoming Christians, Indigenous kept alive their ancestors' beliefs. The mix adds to the complex Peruvian Christian reality. A symbiosis between the Andean imagery and the sacred Christian content coexisted even though

---

14. Vargas Vicuña, *Tayta Cristo*, 10.

15. Jesus is described as "Wamani god." Arguedas, *Todas las Sangres*, 369.

16. Arguedas, *Todas las Sangres*, 216, 217.

17. The Pachamama, the Apus and the Wamanis are gods. The Pachamama is the earth. The Apu and the Wamani are the spirits that inhabit in the hills and mountains; they are one. In the Andean, people respect these spirits. Arguedas uses the word Wamani affirming the sacrality of the mountains. The Wamani provides grass to animals and water to humans. Rojas and Huaco, "Espacio y Tiempo en la Cosmovisió Andina," 3.

the Indigenous fought to accept the cross. Each cross planted at the top of their hills was a burden. The penetration of the sacred Western symbol into sacred hills reveals resistance and welcome. On one hand, relationality allowed participation in their sacred world of the Christian God. On the other hand, suffering prevented rising up to defend their roots and culture because when that happened, they were killed.

The encounter of the two world views was more complex because the Indigenous divinized the conquerors. Being used to divinize their Incas, mythically they recognized the conquerors as Sons of the Sun. Their foreign presence called for respect. But colonizers' disrespect reversed the situation: they possessed their lands, women, and goods. The colonizers structured lordship distinctions based on racial and political factors regarding to the Indigenous and later to African descendants. The social structure of the Andean populations was deeply embedded in socio-economic, racial, and religious factors. Race played an important role primarily because it signified being underestimated. Garcilazo de la Vega, explaining his mixed birth, says that to be Mestizo implies being inferior to Spaniards but, looking from other side, to be Mestizo also implies to be more fully accepted and to have more privileges in relationship to the Indigenous or African descendants. This tension continued to be present across the centuries.

Arguedas, conscious of this human dilemma, addresses the fact of complex mixes in an effort to accept interbreeding and change. Entering the world of the landowner in *Todas las Sangres,* Arguedas describes the colonial nature of the landlord structure. The landlord does not feel his class belongs to the same essence/substance as the Indigenous.[18] They are lords and the Indigenous, animals. To make it more complex, the Indigenous tend to divinize their lords. The landlords use Christianity as an instrument of control reinforcing the conqueror-conquered relationship. For instance, Fermín, one of the landowners, conceives the Indigenous' faith as small and less intellectual. He rejects and despises the Indigenous faith affirming their faith is too emotional; therefore inferior.[19] Arguedas disagreeing with Fermín shows his openness to the Indigenous reality in Matilde:

---

18. Arguedas, *Todas las Sangres,* 235.

19. "I believe that the mountains suffer and they have power to drive them as disgraceful beings because their sensibility is first and the individual almost does not exist" (Arguedas, *Todas las Sangres,* 286).

But as a woman, who has suffered, I cannot share your methods and I cannot approve them. You reconcile, in a very rational way, things that I cannot reconcile . . . your reasoning is too high, and those procedures that are cruel for me, for you are simple methods. I feel God in a different manner.[20]

When Matilde affirms, "I feel God in a different manner," she is not only differentiating herself from her husband's modus operandi. She makes sense of her feelings and connects them to the specific human suffering. This sentient experience awakens her to encompass the Indigenous' suffering. She identifies and enunciates her disagreement with her husband's methods. Her conscious emotions allow her to act in a different manner. The emotional element is one of the central factors in Arguedas' struggle to lead people from the impossible to the possibility to feel and to see God in another way: to find God's presence in the presence of the Indigenous.

Arguedas knows the reality of the Indigenous faith, its mythical elements juxtaposed to Christianity. From the distorted *encomienda* system, Arguedas reverts the responsibility of the landlord; instead of neglecting, he had to save their slaves by bringing into consideration the danger of spiritual dependence. The landlord works as somebody who ensures the morality of his servants.[21] This paradigm, in Christological terms, connects to the idea of a savior who imposes his power even in the moral capacity to ensure that sin does not take part in the servant's lives. Even though the landlord acts as a means of grace, the Indigenous faith guarantees of the landlord's salvation.

Todas las Sangres provides a different notion to landlords[22] and proposes a project based on mixture. Demetrio Rendón Wilca is the prototype who will liberate the Indigenous from the control of their lords. Rendón Wilca, an Indigenous who had lived in the capital city, is educated. He is able to dance in both Spanish and Quechua circles without forgetting his Indigenous roots and changing his values. He continues to

20. Arguedas, *Todas las Sangres*, 236.

21. Portocarrero, *Crítica Literaria*, 160–61.

22. There are different proposals: modernization supporting international capitalism with native partners; a more national modernization preserving autonomy with respect to international capitalism, a feudal project that resists modernization because of its corruptness and national integration, and a project based on the continuous exploitation of the Indigenous' slavery benefiting the landlords. Portocarrero, *Crítica Literaria*, 8.

be poor, obedient to the lord but also autonomous. Rendón Wilca brings healing without confrontation. The mythical figure of Rendón Wilca has a faithful permanence in the Indigenous world enriched by the mixture of the coastal world. For Arguedas, Rendón Wilca is recognized and respected–an example of openness to multiple cultural elements. He is the artistic result of dialectical forces expressed through reincorporation. Wilca creatively offers an alternative by allowing his people to see other worlds, even though he knows that he is the sacrificial victim.[23] In Wilca, Arguedas proposes the encounter of new elements in the present but looking to the future. Like the mountains, Wilca remains solid and resists the landowners' power. He is able to use his wisdom to subvert the landlord's authority. Facing the danger of being killed, Wilca becomes the possibility of survival and self-transformation. In that capacity, Wilca remains faithful to his Indigenous traditions.

In his last novel, *El Zorro de Arriba y El Zorro de Abajo*, Arguedas addresses again survival, change, and transformation. To Andean people living in Chimbote, a small city in the coastal area, Arguedas gives them the potential of ruptures and mixtures. For Arguedas, the Quechua myth continues to be present in the urban and Westernized Chimbote. The fishing industry resembles the Apus for Andean immigrants. It becomes the center of survival and place of connection. Chimbote embraces Andean people, mestizo, creoles, African descendants, and foreigners from the USA. The novel captures the struggle, despair, and hope of common people that, at the same time, is Arguedas' personal struggle. Arguedas lifts up human dilemmas and struggles and remains hopeful about the rebirth of the Andean community. The use of the myth is to remain hopeful and survive in difficult situations. Therefore, Arguedas beautifully represents the mythological force through the fox from up above and the fox from down below.

Chimbote seems to be the promised land: the place where the Andean people reformulate their sacral relationship with the huacas and hills through their connection to industries. Arguedas makes the fishing industry an intense space where the magical presence of the two foxes is to dance. And dancing, they re-elaborate their cultural integration. In their dancing they evaluate the audacity to communicate. Dancing, the foxes challenge and bring wonder to what seems to be

---

23. Portocarrero, *Crítica Literaria*, 12.

insane.²⁴ The flip side is, for Arguedas, a conscious validation of the mythological consciousness in the labyrinth of an urban chaos where sensibilities, solidarity, and cooperation are present.²⁵ The foxes are mythological forces with the strength to be everywhere dancing, mocking, in dialogue. All these elements give continuity and represent the end and the beginning²⁶ for integration.

Integration occurs through the artistic play of the foxes. They enter into the language of the fishing industry owner or by speaking the language of the ducks.²⁷ The ability to dance in two different world views is vigorously reiterated. Diego, a person from Chimbote, uses Andean music to have the privilege to be in dialogue with Angel²⁸ whose rhythms reveal Angel's origins who was corrupted and displaced²⁹ from the Andean world. His corruption subsumes him in the human capitalist system implying that by virtue of being Andean he is not pure. The fox figure, described as a small man, captures this idea of somebody modified. The music to which the Andean fox dances is the element that inspires and connects to Esteban, who has suffered long years of lung damage by working in the mines. Esteban recognizes the mythical. He predicts that the small man will not die³⁰ which announces that the myth of consciousness will continue to live. The prediction reveals that there is hope through heterogeneity. In the middle of the chaotic reality of Chimbote, Arguedas proposes hope connected to his own struggle to live in the face of his multiple attempts at suicide.³¹

The mythical fox also appears as a messenger to the priest Cardoso. Hutchinson, who lived for some years in the Andes, seems to recognize the messenger as somebody he met before. But the messenger corrects

24. The figure of the "negro Moncada," a mad man is the reverse of insanity. Moncada is clearly lucid and conscious of his acts. He preaches change and solidarity because he practices it. Through Moncada, Arguedas pictures the inverse of the paranoia of power, the madness of abandonment, the craziness of individualism and solitude. Arguedas, *El Zorro*, 51–53, 174.

25. Moncada preaches solidarity and acts likewise. Arguedas, *El Zorro*, 210–11.

26. Arguedas, *El Zorro*, 50–51.

27. Arguedas. *El Zorro*, 239.

28. Arguedas. *El Zorro*, 109–10.

29. Arguedas. *El Zorro*, 110.

30. Arguedas. *El Zorro*, 168.

31. In *The Fox from Up Above and the Fox from Down Below*, Arguedas depicts the future as desperation of life which is similar to the fraught reality of the community living in modernity that he desperately tries to move in.

him confirming that he, the fox, had lived for ages in Chimbote.[32] Through this, Arguedas establishes a present myth. The messenger/fox impacts the priest with his invitation to change which does not take place through armed revolution but by turning towards the suffering people. This prophetic invitation reminds the priest about the jubilee of freedom from the oppressor.

Consciousness is the central and mythical element that needs to be present today and tomorrow. Consciousness is Arguedas' deep struggle; he wants the people to be awake, to see the situation, to be aware of the world around them. Despite the violent conditions in Chimbote, dialogue between the Quechua and the Spanish helps finding the mortal problems facing disarticulation. Arguedas, not able to continue writing, proposes dance as potential act of survival, which ironically did not happen for him.

El Zorro de Arriba y el Zorro de Abajo is a Christly attempt to be reminded to live faith through actions and to be a servant to those in need. Moncada, the mad man, is the paradox and the prophet who denounces exploitation and the use of faith by the capitalist system.[33] He calls for change and suggests considering the oppressed rather than continuing to exploit them. The proposal to act in solidarity, rather than to promote false revolutions, locates the oppressed at the center. This proposal reminds one of Jesus as the one who walks in a diverse and complex context. Jesus as one of the people in the struggle for survival, helps to change the color of the Western image of the Christ. Through extraordinary solidarity, Jesus resides in the impact of the message of love, in the fact of seeing God in the Indigenous, in reversing the premise of Western superiority and to encountering God among simple people. How does this discussion intersect with Lutheran identity and the Lutheran Christology?

Entering into Dialogue with the Lutheran Christological Heritage

Christianity in Latin America was inevitably intertwined with practices and faith expressions of Indigenous and African descendants.[34] Spirituality and celebrations continued to be connected to everyday life where

32. Arguedas, *El Zorro*, 234.
33. Arguedas, *El Zorro*, 53–55.
34. González, *Christianity in Latin America*, 132.

Christ became present. Christ's presence, in the Peruvian reality during the end of the seventeenth and eighteenth centuries became closer in the mission enterprise developed by Methodists, Presbyterians, Baptists, or by the presence of Lutherans, Anglicans, and Reformed. From the specific Lutheran Christological perspective, it is necessary to address elements of Lutheran Christology and its impact in multicultural contexts that experienced centuries of colonization.

The Christological Dogma and Luther

The duty to consider Luther's reception of the ancient Christological dogma leads us to consider the tension between the incarnation of God and its philosophical and metaphysical background apparently opposed to the God who indwells the spiritual and sacred Indigenous world guided by the myth. Luther's understanding of Christ as the Son of God is that Christ was truly human and truly divine. The exposition of the faith of the Ancient Church, an explanation of the nature of Christ, moved Luther to affirm that "Jesus Christ was a genuine Jew, the true man and true God, the Messiah that the Jews were waiting for.[35] Jesus was "born of a woman . . . the virgin's flesh and blood . . . was the natural seed of Christ's body. And she too was of the seed of Abraham . . . So this mother is a virgin, and yet a true and natural mother; not, however, by natural capacity or power, but solely through the Holy Spirit and divine power."[36] Luther never engaged in the discussion about the quest for the historical Jesus.

Luther reaffirmed Jesus' humanity and his roots connected to Mary's lineage. This element informs Christology confirming God's incorporation in the world in the real presence of a human who lived in a concrete social cultural, political, and religious reality.[37] With that emphasis, Luther asserts the reality of the divine and human in Jesus. It confirms acceptance of the confession of faith grounded in the Greek and the Latin theology supporting Jesus' two natures. Incarnation, in this sense, emphasized the communication beyond the announcement. God is a vivid and permanent presence expressed through Jesus Christ's deep love in his work on

---

35. Luther, *The Christian in Society*, 229.

36. Luther, *Works of Martin Luther*, 3:196.

37. Luther's position was itself rooted in a specific historical context. He suspected that Jesus had been left in the past and that the church had taken his place. Institutional interests were superseding the proclamation of the gospel. Altmann, *Luther and Liberation*, 16.

the cross and in his resurrection. Luther pursues the traditional way to affirm the true deity of Christ. "The words of God, the Holy Scripture, as well as Jesus' own witness to himself . . . teach that Jesus Christ is true God."[38] The Christological dogma was never a topic in dispute to Luther but "materially correct summary of the Scripture's witness to the Christ. At the same time, [Jesus] always gave . . . a particular interpretation."[39] Reading Luther's interpretation of Jesus Christ one can understand his theology. Luther emphasizes the action of Jesus Christ as communication of God. For Luther, the cross is the major expression and communication of God to followers. This divine presence continues communicating through the invitation to participate in the Lord's Supper.

The Lutheran Christology of Grace

Luther's belief in salvation through faith alone drove him to set forth a Christology based in the works of salvation as the initiative of God's self. Salvation is God's gift initiated in favor of humanity. Jesus Christ "the true Paschal Lamb is an eternal divine Person, Who dies to establish the New Testament (an) eternal and unspeakable treasure, namely, the forgiveness of all sins."[40] The cross invited to faithfully respond embracing Jesus' work of salvation. Explaining salvation, Luther speaks of the enslaved human condition where the human will is not free before God. As soon the will is uncurved upon itself, it can participate in God and can act against sin.[41]

The cross makes evident that in Jesus Christ, God is being revealed, that God comes to walk on the earth to move people to believe in this indwelling in faith. The undeniable love expressed by God on the cross is, according to Luther, only received by faith.[42] God's lovely manifestation through the person and work of Jesus is real in history and that reality reassures a relationship where "Christ is the mirror of God's fatherly heart in whom God himself appears to us . . . Luther, however looks and finds God the Father himself in the person of Jesus Christ."[43] To know

---

38. Althaus, *Theology of Martin Luther*, 180.
39. Lohse, *Martin Luther's Theology*, 221.
40. Luther, *Works of Martin Luther*, 1:300.
41. Luther, *Works of Martin Luther*, 1:65, 1:236–37.
42. Luther, *Works of Martin Luther*, 1:187–88, 1:196.
43. Althaus, *The Theology of Martin Luther*, 182.

God, it is required to know the Son, and to know what love is implies the recognition of God in Jesus Christ. One can understand it by the communication Jesus builds up between the father and human beings opening to faith as doors for relationship. Faith is to know that "we do not offer Christ as sacrifice, but that Christ offers us."[44] The knowledge happening in the communication helps us in faith which helps humans to center in Christ rather than on oneself. It helps overcoming self-glorification.

Luther's Christology is deeply rooted in God incarnated through the Word as redeemer. The Word is a place of reconciliation where God humbles to joyfully join in the table. Luther connects God and humans emphasizing Jesus Christ's proximity. The main emphasis resides in the attention that Luther pays to Christ's suffering and humiliation in order to heal and to communicate things that belong to God:

> If a touch of Christ healed, how much more will this most tender spiritual touch, this absorbing of the Word, communicate to the soul all things that belong to the Word. This, then, is how through faith alone without works the soul is justified by the Word of God, sanctified, made true, peaceful, and free, filled with every blessing and truly made a child of God as John 1 says: "But to all who . . . believed in his name, he gave the power to become children of God.[45]

This promise is for Luther carried out in the framework of the scriptures where Christ continues to reveal and where, through faith, Christians are able to be free. The promise of the Word is a promise that touches the one who faithfully hears. "When God speaks, things can never be the same again. God's Word touches the hearer, condemns, offers forgiveness, appeals and draws."[46] The Word is the expression that counterbalances the ecclesiastical authority exactly because the church was losing its commitment to serve and to promote God's redemption. Luther's Christology is based on the redemptive motif and "is fundamentally soteriology . . . Luther is not so interested in who Jesus *is* as he is in what Jesus *does* and supplies. In the work of Jesus, we discover the person of Jesus and not vice versa."[47] Therefore our faith is the clear expression of Jesus' concrete work in our lives. This recognition is publicly manifested

---

44. Luther, *Works of Martin Luther*, 1:314.
45. Luther, *Martin Luther*, 58, 52–53.
46. Meuser, "Luther as Preacher of the Word of God," 137.
47. Altmann, *Lutheran and Liberation*, 16–17.

in the sacrament of the altar because Jesus' "death is to be realized in me and I am to die with him before I can imitate him."[48] What is singular in Luther's Christology is connected to the cross. Luther understands the theology of glory as the one that drives the believer to ignore the demands of the cross.

The tension between the revealed and hidden God plays a key role in Luther's Christology. Luther confirms that the hidden things of God (Isaiah 45, 15) are revealed on the cross to the faithful; but it is exactly in the suffering on the cross that God remains hidden.[49] This tension helps to make sense of the cross just as Jesus' work reveals what is foolish. Incarnation, therefore, is the complete emptiness of God. Jesus' incarnation represents the total emptiness[50] of which the high point is the cross. On the cross what seems weak is revealed as power. "These are the riches of the boundless mercy of God, which we have received by no merit, but by pure grace."[51]

The Lutheran Christology for the Peruvian Reality

Lutheran Christology needs to be considered within the Peruvian religious environment. The close connection between the Roman Catholic Church and the civil authorities made Catholicism the official religion in Peru. By the year 1897, when Lutherans arrived in Peru,[52] the national authorities informed them that Peru was already evangelized and requesting them to minister only to the Lutheran population. Christ's suffering was deeply rooted in people's minds as well as the image of the sacred heart of Christ that demonstrates Christ's deep love for those in suffering.[53] Along with

48. Lohse, *Martin Luther's Theology*, 222.
49. Von Loevenich, *Luther's Theology*, 27.
50. Luther, *Works of Martin Luther*, 3:128.
51. Luther, *Works of Martin Luther*, 3:192.
52. The German Speaking Lutheran Church started in 1897 in Peru with the goal to serve Lutherans living and working in Lima. Without reaching Peruvians or proselytizing in the bases that Peru was a Christian nation, the purpose of the German Congregation developed its mission in German. By 1964 the social project "Belen House," a kindergarten in a poor area of Lima, was base for mission. See initial letters from 1966 in IL-P's archives.
53. The image of Jesus heart metaphorically symbolizes Jesus' love for humanity. Devotion to the image comes from the Middle Ages. Margarita Maria Alacoque, a religious woman from the "Orden de la Visitación," saw Jesus with an open heart. The image was canonized in May 13, 1920 by Benedict XV.

many other images of Christ, in the subsoil of the population, religious elements survived like Indigenous and African. It evidences that Christ was accepted becoming part of the religious imagery of the people.

Even though Christ continued to be depicted as a white person and the cross was placed on top of the hills; the ancestral gods prevailed. The Pachamama is present in various fests. People persist in giving thanks to the earth for all that she provides. They symbolically drop a bit of their first beverage on the earth to express their gratitude. They also ask for permission during agricultural periods and before putting in the plow indicating the continuing sacred relationship with the earth. While praying before the crosses inserted on their hills, people enter in conversation with the spirits inhabiting them. It demonstrates the ongoing sacred relationship with their ancestors who, after death, have returned to the hills.

This context informs the Peruvian Christology. For some Lutheran pastors and missionaries, it is complex and challenging. The new Peruvian Lutheran population taught pastors and missionaries about a different spirituality where the struggle for survival connects them to the cross and resurrection experience daily. Not surprisingly, a Lutheran person learned easily to pray directly to God. In his/her mind, the dialogue with the ancestral gods is alive. In addition, the same person wears a rosary because the crucified strengthens her/him to face these struggles even though she/he does not know how to pray the rosary.

There are two different moments of Lutheran mission in Peru. First, the church in the Diaspora worshiping God in German and the church was mainly formed by Germans who decided to keep their identity and roots after their arrival in the country. Second, the Evangelical Lutheran Church in Peru (IELP), now known as Lutheran Church of Peru (IL-P), with two mission experiences: a) the mixed marriages and presence of Peruvians moving to develop congregations worshiping in Spanish; and b) mission among Peruvians interested in being Lutherans after living the experience of love and care in the Lutheran Medical Center. Mission initiated around the 1970s.[54] But the Peruvian reality

54. With the presence of Spanish speakers, the congregation Cristo Rey was founded in 1988 linked to the Christus Kirche Church in Lima. Members of Cristo Rey develop mission among friends and family in San Juan de Miraflores founding the congregation Christo Salvador in 1996. In 1998, as an initiative of the mission in Trujillo in the north coastal area of Peru, the congregation San Andes of Trujillo was founded. Later on, San Andres develop its mission establishing the congregation Chocofan in 2003. The four Spanish-speaking congregations engaged in the process to be members of the Iglesia Luterana Evangelica Peruana–ILEP in 2002. The German

and history challenged the Lutheran understanding of Christ's work. It invited a rethinking of the expression of the Christian faith rooted in contexts of survival. The Peruvian perspective is informed by the rich heritage and religious mixtures; their elements motivated the encounter between a very religious population and the very gracious God. This concrete encounter in Peru made the expression of faith different, one where dignity expresses love and it informs faith; one where God incarnates again and many times in a real manner.

Incarnation–The God Who Reintegrates

Salvation in the Lutheran understanding happens continuously in life. It allows recognizing incarnation as an unceasing gift. It distances from the colonizers imposition of faith and salvation where God rules from an inaccessible heaven. Incarnation is the coming of God in Christ to each reality; it helps rediscovering the connection to faith freely offered. Christ incarnates in respect and does not impose unconscious change. Rather, Jesus invites to transformation through relationships that dignify. Respect is expressed through love, central to the Lutheran interpretation of Jesus' work. In circumstances where invisibility, abuse, imposition, possession, and negation of life are constant, respect in love is a singular event where the incarnated resides identifying with women and men in suffering. That identification strengthens hope among vulnerable realities[55] and continues revealing sense to the scriptures.

Confronted by the prevalent theory of atonement based on ransom or economic patronage, salvation needs to be carefully linked to God's closeness–embodying in the middle of circumstances that contradict life. God embodied inspires each person reintegrating[56] and promot-

---

congregation decided to continue its mission in German remaining as Iglesia Evangélica Luterana en Perú—IELP.

55. A family living in the Breña neighborhood was captivated by the love of God after one of their sons received free health care. Along with other families interested in knowing the Lutheran, they requested to develop mission among them. Facing the challenge to evangelize Peruvians, the German leaders invited missionaries from the Lutheran Church in America (LCA) to proclaim the word among Peruvians in 1964. The first missionaries arrived in 1966. Archives ILEP 1966–1973.

56. Reintegration is Arguedas' notion proposed in *Todas las Sangres*. The mythical concept lively depicted by Rendón Wilca points to the return, after years living uprooted in another reality and learning from other contexts, to the Andean practices making possible to belong. The main element in the reintegration is not to loss

ing renewed relationship that are dial-logic: the promotion of sanctity in the other enriched by that environment of sanctity in community. Sanctity is possible just because God's self is embodied in each person. No need to change identity; rather growing in it with the gifts that are genuinely given to each person. God generates life[57] constantly restoring sense in each new day.

In the Peruvian context, women suffer from racial, sexual, and economical oppression. Men suffered as well but still enjoy some privileges given the historical patriarchal-machismo causing greater oppression for women. Suffering of any kind is a reality but when sexism plays a role, the chain of marginalization worsen. Not that the many people suffering under this oppression are invisible, but their strength and dignity were deeply exposed. In these realities Jesus reintegrates uncovering the blindness of insensitivity and covers us with new clothes to act in kind. This change is possible when we, uncovered, see our needs and can be recovered to embrace what is meaningful and brings continued change in others. Incarnation implies emptiness; to be completely worthless and insignificant to embody what is substantial in God's visit: Jesus the Christ with the power to restore.

The incarnation of Jesus in the Peruvian Lutheran perspective calls into question the context where God is incarnated and the Lutheran understanding of God. Christology in the Peruvian Lutheran context resists transplantation of theological dogmas unless they strongly work with solidarity and justice grounded in grace concretely. Peru is one of the poorest countries in Latin America. In the long history of impoverishment, respect needs to regain space and be practiced. Patronal practices together with paternalism needs change, rediscovering the meaning of being accompanied–inspired in the Emmaus road narrative, making both parts equally supported and giving space for learning.

The Incarnated Jesus walks today on the streets, inspiring survival and service through the small Lutheran church. In corrupted and impure realities, the church has the task to recollect the ancestral religions living beneath the Christian faith. The "rejunte" metaphor can inspire moving persons who are very diverse and unique to be seen as God's image. The

---

identity; rather, it is enriched in another cultural experience. The reintegration motif in Christology helps us to capture the coming of God to a tense reality; one known by God, a place of reintegration. This helps understanding incarnation, the embodiment of God in the reality of suffering.

57. Ventura, *Cuerpos Peregrinos*, 235.

impure and pluralistic sphere of Peru is the place where Jesus comes to be real. God's presence is beyond the antithetical corrupted-uncorrupted dualism. In the face of each person God is revealed as sacred. In each person entering freely in the relationship God invites, sanctification is gracious, making the impure holy, redeeming life in its integrity.

Christian elements or rituals seen with suspicion because of what is determined by the official church, need to be restored. They have survived as silent or invisible marks of a rich past where God embodied. Even hidden rituals and dissident practices struggle for belonging; God is able to reintegrate and bless aspects defined as idolatry[58] giving new meaning. God empties to liberate and rebuild connection to practices that enrich faith and service: "the path of the cross. Our rediscovery of the value of the historical Jesus, in particular his active identification with the poor and the oppressed, ought to be integrated into the theology of the cross and of the kenosis of Jesus."[59]

In Christ, God reintegrates and continues recreating life in realities that contradict the vision of new life. It embraces symbols, myths, and representations[60] blessing the fruits of love expressed in the Pre-Inca, Inca, and African cultures. The ancestors were known by God since they were conceived and the Spirit of God continues to move among their descendants. God's incarnation is a process of integration to a familiar place like the religious Peruvian context where a more human word can take place. God reintegrates among many persons in the communities; then, incarnation never becomes a "private and hidden worship,"[61] but public where God's presence affirms diversity. The God who incarnates enters into the alienated reality of the other, offering the strength and capacity for resilience and recreation. In a long history of injustice and exigencies for change, God recognizes the value of past beliefs and the value of the identity of each human being.

Entering in relationship, Christ stays side by side as companion, in a relationship of equals grounded in the capacity to feel the suffering of people. By walking among the displaced and the wanderers God not only

---

58. The colonizers struggled against the infidels: Islam people and Indigenous—both seen as idolaters. Infidelity and idolatry are valid in the incarnation God but God embraces all persons communicating them how love is close rather than legitimizing a projected image of celestial monarch.

59. Altmann, *Lutheran and Liberation*, 23.

60. Ventura, *Cuerpos Peregrinos*, 247–48.

61. Althaus-Reid, *From Feminist Theology*, 162.

knows their sorrows but promotes meaningful experiences grounded in past memories[62] to nourish the present and fertilize the future. This sentient knowledge[63] is possible for the miracle of life and resurrection.

Incarnation as embodiment calls for the intentional action of social justice. Jesus' works promoted justice that in ecclesiological terms is the "call for *commitment* to justification with an unwarranted *confidence* in the social institutions that rule our everyday existence."[64] Incarnation closely reconnects with resurrection; with elements that make sense to peoples' life-like language. Christology has the wisdom–the Holy Spirit "to enter into the language (of people in a) joyful way;"[65] to get in touch with people's meaning by looking at and feeling their hearts through their own language. This fantastic task allows reconnection and is what Jesus did through his ministry; these acts of love are tools to renew relationships and therefore, life.

Cross–Conversion–Salvation or Cross–Resurrection

The personal and individual change that the plan of salvation proposes is challenged by the notion of renewal and reintegration. Rethinking salvation from the communal perspective prompts us to reorganize our way of approaching the cross. Salvation was never meant to make people's experiences uniform. Salvation through the cross looks beyond the dichotomy of sacred and profane[66] because it is a provocation to overcome what really becomes foolish, imprudent, and superficial. Salvation is the provocation to make possible the active communication of God's love. To walk with the God who reintegrates in a personal experience which is evident in community and not in the institution.[67]

62. Ventura, *Cuerpos Peregrinos*, 261.

63. Mary Solberg proposes the disembodiment of knowledge as requisite to know what people who are suffering feel. Knowing has a strong subjectivity and looks for fidelity. Solberg, *Compelling Knowledge*, 24–25, 54.

64. Westhelle, "The Dark Room," 326, 327.

65. Arguedas, *El Zorro*, 107.

66. "The homogenization of earth came as a result of the establishment of its spherical nature and the actual conquering of it through navigation since the fifteenth century. The chaotic, the uncanny was cosmicized. Since then, the profane is separated from the sacred by an abstract act of the mind that sets these spaces, the sacred and the profane, against each other . . . the *idea* of the holy, of the sacred, and the *idea* of the profane is quite a recent creation" (Westhelle, *The Scandalous God*, 152–53).

67. "there was the confidence in the gift that was gained through faith and a

The cross values and welcomes the impure, contaminated, and the beautiful. Beauty has the potential to promote idolatry;[68] therefore, the cross includes both sacred and profanes sacred. It is a place where, once and for ever, the idolatry, in its beauty or ugly expression tried to prevail. It is a place for irreverence; it continues to be a major rejection of death. As long as cross will mean death, imprudently people daily will continue to be resurrected by the force the Wisdom in life that brings new meaning. The crosses placed at the top of the mountains as signs of control, were also signs of freedom. God reintegrating into the community gives new sense to the cross. Jesus' crucifixion continues to be real but the question that remains is what happens to Andean, African descent or other people "who enters this tale (of salvation) having not in the space of narcissistic self-definition (an individual inability to save) but in space of fragmentation and dissolution?"[69] What do the cross and resurrection mean today? In fragmented societies, the cross makes life visible.

The cross invites to see suffering as an invitation to create a miracle of identification between people who experience the cross. Ironically, today people continue to be crucified. This multiple crucifixion wants to kill the dreams and identities of different people. It wants to create more margins, diminish dignity, pushing the cross to become fiction.[70] Nevertheless, life prevails, identity is reshaped, and hope is strengthened. Women and men who carry in their bodies the marks of crucifixion are the "co-existence (with God that in gracious relationship) reauthorize(s) to move through the world as an agent, a self-responsible for the actions it initiates. We see, therefore, how agentic identity is reconfirmed and created, ever anew."[71]

The driving force reintegrates, allowing people to practice dissidence against prevailing opinions that condemn to crucifixion. There is real crucifixion when the continuum is broken, when survival takes

---

commitment to discipleship as an expression of the gift received. How did we ever get the two attitudes confused with each other?" (Westhelle, "The Dark Room," 327).

68. "Beauty suggests a univocal epiphany, a direct manifestation of God. This leads to idolatry. Not because beauty and goodness are false instructors, but because they arrest our gaze and blind us to suffering and evil" (Westhelle, *The Scandalous God*, 101).

69. Jones, *Feminist Theory and Christian Theology*, 62.

70. Arguedas understands negation of life in the figure of Rendón Wilca capturing it as real fiction. One must die in order to open paths for others. Arguedas, *Todas las Sangres*, 443–45.

71. Jones, *Feminist Theory and Christian Theology*, 67.

place, when dissident practices contradict the meaning of suffering on the cross. The cross connects to incarnation because the different meets God. Jesus' death corroborates that the religious and political authorities of his time found Jesus a dissident and completely indecent because Jesus accepted differences. Again, women and other minorities' crucifixions are rooted in what the institutional rule determines as indecency. Before that desire to control, Jesus built up a prophetic-Christly-community denouncing oppression, misery, and promoting resurrection and hope. The prophetic-Christly-Community promotes daily resurrection. They share through their experiences the re-signification of their dreams.[72]

A Relational Christology Based on the Mythological Consciousness

As José María Arguedas struggles to reconcile the two strong elements of his Mestizo heritage, Indigenous Quechua and the Spanish, he is able to see and feel a solution: the possibility of being different and to be enriched by one another. The Peruvian Christology, that is not official, does not affirm a dualistic system, an opposition between Christianity coming from Europe and the mix with the Indigenous and African descendants' beliefs. The history of salvation in this worldview is not linear; rather, it is cyclical. Salvation allows returning to the people's history and recovering faith that has been marginalized: the communal rituals and expressions of divinity.

Salvation is never one event; it is part of the identity that embraces in respect the difference. "When God, in an act of unmerited love, imputes to woman (and men) the identity *forgiven*, God meets her as truly *other* and does not reduce her to a function to God's desires."[73] The Indigenous and African descendants struggle to keep their faith identity as they are a source of hope that assures convivial relations hips.

---

72. To be poor does not mean the privation of education, food, or economic wellness. The real poor are the ones whom fail people's trust. The poor do not enjoy life because abundance and wealth do not permit enjoyment. Thinking and rethinking about poverty, Consuelo ironically prefers to be poor. As a poor person she finds hope and answers; she is able to open hands to give and to receive. Trigo and Chirinos, *To be Poor?*, 22.

73. Jones, *Feminist Theory and Christian Theology*, 67.

Mythological Consciousness and Identity

For the Indigenous, space and time are related. Arguedas used this notion to explore myth that is never connected to a simple tale of an illusory invention. Arguedas proposes myth as rooted in actions and efforts for resistance and survival. The myths stay in tune with people's reality and history. The "mythological consciousness . . . allows for variety, diversity, and change (and) it is inconclusive, its interest lies not in the known but in its search for what may come into being from the vastness of the unknown, liminal familiar, like the rhythm of our bodies."[74] Matto values the visible spaces where God was incarnated. In her commitment and solidarity, she reintegrates herself into the suffering of the Indigenous people. Even though Matto's proposal to leave Killac was criticized, her suggestion encompasses a visionary understanding of the future. Matto is able to read the inevitable transgression of frontiers that modernization proposes predicting the immigration from the rural areas to big cities. This visionary proposal addresses the audacity of crossing and transgressing borders; a movement that invites to encounter the unknown.

Conversion during the conquest worked continuously to reshape and change people's identity. The duty to reverse that fatal process comes all together through new means of communication that generates reintegration and moves people to their past to transgress finding in respect their faith that was scandalously taken as unsacred. Institutionalized Christologies continues to manipulate and mutilate peoples' faith. But Christ in Church aims at liberating and building actions based on consciousness and grace.[75] Transgression may lead to contravene the official uniformity but it uncovers the violence it brings. "In societies where poverty and marginalization abound, (the sense of superiority and the right to control) can be inappropriate or violent."[76]

Here the need for reconciliation, which also involves reintegration, implies a reopening to a more holistic way to get in contact with God that taking the initiative relates with each person and community. Relationship is involvement and the possibility to discover how Jesus Christ incarnates

---

74. Kemper Columbus, *Mythological Consciousness*, 15, 73.

75. "The problem is rooted in the fact that in Latin America the usual meaning of justification is confusing or misplaced. The historical dimension, which is capable of challenging both conscience and concrete practice, is absent" (Tamez, *Amnesty of Grace*, 21).

76. Tamez, *Amnesty of Grace* 23.

in their realities where many divinities subsist underground. The relationship people had with the hills, animals and other elements affirmed the relational function in communal way happening on the streets[77] where solidarity becomes possible. Theologian Tamez works on the concept of nakedness inviting women to know themselves by rediscovering their potential. She empowers to leave aside privileges "laying aside the *clothing* that the church and society have designed for women." [78] This rebellious act of nakedness will be the same Indigenous and African populations embrace in order leave aside what society and church still affirm of their understanding of Christ, one more person in the community.

Conversion-Resurrection in the Lutheran Peruvian Context

The process of marginalization and abjection is never ending. Resistance is therefore ever present. In resisting, the act of resurrecting takes place. The discovery of self-strength, the power to fly, to transgress is a gift. Even in dark silence or clear invisible places, marginalized women and men have the capacity to continue and to live in community being witness to their own and their neighbor's resurrection. In a society where abjection is present, poor women and men have the capacity to identify and to re-create themselves in the "caminata."[79] The inspiration to be more conscious of their resurrection happens also through surprise and sensitivity to others. The ones in misery invite us to solidarity:

> Maria, an activist and health promoter, grew enormously in knowledge and care through service: "I did not know into what I was entered. The organization was strange for me. It was so big. Later I found that it involved more than just giving away milk to people. I realized I had entered another school of life." Together with other women she became involved in classes on topics such

---

77. Justice starts with the serious consideration of personal experience. "I have suffered in my own flesh together with the women in the community. We need to recognize that people on the street also make theology which comes from our daily experiences" (Chirinos, *A Thousands Marias*, 15).

78. Tamez, "The Power of Nudity," 188–89

79. "The excluded are not simply human beings who stand forgiven before God, and who are thus empowered to do justice. They are also worthy historical subjects re-created for life, with the power to transform their history that has tended to marginalize the majority of the people. They are persons whose sins are not counted against them, because the will of God in Jesus Christ was precisely to liberate all people for life" (Tamez, *Amnesty of Grace*, 165).

as women's rights, health issues, and using popular protests such as marches to pressure the government.[80]

The discussion about the nature of Jesus Christ is important for the Peruvian context but even more relevant is the dialogue and practice of the nature of Jesus' ministry. Jesus' ministry starts with his gracious incarnating. Jesus is a gift to all but especially to the poor in suffering. People who experience abusive authorities and have a distorted concept of sin and salvation are often oppressed; "I did not know that it was good to struggle for my rights. I am afraid but I will try."[81]

Christology should never be detached from the multiple oppressions people experience because its goal is to empower persons and to affirm Christ presence among their daily struggles. Christology in that sense is enriched by diverse life experiences. Christology is Christ-telling, Christ discoursing through a ministry of love and justice, through a ministry of accompaniment.[82] When Jesus walks among women and men, among Indigenous and African descendant populations, he is a God who is alive, a God who understands each person and their communities because he feels their oppression. The closeness of God in Christ move people to sincerely confess their faith to Jesus' self, a confession that is felt and brings sense in the hope that their life of faith has solid ground: they are accompanied in life and the journey is less difficult.

---

80. Trinidad, *Thousand Marias*, 12.

81. This was the experience of my mother who after almost fifteen years of work was invited to resign and was offered a ridiculously small amount of money to end her employment. When she found that her rights meant to fight for justice, she entered a new theological world. Struggling to re-conceptualize her understanding of sin, salvation, and love of God, my mother asked many times if that way of justice was not sin. She, an Andean Quechua woman was slowly empowered and changed her vision of a judging Christ to the companion one.

82. Trigo and Chirinos Trinidad, *To Be Poor?*, 15.

Conclusion

THIS RESEARCH, DRAWN TO the action of Jesus Christ, seeks to focus on the various Christological perspectives in Latin America in order to discover elements for a more contextual Christological reflection. In order to study Latin American Christologies, it goes back to the period of the conquest of the Americas in order to study the roots of evangelization during the period of conquest and colonization. During the process of evangelization, the cross and the image of Christ were used in the service of the colonial agenda. These images, linked to the Lordship motif, supported the dominion of the conquerors over the Indigenous and those of African descent. The degradation that the Indigenous suffered established a singular relationship between conquerors and conquered.

The Indigenous were considered idolaters because they worshiped a variety of gods, unlike the monotheistic conquerors. The main reason to consider the Indigenous as idolaters was that the conquerors knew that the Indigenous were, in various areas of the continent, religiously organized. For instance, the Inca was worshiped as God and in the Incan organization the religious authorities were also the political authorities. The religious environment, different from the Iberian one, was a challenge in terms of conquest and colonization. The conquerors needed to make the inhabitants subject and to possess their lands. The conquest was similar to the expulsion of the Muslim and Jewish populations from Spain. The reason for these expulsions was not only the recovery of the Southern areas of the Iberian Peninsula, but also religious control. The two religions, Islam and Judaism, were culturally and politically organized. They could undermine the supremacy of the Roman Catholic faith. Discrediting other religions as infidel or idolatrous was a strategy that helped the Spanish to expel Muslims and Jews and to conquer the new lands in America.

The encounter between Spaniards and the Indigenous was an un-encounter, a failure. The conquerors imposed the Christian faith using the "repartimiento" and "encomienda" systems. Behind those systems was an economically driven project in which the conquerors would subjugate and support human abuse. An anthropology based on differences supported the narrow understanding of the Indigenous as "bruta animalia." The Indigenous' acceptance of the Christian faith implied death for many of them. Survival implied accepting the new faith but to keep, behind the walls of Christianity, their own beliefs. The organization of the Indigenous and the role of women in the Incan society are central topics in the engagement between these two worlds, but are beyond the scope of this study.

Roman Catholic hegemony, in both religious and political terms, was challenged by the presence of Protestants. Protestants arrived with the spread of European emigration during the second half of the eighteenth century. Immigrants brought their faith and culture. The Protestant presence functioned for some Peruvians as an intermediate space because they preached God's grace and addressed people's needs. Protestantism in Latin America has its own characteristics connected to immigration or mission.

In the context of oppression and poverty, Latin American Christology reflects on the scandalous historical subjugation in which the continent lived. In this respect, the European study of the historical Jesus influenced Latin American theologians. The relevance of Jesus' historicity for Latin American theologians was linked to Jesus' compassionate actions that lead to a revelation of his divinity. Jesus' ministry of justice and compassion became relevant for a poor continent. In the context of this struggle for justice, the reality of poverty signified that millions of people continued to hang on the cross. The crucified people are the place of conversion and life that clamors for justice as well. The conversion toward the poor signified a commitment to walk in justice by making them a priority; i.e., a theological option for the poor. In terms of approaching the scriptures, the reciprocity between people's struggles and the scriptures revealed a new horizon of reinterpretation. This reciprocity was also present in Christology because Christ is not other than Jesus of Nazareth. In a colonial and capitalist system, the acts of Jesus of Nazareth continue to be acts of economic justice. Within liberation theology, women theologians, aware of the relationships of power, denounce economic disparities and gender/sexual disparities. Women assert that Christology is not a friendly topic. Many centuries of patriarchal dominion and a strong patriarchal religious structure did not welcome women's leadership. The experience of women in re-reading the scriptures engaged them to establish different and contextual Christologies.

The many experiences of women's marginalization in Latin America challenged liberation theology. Women's struggles were grounded in hopeful experiences that allow them to see the correlation between crucifixion and resurrection. Women's bodies as crucified bodies found their sacrality because they have been inscribed and know how to survive in the face of suffering and subjugation. Women turned to reflect on their "caminata" in order to know how to live. Women's daily experiences became the essence of their epistemology. Women engaged in survival embraced the suffering of children and the earth because they knew the meaning of possession and control. The cross could not mean remaining in despair. Women had to walk together in order to promote hope. Following Jesus, women discovered the power to transgress and to live hope even though their acts were seen as wrong.

Christology was ground for indecent motif. Indecency focuses on transgression of what is official, in the act of disobeying strict norms and rules that fix the concept of family, church, and relationships in community. The death of a lesbian or gay person signifies the continued death of Christ. In gays' and lesbians' struggle for survival, they return to past relationships which enhance the concept of community and family.

In Peru, Christological expressions abound and all are based in real experience of suffering and in experiences of overcoming suffering. There is a reinterpretation of Christ in Peru. A detailed study of the historical roots and reasons for that phenomenon and devotion invites further investigation. But these expressions of faith through the different images of Christ clearly lead to the conclusion that people believe that Christ continues to suffer with them. Devotion to Christ gives the impression that people's faith is Christ-centered; in fact, it confirms that their faith is more ritualistically centered. The prominent place occupied by Peruvian Christology demonstrates that the so-called idols were not and never have been exterminated. Even given the imposition of the glorification of suffering, Indigenous' rituals and ancestral religious expressions survived beneath Christianity.

Novels offer rich elements to capture some aspects of that Christological reality. The use of literature responded to the fluid recounting of past and present dilemmas and events. Writers who engaged these concerns did so in light of the most concrete human dilemmas. But these novels also grasp significant perceptions in the imaginary realm. They include beliefs, feelings, frustrations, and dreams, and they develop chains of relationships and social organizations. Novels have the power to push artfully at relevant notions and experiences. They are vigilant eyes and critical reflections full of gifts for theology. Therefore, the use of Clorinda Matto de Turner's novels work exactly to capture what the author already understood: the religious, economic, and juridical oppression of the Indigenous people in Killac.

Matto offers solutions through the presence, affections, and actions of the Marin family, and through education and emigration. Even while that proposal may seem simplistic, she stood as a vanguard. Matto's proposal can also seem paternalistic, but she establishes elements to understand the Christology of her time. She is a pioneer in denouncing the use of cultural elements to support the Indigenous' oppression. She denounces the sexual abuse that the Indigenous women suffer at the hands of some priests. In this aspect, Matto is a forerunner in the critical review of celibacy within the Roman Catholic Church.

José María Arguedas, Eleodoro Vargas Vicuña, and Samuel Scorza propose resistance and the raising of consciousness. This present research does not develop a deep analysis of these elements, but it opens paths for continuing to study the connection between theology and literature. Arguedas and Scorza pay attention to ordinary events and to myth. They invite Christology to see the dance and the artistic way of dealing with people's dilemmas. Therefore, to comprehend how people resist and continue to be crucified, they propose dialogue between religious experiences regardless of dogmatic affirmations in order to make life possible.

To renew, re-envision, and rebuild Christology from the resources that this research offers means to recover the foundation of myths that heal the self, key concepts like transgression, rejunte, and reintegration and to contextualize concepts like incarnation, resurrection, and salvation. Because incarnation is an ongoing manifestation of God, the cross offers elements to continue being aware of the love of the incarnated who considers the multiple oppressions of marginalized people. This Christology points to the daily crucifixions and resurrections and therefore to the creative and lovely acts of God through Jesus the Christ. This Christology is still at the beginning; further dialogue with marginalized people, through an ethnographic research, will provide rich concepts and fresh conceptions of Christ and Christ's ministry.

Bibliography

Althaus, Paul. *The Theology of Martin Luther*. Philadelphia: Fortress, 1966.
Althaus-Reid, Marcella. *From Feminist Theology to Indecent Theology: Reading in Poverty, Sexual Identity and God*. London: SCM, 2004.
———. *Indecent Theology: Theological Perversions in Sex, Gender and Politics*. London: Routledge, 2000.
Althaus-Reid, Marcella, and Luisa Isherwood. *Controversies in Feminist Theology*. London: SCM, 2007.
Altmann, Walter. *Luther and Liberation: A Latin American Perspective*. Minneapolis: Fortress, 1992.
Álvarez, Raúl. "Ideologización del espacio en *Doña Perfecta* y *Ave sin nido*: La oposición campo-ciudad." *Decimonónica* 1/1 (Fall 2004) 1–15.
Alves, Rubem A. *The Poet, the Warrior, and the Prophet*. London: SCM, 1990.
Amezcua Pérez, Francisco. *Arguedas: Entre la Antropología y Literatura Revista de Antropología y Literatura*. México: La Feria, 2000.
Aquino, María Pilar. *Our Cry For Life: Feminist Theology from Latin America*. New York: Orbis, 1993.
Aquino, María Pilar, and Elsa Tamez. *Teología Feminista Latinoamericana*. Quito: Pluriminor, 1998.
Arellano, Luz Beatriz. "Women's Experience of God in Emerging Spirituality." In *With Passion and Compassion: Third World Women Doing Theology*, edited by Virginia Fabella and Mercy Amba Oduyoye, 135–50. Eugene, OR: Wipf & Stock, 2006.
Arguedas, José María. *The Fox from Up Above and the Fox from Down Below*. Pittsburgh: University of Pittsburgh, 1990.
———. *Los Ríos profundos*. Madrid: Cátedra, 1995.
———. *Todas las Sangres*. Lima: Horizonte, 1983.
———. *El Zorro de Arriba y el Zorro de Abajo*. Lima: LLCA XX, 1996.
Armas, Julio. *Las Lágrimas de Caxamarca. La Epopeya de Pizarro y Atahualpa en el Perú*. Madrid: Carrogio, 2002.
Athanasooulou-Kypriou, Spyridoula. "Beyond the Death of the Christian Novel: Literature as Theology." *Philotheos* 6 (2006) 48–60.
Barnes, Tatum. *In Quest of Jesus*. Nashville: Abingdon, 1999.
Bedford, E. Nancy. "Hacia una cristología saludable para mujeres pertinaces: la doctrina de la expiación bajo la lupa de la crítica feminista." *Cuadernos de Teología* 5/22 (2003) 105–21.
Benito, José Antonio. "Historia del Señor de los Milagros de las Nazarenas." In *El Rostro de un Pueblo. Estudios sobre el Señor de los Milagros*, edited by Gian Corrado Peluso, 253–60. Lima: Fondo Editorial de la Universidad Católica Sedes Sapientiae, 2005.

Bennani, Aziza. "Fundamental Values of *the Golden Age of Al-Andalus* and Modernity." In *Judeus and Árabes da Península Ibérica*, edited by Jorge Casimiro, 74–89. Monsaraz: Comissão Nacional da UNESCO, 1993.

Berg, Mary G. "Writing for Her Life: The Essays of Clorinda Matto de Turner." In *Reinterpreting the Spanish American Essay*, edited by Doris Meyer, 80–89. Austin: University of Texas, 1995.

Bingemer, María Clara Luchetti. "La Trinidad desde la Perspectiva de la Mujer: Algunas Pautas para la Reflexión." In *El Rostro Femenino de la Teología*, edited by Maria Clara Luchetti Bingermer, 135–66. San José: Departamento Ecuménico de Investigaciones, 1986.

Boff, Clodovis, "Epistemology and Methodology of the Theology of Liberation." In *Mysterium Liberationis: Fundamental Concepts of Liberation Theology*, edited by Jon Sobrino and Ignacio Ellacuría, 57–85. Maryknoll, NY: Orbis, 1993.

Boff, Leonardo. *Em busca dos Pobres de Jesus Cristo*. São Paulo: Paulis, 1995.

———. *Jesucristo el Liberador: ensayo de Cristología crítica para nuestro tiempo*. Santander: Sal Terrae, 1980.

———. *Pasión de Cristo, Pasión del Mundo: Hechos, interpretaciones y significados ayer y hoy*. Santander: Sal Terrae, 1980.

Bravo, Wilder. "La Pobreza y Extrema Pobreza." http://www.monografias.com/trabajos26/pobreza/pobreza.shtml.

Burga, Manuel. "¿Cuándo se jodió el Perú?" In *En qué momento se jodió el Perú*, edited by Carlos Milla Batres, 75–83. Lima: Milla, 1990.

Cardoso, Nancy. "The Body as Hermeneutical Category: Guidelines for a Feminist Hermeneutics of Liberation." *The Ecumenical Review* 54 (2002) 1–5.

———. "The Immobile Dance: The Body and the Bible in Latin America." *Concilium* (2002/2) 76–83.

Carrión, Benjamín. *Atahualpa*. Quito: El Conejo, 1986.

Casimiro, Jorge, ed. *Judeus e Árabes da Península Ibérica*. Monsaraz: Comissão Nacional da UNESCO, 1993.

Castillo, Victoria A. "Indigenous 'Messengers' Petitioning for Justice: Citizenship and Indigenous Rights in Peru, 1900–1945." PhD diss., The University of Michigan, 2009.

CCCP. *Marxism, Mariategui and the Feminist Movement*. Lima: Central Committee Communist Party of Peru, 1976.

CELAM (Consejo Episcopal Latino Americano). *Medellín Conclusiones: La Iglesia en la Actual Transformación de América Latina a la luz del Concilio*. Bogotá: CELAM, 1990.

CELAM III. *Conferencia General del Episcopado Latinoamericano: Puebla, la Evangelización en el presente y en el futuro de la Iglesia de Latino América*. Puebla: CELAM, 1979.

Chirinos Soto, Enrique. *Historia de la República*. Lima: Ediciones Andinas, 1977.

Chirinos Trinidad, Maria Luz. *A Thousand Marias: The Life and Poetry of Maria María Luz Chirinos Trinidad*. Chicago: Women of the ELCA, 1997.

Columbus, Claudette Kemper. *Mythological Consciousness and the Future: José María Arguedas*. Frankfurt am Main: Lang, 1986.

Cometta Manzoni, Aida. *El Indio en la Nivela de América*. Buenos Aires: Futuro, 1960.

Congregation For the Doctrine of the Faith. *Notification on the Works of Father Jon Sobrino, SJ*. November 26, 2006. http://www.vatican.va/roman_curia/congre

gations/cfaith/documents/rc_con_cfaith_doc_20061126_notification-sobrino_en.html.
Cornejo Polar, Antonio. *Clorinda Matto de Turner, Novelista. Estudios sobre Ave sin Nido, Índole y Herencia*. Lima: Lluvia, 1992.
———. *Escribir en el aire: Ensayo sobre la heterogeneidad socio-cultural en las literaturas andinas*. Lima: Horizonte, 1994.
———. *La Novela Peruana*. Lima: Horizonte, 1989.
———. *Sobre Literatura y Crítica Latinoamericana*. Caracas: Humanidades y Educación Universidad Central de Venezuela, 1982.
Culp, Kristine A. "Appropriation, Reciprocity, and the 'Use' Fiction." *Annual of the Society of Christian Ethics* (1993) 197–203.
Cusi Yupanqui, Tito Inca. *Relación de la Conquista del Perú*. Lima: Biblioteca Universitaria, 1973.
Deifelt, Wanda. "Can Christology Be Freed from Patriarchy?" In *Justification and Justice*, edited by Viggo Mortensen, 37–50. Geneva: FLM, 1992.
———. "Feminist Theology as a Critic and Renewal of Theology." In *Feminist Theology: Perspectives and Praxis*, edited by Prasanna Kumari, 198–208. Gurukul: Summer Institute, 1998.
———. "The Recovery of the Body: Jesus in a Feminist and Latin-American Perspective." In *Discovering Jesus in Our Places: Contextual Christologies in a Globalized World*, edited by Sturla J. Stålsett, 24–44. Dehli: ISPCK, 2003.
Delgado, Washington. "¿Cuándo se jodió el Perú?" In *En qué momento se jodió el Perú*, edited by Carlos Milla Batres, 29–74. Lima: Milla, 1990.
Dewey-Montefort, Jamie Arlene. "Entre la Literatura Indianista y la Narrativa Neo-Indigenista: Identidad y Modernidad." MA thesis, Bowling Green State University, 2006.
Dias Farinha, António. "*Ahl Al-Kitab* or the People of the Book." In *Judeus e Árabes da Península Ibérica*, edited by Jorge Casimiro, 66–73. Monsaraz: Comissão Nacional da UNESCO, 1993.
Díaz del Castillo, Bernal. *Historia verdadera de la conquista de la Nueva España*. Madrid: Historia 16, 1985.
Dressendörfer, Meter. "Acercándose a una realidad opaca: el sincretismo latinoamericano. Apuntes teóricos." In *Estudios sobre el sincretismo en América Central y en los Andes*, edited by Bernd Schmelz and N. Ross Crumrine, 23–32. Bonn: Estudios Americanistas de Bonn, 1996.
Dussel, Enrique. "Theology of Liberation and Marxism." In *Mysterium Liberationis: Fundamental Concepts of Liberation Theology*, edited by Jon Sobrino and Ignacio Ellacuría, 85–102. Maryknoll, NY: Orbis, 1993.
Echegaray, Hugo. *La Práctica de Jesús*. Lima: CEP, 2003.
Eckholt, Margit. "Creative on New Ways: Women Theologians in Latin America." *Herder Korrespondenz*, October, 2007. http://www.con-spiration.de/texte/english/2007/eckholt-e.html.
Estermann, Josef. *Filosofía Andina. Estudio Intercultural de la Sabiduría Autóctona Andina*. Quito: Abya Yala, 1998.
———. "Religión como Chakana. El Inclusivismo Religioso de los Andes." *Chakana* 1/1 (2003) 69–93.

Ferreira, Rocío. "Clorinda Matto de Turner, Novelista y los aportes de Antonio Cornejo Polar al estudio de la novela Peruana del siglo XIX." *Revista de Crítica Literaria Latinoamericana* 31/62 (2005) 27-51.

"Final Document: Latin American Conference on Theology from the Perspective of Women." In *With Passion and Compassion: Third World Women Doing Theology*, edited by Virginia Fabella and Mercy Amba Oduyoye, 181-83. Eugene, OR: Wipf & Stock, 2006.

"Final Statement: Intercontinental Women's Conference." In *With Passion and Compassion: Third World Women Doing Theology*, edited by Virginia Fabella and Mercy Amba Oduyoye, 184-90. Eugene, OR: Wipf & Stock, 2006.

Freire, Paulo. *Pedagogía del Oprimido*. México City: Siglo Veintiuno, 2000.

Fuss, Diana. *Essentiality Speaking: Feminism, Nature and Difference*. New York: Routledge, 1989.

Galilea, Segundo. *El seguimiento de Cristo*. Bogotá: Paulinas, 1986.

García Fitz, Francisco. "Las Minorías religiosas y la tolerancia en la Edad Media Hispánica: ¿Mito o Realidad?" In *Tolerancia y Convivencia Étnico Religiosa en la Península Ibérica durante la Edad Media*, edited by Alejandro García Sanjuán, 13-56. Huelva: Universidad de Huelva, 2003.

García Miranda, Juan José. *Racionalidad de la Cosmovisión Andina*. Lima: CONCYTEC, 1996.

Garcilaso de la Vega, Inca. *Comentarios Reales: El origen de los Incas*. Barcelona: Bruguera, 1968.

Gaylord Warren, Harris. *Paraguay and the Triple Alliance*. Austin: University of Texas, 1978.

Gebara, Ivone. "A Feminist Theology of Liberation: A Latin American Perspective with a View toward the Future" In *Toward a New Heaven and a New Earth: Essays in Honor of Elizabeth Schüssler Fiorenza*, edited by Fernando F. Segovia, 249-68. Maryknoll, NY: Orbis, 2003.

———. *Intuiciones Ecofeministas. Ensayo para repensar el conocimiento y la religión*. Madrid: Trotta, 2000.

———. *Out of Depths: Women's Experience of Evil and Salvation*. Minneapolis: Fortress, 2002.

———. *Reflexiones ecofeministas*. San José: Universidad Bíblica Latinoamericana, 2006.

———. *Teología a ritmo de mujer*. Mexico City: Dabar, 1992.

———. "What Scriptures Are Sacred Authority? Ambiguities of the Bible in the Lives of Latin American Women." *Concilium* 3 (1998) 7-19.

———. "Women Doing Theology in Latin America." In *With Passion and Compassion: Third World Women Doing Theology*, edited by Virginia Fabella and Mercy Amba Oduyoye, 125-34. Eugene, OR: Wipf & Stock, 2006.

González, Ondina E., and Justo González. *Christianity in Latin America, A History*. Cambridge: Cambridge University Press, 2008.

González Faus, José I. *La Humanidad Nueva, Ensayos de Cristología*. Santander: Sal Terrae, 1984.

Grau, Marion. "Divine Commerce: A Postcolonial Christology for times of Neocolonial Empire." In *Postcolonial Theologies: Divinity and Empire*, edited by Catharine Keller, Michael Nausner, and Mayra Rivera, 164-85. St. Louis, MO: Chalice, 2004.

Gutiérrez, Gustavo. *The Density of the Present: Selected Writings*. Maryknoll, NY: Orbis, 1999.
———. *El Dios de la vida*. Lima: Pontificia Universidad Católica de Lima, 1989.
———. *The Power of the Poor in History: Selected Writings*. Maryknoll, NY: Orbis, 1983.
———. *A Theology of Liberation: History, Politics and Salvation*. Maryknoll, NY: Orbis, 1973.
———. *The Truth Shall Make You Free*. Maryknoll, NY: Orbis, 1990.
Gutiérrez, Gustavo, and Richard Shaull. *Liberation and Change*. Atlanta: John Knox, 1977.
Haliczer, Stephen. "The Expulsion of the Jews as Social Process." In *The Jews of Spain and the Expulsion of 1492*, edited by Moshe Lazar and Stephen Haliczer, 237–50. Lancaster, CA: Labyrinthos, 1997.
Hess Lakey, Carol. "Fiction Is Truth, and Sometimes Truth Is Fiction." *Religious Education* 103 (May-June 2008) 280–85.
Hudson, Rex A., ed. "The Fujimori Government." 1992. http://countrystudies.us/peru/69.htm.
Iglesia Luterana Evangélica Peruana–ILEP. Initial letters from 1966. ILEP's archives.
———. Archives 1966–1973.
Intipampa Alinga, Carlos. "Lo divino en la concepción andina." In *Teología Andina. El tejido diverso de la fe indígena*, edited by Josef Estermann, 2:51–84. La Paz: ISEAT, 2006.
Jones, Serene. *Feminist Theory and Christian Theology: Cartographies of Grace*. Minneapolis: Fortress, 2000.
Kort, Wesley A. "Doing 'Religion and Literature' in a Postmodenist Mode." *Christianity and Literature* 39/2 (Winter 1990) 193–98.
Lambright, Anne. *Creating the Hybrid Intellectual: Subject, Space, and the Feminine in the Narrative of José María Arguedas*. Cranbury, NJ: Bucknell University Press, 2007.
Lara, Jesús. *Mitos, Leyendas y Cuentos de los Quechuas. Antología*. La Paz: Los Amigos del Libro, 1987.
León-Portilla, Miguel. *The Broken Spears: The Aztec Account of the Conquest of Mexico*. Boston: Beacon, 1992.
Lessing G. E. *Brief Critical Reimarus on the Object of Jesus and His Disciples as Seen in the New Testament*. Edinburg: Williams and Norgate, 1879.
Linehan, Peter. *History and the Historians of Medieval Spain*. Oxford: Clarendon, 1993.
Lohse, Bernhard. *Martin Luther's Theology: Its Historical and Systematic Development*. Minneapolis: Fortress, 1999.
Lois, Julio. "Opción por los Pobres. Síntesis Doctrinal." In *La Opción por los Pobres*, edited by José María Vigil, 9–18. Santander: Sal Terrae, 1991.
López Lozano, Carlos. *Precedentes de la Iglesia Española Reformada Episcopal*. Madrid: Iglesia Española Reformada Episcopal, 1991.
Lunenfeld, Marvin. "Facing Crisis: The Catholic Sovereigns, the Expulsion, and the Columbian Expedition." In *The Jews of Spain and the Expulsion of 1492*, edited by Moshe Lazar and Stephen Haliczer, 253–62. Lancaster, CA: Labyrinthos, 1997.
Luther, Martin. *The Christian in Society II*. Edited by Walter I. Brandt. Translated by Helmut T. Lehmann. Luther's Works 45. Philadelphia: Muhlenberg, 1962.
———. *Martin Luther: Selections of His Writings*. Edited by John Dillengerger. New York: Anchor, 1961.

———. *Works of Martin Luther. The Philadelphia Edition.* Vol. 1. Philadelphia: Muhlenberg, 1915.
———. *Works of Martin Luther. The Philadelphia Edition.* Vol. 2. Philadelphia: Muhlenberg, 1915.
———. *Works of Martin Luther. The Philadelphia Edition.* Vol. 3. Philadelphia: Muhlenberg, 1915.
Mackay, Juan A. *El Otro Cristo Español.* Lima: San Andrés, 1991.
Mariátegui, José Carlos. *Siete Ensayos de Interpretación de la Realidad Peruana.* Lima: Biblioteca de Marcha, 1970.
Marzal, Manuel. "La Religión Quechua Sur Andina Peruana." In *El Rostro Indio de Dios,* edited by Manuel M. Marzal, 197–271. Lima: Pontificia Universidad Católica del Perú, 1991.
———. *Tierra Encantada, Tratado de Antropología Religiosa de América Latina.* Madrid: Trotta, 2002.
Matto de Turner, Clorinda. *Aves sin nido.* Buenos Aires: Stockcero, 2004.
———. *Herencia.* Buenos Aires: Stockcero, 2006.
———. *Índole.* Buenos Aires: Stockcero, 2006.
———. *Tradiciones Cuzqueñas; leyendas, biografías y hojas sueltas.* Cuzco: Universidad Nacional de Cuzco, 1954.
McAlister, Lyle N. *Spain and Portugal in the New World, 1492–1700.* Minneapolis: University of Minnesota Press, 1984.
McCarter, J. Parnell, ed. "Protestantism in North and South America." In *Thy Kingdom Come: A Sketch of Christ's Church in History.* 2004. http://www.puritans.net/curriculum/Thy%20Kingdom%20Come%20II/chapter40.pdf.
McGrath, Alister E. *The Christian Theology Reader.* Malden, MA: Blackwell, 2007.
Meléndez, Concha. *La Novela Indianista en Hispanoamérica.* Río Piedras: Universidad de Puerto Rico, 1961.
Menocal, María Rosa. *The Ornament of the World: How Muslims, Jews, and Christians created a Culture of Tolerance in Medieval Spain.* Boston: Little, Brown, 2002.
Meuser, Fred W. "Luther as Preacher of the Word of God." In *The Cambridge Companion to Martin Luther,* edited by Donald K, McKim, 136–48. Cambridge: Cambridge University Press, 2003.
Migliore, Daniel L. *Faith Seeking Understanding: An Introduction to Christian Theology.* Grand Rapids: Eerdmans, 2004.
Míguez Bonino, José. *Jesús: ni vencido ni monarca celestial.* Buenos Aires: Tierra Nueva, 1977.
Miranda Luizaga, Jorge, and Viviana Del Carpio Natcheff. "Fundamentos de las espiritualidades panandinas." In *Teología Andina. El tejido diverso de la fe indígena,* edited by Josef Estermann, 1:21–38. La Paz: ISEAT, 2006.
Murray, Pauli. "The Liberation of Black Women." In *Feminist Theory: A Reader,* edited by Wendy K. Kolmar and Frances Bartkowski, 232–38. New York: McGraw Hill, 2005.
Nieto Velez, Armando. "La Transformación Religiosa Peruana." In *Perú: Presencia e Identidad,* edited by Ariel Comunicaciones para la Cultura, 85–102. Lima: Ariel, 1992.
Penyak, Lee M., and Walter J. Petry. *Religion in Latin America: A Documentary History.* Maryknoll, NY: Orbis, 2006.

Pérez Alvarez, Eliseo. "Teoría del Destino Manifiesto en Cortés." In *Desde el Reverso: Materiales para la Historia de la Iglesia*, edited by Justo Gonzales, 97–127. Mexico City: El Faro, 1993.

Petrella, Ivan. *The Future of Liberation Theology: An Argument and Manifesto*. Hampshire, UK: Ashgate, 2004.

Pini, Francesco. "La Devoción a la Cruz y al Cristo crucificado en la Tradición Histórica de América." In *El Rostro de un Pueblo. Estudios sobre el Señor de los Milagros*, edited by Gian Corrado Peluso, 23–129. Lima: Universidad Católica Sedes Sapientiae, 2005.

Porcile, María Teresa. *La Mujer espacio de salvación: Misión de la Mujer en la Iglesia, una perspectiva antropológica*. Mexico City: Instituto Mexicano de Doctrina Social Cristiana, 1993.

Portocarrero, Gonzalo. *Racismo y mestizaje y otros ensayos*. Lima: Congreso del Perú, 2007.

Quijano, Anibal, ed. *¿He vivido en vano? Mesa redonda sobre Todas las Sangres 23 de junio de 1965*. Lima: IEP, 1985.

Quispe-Agnoli, Rocio. *Geopolitics, Race, and Ethnicity in the Andes*. http://www.google.com/search?hl=en&rlz=1T4TSHB_enUS213US213&q=mulato+siglo+xvi+en+peru&start=10&sa=N.

Ramírez V., Elicenia. "La presencia y significado del mito en *Garabombo el Invisible* de Manuel Scorza." *Poligramas* 27 (October 2011) 1–19. http://hdl.handle.net/10893/2972.

Ress, Mary Judith. "Feminist Theologians Challenge Churches." In *Liberation Theology: A Documentary History*, edited by Alfred T. Hennelly, 385–89. Maryknoll, NY: Orbis, 1990.

Ritchie, Nelly. "Mujer y Cristología." In *El Rostro Femenino de la Teología*, edited by Maria Clara Luchetti Bingemer, 119–34. San José: DEI, 1986.

———. "Women's Participation in the Church: A Protestant Perspective." In *With Passion and Compassion: Third World Women Doing Theology*, edited by Virginia Fabella and Mercy Amba Oduyoye, 151–64. Eugene, OR: Wipf & Stock, 2006.

Rivera Pagán, Luis N. *Mito, Exilio y Demonios, Literatura y Teología en América Latina*. Hato Rey: Publicaciones Puertorriqueñas, 1996.

———. *Los Sueños del Ciervo: Perspectivas Teológicas desde El Caribe*. Quito: CLAI, 1995.

———. *Teología y Cultura en América Latina*. Heredia: Universidad Nacional de Costa Rica, 2009.

———. *A Violent Evangelism: The Political and Religious Conquest of the America*. Louisville: Westminster/John Knox, 1990.

Rocha Areas, Violeta. "Bodies, Discourse, Emotions, and Symbols in the Middle of the Empire." In *Feminist Intercultural Theology: Latina Explorations for a Just World*, edited by María Pilar Aquino and Maria José Rosado-Nunez, 218–30. Maryknoll, NY: Orbis, 2007.

Rodríguez, Daniel R. "Los Movimientos Misioneros y Colonialismo en las Américas." In *Desde el Reverso: Materiales para el Estudio de la Historia de la Iglesia*, edited by Justo Gonzales, 56–72. Mexico City: El Faro, 1993.

Rodríguez, José David, and Nelson Kirst, eds. *Relectura de la Teología de Lutero desde el Contexto del Tercer Mundo*. Mexico City: El Faro, 1995.

Rojas, G. A., and Ángel Y. Huaco. "Espacio y Tiempo en la Cosmovisión Andina." www.lateinamerika-studien.at/content/lehrgang/lg_mader/lg_mader-467.html.

Rollason, Christopher. "Voces Subalternas en el Perú del siglo XIX: reseña de Clorinda Matto de Turner, *Ave Sin Nido*, novela de 1989; edición crítica de Dora Sales Salvador, 2006." *Boletín de la Academia Peruana de la Lengua*, Lima (2007).

Roth, Norman. "Coexistence and Confrontation: Jews and Christians in Medieval Spain." In *The Jews of Spain and the Expulsion of 1492*, edited by Moshe Lazar and Stephen Haliczer, 1–24. Lancaster, CA: Labyrinthos, 1997.

Ruether, Rosemary Radford. *Women and Redemption: A Theological History*. Minneapolis: Fortress, 1998.

Ruether, Rosemary Radford, and Marion Grau. *Interpreting the Postmodern: Response to "Radical Orthodoxy."* New York: T. & T. Clark, 2006.

Segundo, Juan Luis. *El hombre de hoy ante Jesús de Nazaret*. 2 vols. Madrid: Cristiandad, 1982.

———. *Liberation of Theology*. Maryknoll, NY: Orbis, 1976.

———. *Signs of the Times: Theological Reflections*. Maryknoll, NY: Orbis, 1993.

Schüssler Fiorenza, Elizabeth. *Pero Ella Dijo*. Madrid: Trotta, 1996.

Schweitzer, Albert. *The Quest of the Historical Jesus: A Critical Study of Its Progress from Reimarus to Wrede*. London: A. & C. Black, 1926.

Scorza, Manuel. *Garabombo El Invisible*. Barcelona: Plaza & Janes, 1984.

Siemsen, Eliane. "Through the Eyes of the Artist: Joseph Sittler, Theology and Literature." *Dialog: A Journal of Theology* 42/2 (Summer 2003) 126–30.

Silva, Silvia Regina De Lima. "Dialogue of Memories: Ways Toward a Black Feminist Christology from Latin America." In *Feminist Intercultural Theology: Latina Explorations for a Just World*, edited by María Pilar Aquino and Maria José Rosado-Nunez, 166–78. Maryknoll, NY: Orbis, 2007.

———. "Latin American Feminist Theology and Gender Theory." In *Global Voices for Gender Justice*, edited by Ramathate T. H. Dolamo, Ana Maria Tepedino, and Dwight N. Hopkins, 62–78. Cleveland: Pilgrim, 2003.

———. "Por Caminos y Senderos: Las Teologías de la Liberación y Nuevos Sujetos Teológicos en América Latina." *Pasos* 110 (November–December 2003) 15–19.

Slade, David F., and Jerry M. Williams. *Bajo el Cielo Peruano: The Devout World of Peralta Barnuevo. La Galería de la Omnipotencia* and *Pasión y Triunfo de Christo*. Chapel Hill: University of North Carolina Press, 2003.

Smith, Andrea. *Conquest, Sexual Violence and American Indian Genocide*. Cambridge, MA: South End, 2005.

Sobrino, Jon. *La fe en Jesucristo: Ensayo desde las víctimas*. Madrid: Trotta, 1999.

———. *Fuera de los Pobres no hay Salvación: Pequeños ensayos Utópico-Proféticos*. Madrid: Trotta, 2007.

———. *Jesús en América Latina: Su significado para la fe y la cristología*. Santander: Sal Terrae, 1982.

———. *Jesucristo Liberador*. Madrid: Trotta, 1991.

———. *La oración de Jesús y del cristiano*. Mexico City: Aportes, 1981.

———. *El Principio Misericordia. Bajar de la Cruz a los Pueblos Crucificados*. San Salvador: UCA, 1993.

———. *The True Church and the Poor*. Maryknoll, NY: Orbis, 1984.

Sullivan, Francis. *Indian Freedom: The Cause of Bartolomé de las Casas*. Kansas City, MO: Sheed & Ward, 1995.

Tamez, Elsa. *The Amnesty of Grace*. Nashville: Abingdon, 1993.
———. *Bajo un Cielo sin Estrellas. Lecturas y meditaciones bíblicas*. San Jose: DEI, 2001.
———. "Cultural Violence against Women in Latin America." In *Women Resisting Violence: Spiritual Life*, edited by Mary John Mananzan and Mercy Amba Oduyoye, 11–19. Maryknoll, NY: Orbis, 1996.
———. "Gracia sin desquite." In *Gracia y Ética*, edited by Mary John Mananzan and Mercy Amba Oduyoye, 49–57. Buenos Aires: CLAI, 2006.
———. "Hermenéutica Feminista Latinoamericana, Una mirada retrospectiva." In *Religión y Género*, edited by Silvia Marco, 43–65. Madrid: Trotta, 2004.
———. *Jesús y las Mujeres valientes*. New York: Ministerios Globales Iglesia Metodista, 2001.
———. *Las Mujeres en el Movimiento de Jesús el Cristo*. Quito: CLAI, 2004.
———. "The Power of Nudity." In *Faith Born in the Struggle for Life*, edited by Dow Kirkpatrick, 181–92. Grand Rapids: Eerdmans, 1988.
———. *Through Her Eyes: Women's Theology from Latin America*. Maryknoll, NY: Orbis, 1989.
———. *Struggle for Power in Early Christianity: A Study of the First Letter to Timothy*. Maryknoll, NY: Orbis, 2007.
———. "Women's Lives as Sacred Text." *Concilium* 3 (1998) 57–64.
———. "Women's Rereading of the Bible." In *With Passion and Compassion: Third World Women Doing Theology*, edited by Virginia Fabella and Mercy Amba Oduyoye, 173–83. Eugene, OR: Wipf & Stock, 2006.
Tancara Chambe, Juan Jacobo. "Tuve una Importante Revelación: Revelación en la experiencia evangélica andina." In *Teología Andina. El tejido diverso de la fe indígena*, edited by Josef Estermann, 2:11–50. La Paz: ISEAT, 2006.
Tatum, W. Barnes *In Quest of Jesus*. Nashville: Abingdon, 1999.
Tauro, Alberto. *Clorinda Matto de Turner y la Novela Indigenista*. Lima: UNMSM, 1976.
Taylor, Gerald. *El sol, la luna y las estrellas no son Dios . . . La evangelización en Quechua (siglo XVI)*. Lima: IFEA/PUCP, 2003.
Tazi, Abdelhadi. "Dialogue of Civilization on the Iberian Peninsula." In *Judeus e Árabes da Península Ibérica*, edited by Jorge Casimiro, 62–63. Monsaraz: Comissão Nacional da UNESCO, 1993.
Tepedino, Ana María. "Feminist Theology as the Fruit of Passion and Compassion." In *With Passion and Compassion: Third World Women Doing Theology*, edited by Virginia Fabella and Mercy Amba Odoyoye, 165–72. Eugene, OR: Wipf & Stock, 2006.
Tepedino, Ana María, and Margarida Brandão. "Women and the Theology of Liberation." In *Mysterium Liberationis: Fundamental Concepts of Liberation Theology*, edited by Jon Sobrino and Ignacio Ellacuría, 221–31. Maryknoll, NY: Orbis, 1993.
Torres-Calderón, Alvaro M. "Mujer, Nación y Progreso en el discurso del exilio de Clorinda Matto de Turner y Juana Manuela Gorriti." PhD diss., Florida State University, 2006.
Trigo, Pedro. "Teología narrativa en la nueva novela Latinoamericana." In *Raíces de la Teología Latinoamericana*, edited by Pablo Richard, 263–343. San José: DEI, 1987.
Trigo de Breiding, Consuelo, and Maria Luz Chirinos Trinidad. "I Love Life." In *I Love Life: Poetic Reflections from Peru*, edited by Barbara Hofmaier. Translated by Magdalena Meza, María Paiva, and Carmen Rodríguez Rivera. Chicago: Women of the ELCA, 2003.

———. *To Be Poor?* Chicago: Women of the ELCA, 1994.
Urbano, Enrique. "Rituales andinos y discursos antiidolátricos." In *Estudios sobre el sincretismo en América Central y en los Andes*, edited by Bernd Schmelz and N. Ross Crumrine, 137–52. Bonn: Estudios Americanistas de Bonn, 1996.
Valdeavellano, Luis G. de. *Historia de España Antigua*. Barcelona: Norma, 1989.
Vargas, Virginia. *Feminismo: Una respuesta frente al Capitalismo Patriarcal*. Lima: Flora Tristán, 1982.
———. "Los Feminismos Latinoamericanos en su tránsito al Nuevo milenio (Una lectura político personal)." *CLACSO, Consejo Latinoamericano de Ciencias Sociales* (2002). http://bibliotecavirtual.clacso.org.ar/ar/libros/cultura/vargas.doc.
Vargas Vicuña, Eleodoro. *Tayta Cristo*. Lima: Publilibros, 1960.
Ventura, Tirsa. *Cuerpos Peregrinos: Un Estudio de la Opresión y la Resistencia desde el Género, Clase y Etnia*. San José: DEI, 2008.
Von Loevenich, Walter. *Luther's Theology of the Cross*. Minneapolis: Augsburg, 1976.
Walton, Heather. *Literature, Theology, and Feminism*. Manchester: Manchester University Press, 2007.
Westhelle, Vitor. "Cross, Creation, and Ecology: The Meeting Point between the Theology of the Cross and Creation Theology in Luther." In *Concern for Creation: Voices on the Theology of Creation*, edited by Viggo Mortensen, 159–67. Uppsala: Tro & Tanke, 1995.
———. "The Dark Room, the Labyrinth, and the Mirror: On Interpreting Luther's Thought on Justification and Justice." In *By Faith Alone: Essays on Justification in Honor of Gerhard O. Forde*, edited by Joseph Burgess and Marc Kolden, 316–31. Grand Rapids: Eerdmans, 2004.
———. "Invisibility and Dissimulation: The Problem of the Other in Latin American Theologies." In *Prejudice: Issues in Third World Theologies*, edited by Andreas Nehring, 141–60. Gurukul: Gurukul Summer Institute, 1996.
———. "Liberation Theology: A Latitudinal Perspective." In *The Oxford Handbook of Eschatology*, edited by Henry L. Walls, 311–27. New York: Oxford University Press, 2008.
———. *The Scandalous God: The Use and Abuse of the Cross*. Minneapolis: Fortress, 2006.
———. *Voces de Protesta en América Latina*. Chicago: Lutheran School of Theology, 2000.
Westhelle, Vitor, and Hanna Betina Götz. "In Quest of a Myth: Latin American Literature and Theology." *Journal of Hispanic/Latino Theology* 3/1 (1995) 5–22.
Wood, Ralph. *Literature and Theology*. Nashville: Abingdon, 2008.
Zahl, F. M. Paul. "The Historical Jesus." *Christless Christianity* 16/3 (May–June 2007).

Index

Abba Father, 76–77
abjection, as motif in Matto's novels, 119–23, 120n20, 127. *See also* poverty; resistance; suffering
Acosta, José de, 108
activism, social action. *See* liberation theology; resistance; service, active
Ad Gentes, and liberation theology, 42n68
affection praxis, 69
African slaves. *See* black women; enslaved people
"Agreement of Capitulation. . .," 2
Alacoque, Margarita Maria, 144n53
Al-Andalus, Southern Spain, religious structures, 3–4
Alberdi, Juan Bautista, 32, 34
Alejandro (character in *Tayta Cristo*), suffering by, 135
al-Mandaris al-Mushtarak (Common Teaching Establishments), 3–4
Althaus-Reid, Marcella, 82n108, 85, 88–89. *See also* Queer Christology
Anglicans, missions in Latin America, 32–33
ánima (soul), introduction of concept to Indigenous people, 96, 96n17
anti-kingdom, 53–54, 54n156
Antuñano, Sebastián, and the "Lord of the Miracles," 111
apostolic preaching. *See kerygma*
Apus, 135n17
Argentina, immigration into, 32
Arguedas, José María, 141, 131n1, 135–139, 146–47n56, 152, 158
Aristotle, 73–74

ascension, as a concept, 133
Atahualpa, xiii, 13, 13, 18–21, 132
atonement theory of satisfaction, 114–15
Augustine, 73
Aurelia Ramos (character in Tayta Cristo), compassionate suffering of, 135
Aves sin nido (Matto)
    approaches to transformation, 117–18, 118n14, 122–23
    and challenge to concept of priestly celibacy, 116n9
    Christology in, xviii
    criticisms, controversies surrounding, xviiin22, 126–27
    depiction of the mita system, 116, 116n7
    ecclesiastical interdiction against, 126n36
    issues raised in, 113–14
    salvation and purification in, 123–24, 127–29
    theme of abject servitude, 120–21, 120n20
    theme of Indigenous suffering, 117
    theme of sexual abuse by priests, xvii, 116–17, 116n9
Ayllu (community), 106, 106n65

baptism, 14, 98, 98n25
beauty, as manifestation of God, 150, 150n68
the Bible, Holy Scripture. *See also* God; Jesus Christ; Jesus, historical
    authority of, 37–38
    as confession of faith, 35, 35n32, 55

170 INDEX

the Bible, Holy Scripture *(continued)*
  feminist reinterpretations, 68–69, 83n112
  mythic aspects, 38
  portrayal of Jesus in, 38–39
  reinterpretation of through liberation theology, 45–46, 71–72, 72n62, 157
  role in Lutheran Christology, 143–44
  as source of connection between God and humans, 143 146
  transgressive readings, 88–89
Bingemer, María Clara Luchetti, 89
bishops, Roman Catholic
  authority given to, 9, 14n58, 21, 31, 31m13
  policies in Latin America, 42–43, 64
  qualifications, 8n32
black women. *See also* women
  exclusion from democratic systems, 72–73
  and liberation movements, 62n11
  mass sterilizations, 70–71, 70n54, 71n55
  Matto's depictions of, 122–23
bodies, female as locus of revelation, 80–81, 81n101, 83–85, 83n110, 84n112, 84n115, 90. *See also* women
Boff, Leonardo, 68
borders, Matto's focus on, xvii
Brazil, Protestant colonies in, 32
Bultmann, Rudolf, 39–40

cabildo (municipal authority), 5n21, 21–22
camac (vital force), 93, 95n15
caminata (path) of women theologians, xv, 79, 153, 157
capitalism
  colonial, Arguedas's depiction, 131n1
  and dependency among Indigenous peoples, 29–30
  feminist challenges to, 60–61
  ideas for transforming, 137n22
  and structural sin, 46
Cardoso Pereira, Nancy, 84n111, 90

Casas, Bartolomé de las, 26
Castellano/Spanish, xvi, 95n12
Catholic Church. *See* Roman Catholic Church
chakana (relationality). *See* relationship
Chile, Protestants in, 33
Chimbote (fictional city in *El Zorro de Arriba y El Zorro de Abajo*), intermixing of myth and reality in, 137–38
cholo (the mix of mestizo and Indian), 101–2
Christ. *See* Jesus Christ
The Christian Doctrine for the Instruction of the Indians, xvi, 96
Christ of the faith, 39, 39n58. *See also* Jesus, historical; Jesus Christ
Christology, Latin American. *See also* Christology, Lutheran; the cross; faith; Jesus, historical; liberation theology; *rejunte* (re-joining) theology; women theologians
  Catholic vs. Protestant understandings, 33–34
  and the crucified people concept, 43, 49–50, 49n129, 158
  emphasis on communal inclusion and relatedness, 79, 89
  emphasis on the historical Jesus, 41–42, 47, 82n106, 156
  historical evolution, 54–55
  and the hypostatical essence of the incarnated, 89
  and the incorporation of Christ into Indigenous culture, 89, 103, 135–36, 135n15, 135n17, 137, 145, 151
  and interactions with European Christology and the historical Jesus, 35, 35n31
  and Jesus' teachings about love, 54
  and the kingdom of God, 52–54, 53n145, 56
  and mythic-religiosity, xviii–xix
  recognition of the Abba Father, 76–77
  recognition of the indwelling, embodied Christ, 47

reintegration motif, 86–87, 86n123, 146–53, 146–47n56, 158
and the resurrected Christ as the crucified Christ, 54, 54n157
and the spirituality of daily life, 44, 51, 51nn138–140, 139n31
and the unofficial Quechua church, 108–10
and the sin associated with injustice, 45–46, 45n98, 49, 45n98, 50, 50n135
Christology, Lutheran. *See also* faith; incarnation; Luther, Martin
and active promotion of social justice, 149
and direct relationship with God, 145
and the importance of the cross, 142, 144
and salvation through faith, 141–42, 146
and the Word as connection between God and humans, 143
Christology, Peruvian, as ritual-centered, xvii, xviin18
Christology, traditional
and the church as state, 8, 8n32
and the coercive elements of marriage, 86–87, 86n124
limitations on female participation, 61, 70
and the position of women, 83
re-imagining, xi
reinforcement of patriarchal church structures, 60–61, 73
reinforcement of suffering of Indigenous peoples, 125–26
Christo Salvador congregation, San Juan de Miraflores, Peru, 145n54
Christ the Victor theory, 22n87, 114. *See also* Jesus Christ
Christus Kirche Church, Lima, 145n54
colonialism. *See* Spanish conquerors
Columbus, Christopher, 7–8, 10–11
Common Teaching Establishments (*al-Mandaris al-Mushtarak*), 3–4
Communist Party of Peru, 60–61, 61n7

compassion, and service to the suffering, xix, 41, 52n145, 66–67, 69, 75, 135. *See also* liberation theology; love
confession of faith. *See* faith; hope
Congregation for the Doctrine of the Faith, 68
Congress of Theology, 1999, 70n51
conversion
and commitment to struggle against oppression, xix, 51–54, 52n148, 53n149
forced, as tool for conquest, 3, 26, 93–98, 131
purposes of, 13
conversos, 5
corregidores (royal assistants), 6, 21, 21n84, 26
Cortés, Hernán, xiii, 8, 14–18, 16n67
Concilio Limense (Third Council of Lima), pastoral guidelines, xvi–xvii, 95, 108
Council of Trent, 97
criollo (Creoles), social status, 31, 101–2
Cristo Rey congregation, 145n54
the cross, crucifixion. *See also* crucified people; evangelization
association with daily life and suffering, xix, 43–44, 84, 89–90, 99–100, 134–35, 139n31157
and Atahualpa's questioning of Jesus' death, 132
centrality in Latin American Christology, 99–101, 107–8, 111–12, 111n85, 132–33, 142, 144
communicating meaning of to Indigenous peoples, 97–98
as form of human sacrifice, 132
importance in liberation theology, 57–58, 57n166
and integration of the sacred and profane, 149–51
and the reality of Jesus' suffering, 48
role in Queer Theology, 87
as substitute for Indigenous sacred places, 108

Crossing the Threshold of Hope (John Paul II), 44
crucified people. *See also* hope; poverty; suffering
  active hope, and the possibility of change, 51, 51nn138–39, 151n72, 157
  Christ's presence among, 57–58, 57n167
  as the church, 57–58
  as a concept, 49–50, 49n129
  and daily economic survival, xii, 50–51, 51n138, 57n166
  and focus on the poor, 156
crucifixion. *See* the cross, crucifixion

Deifelt, Wanda, 78, 89–90
Delante de una Imagen de Christo Crucificado (Peralta), 98
de la Parra, José, 110–11
Demetrio Rendón Wilca (character in *Todas las Sagres*), as symbol of reintegration, modernization, 137–38, 146–47n56, 146n56
democracy, 30, 34, 72–73
De Soto, Fernando, 19
deunmes, 3
dhimmins (People of the Book), 3
Diaz de Castillo, Bernal, 11, 14n55, 16n67
Dios, as a term, 95, 95n16. *See also* God; Jesus Christ
divine commerce, 72, 72n66
Domingo de Santo Tomás, xvin17, 93–94, 93n4

ecclesial base communities, 68–70
economic progress, development. *See also* poverty; suffering
  and the confession of faith, xii
  and economic shock, xii, xiin4
  limitations of, for women, 61
  and the suffering of Indigenous peoples, 126
  as tool for redressing injustice, 123–24
Ecumenical Association of Third World Theologians (EATWOT), 63–64

education, Matto's emphasis on, xvii, 117–18, 123–24, 125n34
Ellacuría, Ignacio, 49n129
El Zorro de Arriba y El Zorro de Abajo (Arguedas), xviii, 138–39, 139n31
encarnakorqa (has been incarnated), 23n89
encomienda system, xiii, 6–7, 21, 24–26, 156
enslaved Africans, importation into Latin America by Spanish colonizers, 101
Espíritu Cadenas (character in *Herencia*), suffering of, 121–23
Eulalia (character in *Índole*), love of priest for, 117n10, 121
Evangelical Lutheran Church in Peru (IELP), 145n54
evangelization, Spanish approaches. *See also* the cross, crucifixion; idolatry
  The Christian Doctrine for the Instruction of the Indians, 95–98
  and the Christianizing of the Pachamana, 105
  and conversion as tool for conquest, 3, 14–15, 26, 23–98, 131, 152
  ánd Cortés' conversation with Moctezuma, 15–18, 16n67
  delegitimizing of Indigenous culture and beliefs, 1–14, 27, 27n110, 136
  and the divine mission to eradicate idolatry, 8, 12–14, 20, 24–25, 108, 124–25
  efforts of Pedro de Peralta Barnuevo, 98–101
  emphasis on the cross, crucifixion, suffering, 132
  impact on Indigenous spiritual beliefs and practices, xiv, 12–14, 97, 103–4, 108–9, 109n75
  Plática para todos los Indios, 93–96, 93n4
  renaming Indigenous people with Christian names, 14

as tool for Spanish dominance, xiii–xiv, 11–12, 14, 24–28, 104, 131–32, 156
violence associated with, 25–26, 26n103
Eve, body of, 73–74

faith. *See also* Christology, Latin American; crucified people; hope
and the arrival of Protestantism, xi–xii, xiv, 35, 35n32
as basis for activism, 153–54, 153n79, 154n81
and the Christian communion, 37
daily confession of, xi–xii , xix, 46–47, 78–79, 78n88, 89–90, 147–48, 151, 151n72, 157–58
and Lutheran Christology, 141–42
levels of, 57–58, 57n164
and moral action, 139–40
praxis of, characteristics and purpose, 40–41, 44–46, 45n94, 47n112, 55, 55n160, 55n164, 65, 147–49
and recognizing God as merciful, 76
role of the gospels, 35, 35n32
salvation through, 51n140, 141n72, 142, 146, 151n72
and the struggle for survival, xii–xiii
"Fe en Jesucristo: Ensayo desde las víctimas" (Sobrino), 57–58n167
Felipe (Puná translator), 13, 19
feminism, Latin American. *See also* women; women theologians, Latin American
and approaches to theology, 63–64, 74–75, 75n78
and changing gender constructs, 63, 68–70
and ecofeminism, 61, 69–71
focus on justice, 63
hermeneutics promoted by, 65, 72n62
and Queer Theology, 87
questions raised by, 59n1
racial component, 62n11
and the religious-patriarchal system, 60
and resistance, 62
and the special challenges of peasant women, 60–61
Ferdinand (king of Castile), 5, 5n19, 5n21
the fox, symbolism of in *El Zorro de Arriba y El Zorro de Abajo*, 138–40
"Fragments" (Reimarus), 36, 36n34
French Huguenots, 32
Fujimori, Alberto, xii, xiin4

Garabombo el Invisible (Scorza), xviii, 133–34, 134n10
Garcilaso de la Vega, Inca, 136
Gebara, Ivone, 70
German Speaking Lutheran Church, 144n52
God. *See also* Jesus Christ; the Bible, Holy Scripture
as Abba-Father, 76–77
as creator, feminine and masculine aspects, 74, 74n74, 75n78
explaining to the Quechua, 93–94
intimate connection with the creation, 75–76
kingdom of, 52–53
as merciful, 72–73
satisfaction required by, 23, 23n90
women's theological understanding, xv–xvi, xvn15
the Gospels. *See* the Bible, Holy Scripture
Greece, ancient, and patriarchy, 72–73
Gutiérrez , Gustavo. 42–43n71, 44, 45n98, 46

heaven, Quechua word for, 93–94, 93n6
Herencia (Matto)
absence of a savior in, 122–23
Christology in, xviii
depiction of the marginalized poor in, 121, 127
education and modernity as transformative goals in, 117–118, 118n14

Herencia (Matto) *(continued)*
    focus on women of African descent, xvii
    salvation and purification in, 123–24
Holy Brotherhood (Santa Hermandad), 5, 5n21
hope. *See also* faith; liberation theology; women theologians, Latin American
    active, and the possibility of change, 51n140, 58, 151n72, 157
    in Arguedas' novels, 138–39
    and day-to-day survival, xii, xvii, 50–51, 51n138
    Jesus' offering of, 36–37, 47n112, 48, 52–54, 52n145, 56, 146
    in Matto's novels, 125–26, 129
    and the prophetic-Christly-community, 151
Huascar, 18–19
Huayna Capac Inca, 18n75
huecas (sacred stone or places), 94–96, 94n9, 95n14

Iberian Peninsula, religious upheavals in, 1–2, 5–6. *See also* Spanish conquerors
idolatry. *See also* evangelization, Spanish approaches
    and the anti-kingdom, 54, 54n156
    and beauty, 150
    and commitment to the Christian God, 54, 148
    among Indigenous people, Spanish view, xiii, 2, 11, 22, 24–25, 148n58, 155
    among Muslims and Jews, xiii
Ildefonso (character in *Índole*), ongoing servitude, 121, 122n22
incarnation. *See also* Christology, Latin American; Jesus, historical
    and Christ's integration of the masculine and feminine, 89
    daily experience of, xix, 83, 83n110, 158
    lack of Quechua word for, 23, 23n89

    and Latin American Christology, 47–48
    links of the cross with, 142, 144, 150–51
    links to the reality of the poor, 56
    as manifestation of God's loving mercy, 76–77
    and Queer Christology, 90
    and the redemptive Christ, 76–77, 89, 143, 146
Incas, 18, 23, 27, 92–93, 132. *See also* Indigenous people
indecency, indecent theology, 85–88, 85n120, 157
Indigenous people. *See also* idolatry; land, Indigenous; poverty; Quechua people; Spanish conquerors; spirituality Indigenous
    challenges understanding Christological concepts, 132–33
    dehumanizing and marginalizing of, 27, 27n110, 72–73, 77–78, 119–22, 132
    diversity of cultures among, 13
    economic dependence, 26
    embrace of Christianity, 93, 108
    ethnic hierarchies, intermixing, 101–3, 136
    liberty from the Spanish, 29
    mass sterilizations, 70–71, 70n54, 71n55
    military service, 5n21, 125, 125n35
    and multicultural approaches to modernization, 137–38, 137n22
    and the myth of invisibility, 134, 134n10
    as objects, 104
    and the Peruvian Constitution of 1928, 103n52
    spiritual world view, religious practices, xiv, xviii, 11, 24, 27, 135, 135n17, 152
indissolubility, doctrine of, 8, 8n32
Índole (Matto)
    challenges to idea of priestly celibacy, 116–17, 117n10
    Christology in, xviii

themes, didactic purpose, 121, 121n25
injustice, inequality, oppression. *See also* crucified people; liberation theology; resistance
  as the context for confession of faith, 79–80
  and the daily presence of the incarnated Jesus, 147, 153–54
  focus on, among Latin American feminists, 60, 63, 69–70, 75, 134n10
  and global capitalism, 46, 46n100
  and Jesus' embodiment of God's love, 77
  Matto's focus on, 115, 117
  as never-ending oppression, 153
  and Queer Christology, 85
  religious-patriarchal system, 60–61, 81–82, 125–26
  as sin, 45–46, 45n98, 49, 45n98, 50, 50n135
  and survival skills, xii
International Women's Year, 60
Invisibility, myth of, 134, 134n10
Isabella (queen of Castile), 5–6, 5n19, 5n21, 18

Jacinto Navarro (character n *Tayta Cristo*), awareness of Indigenous suffering, 135
"Jesucristo Liberador, Lectura Históriógica de Jesús de Nazaret" (Sobrino), 57–58n167
Jesus Christ. *See also* the cross, crucifixion; Jesus, historical *and the various Christological perspectives*
  acceptance as another Indigenous god, 35n17, 109–10, 135–36, 135n15
  as both conquered and conqueror, 35n33
  and Christ of the faith, 39, 39n58
  and Christ the Victor, 22n87, 114
  communal emphasis, 79, 89
  as communicator of God to humans, 141–42
  continuing suffering of, as reflected in people's daily lives, 131–32, 133n5, 157–58
  death and resurrection, 99–101
  depictions of, 110–11
  as divine redeemer, xvn11, 37
  and divine Sonship, 38
  Indigenous acceptance as the lord savior, xvi, 22, 108, 135, 141–42
  integration of the human and the divine, 54, 54n157, 99, 141
  integration of masculine and feminine, 89
  knowledge of, as basis for knowing God, xi, xin2, 142–43
  as liberator, 57–58
  ministry of love, 153–54
  presentation to Indigenous peoples, 22, 133
  and the two natures formula, 82, 82n107
Jesus, historical. *See also* Jesus Christ; liberation theology
  continuity with the kingdom of God, xiv, 53n145
  defined, xivn10
  as the embodiment of love, 77
  and European Christology, xiv, 35, 35n31
  experience as a Jewish man, 48–49
  humanity of, 48–49, 48n117, 141n37, 147
  messianic ideal, 36–38
  mission and intention, xvi, 36–39, 41–43, 42n66, 55–58
  poverty of, and prophetic ministry, xiv–xv, 49, 52–53, 148
  relevance for Latin American Christology, 35, 35n31, 41–42, 47–48, 82n106156
  respect for women, 80
  scholarly quest for, 36, 39–40
  and sexuality, 87–88
Jews, Spanish, xiii, 1–5, 5n19
John 14:15, 76
justice. *See* injustice, inequalities, oppressions; social justice

justification, and commitment to follow Jesus Christ, 97, 149, 152n75

Käsemann, Ernst, xiv, 40–41
kerygma (apostolic preaching), 39–40
land, Indigenous
    appropriation by Spanish conquerors, 1, 10, 13n49, 10, 29
    and Indigenous spirituality, 27, 93–94, 104–5, 104n55
landlords, landlord structure, 136–37, 137n22
language. *See* Quechua language; Spanish language
Latin America. *See* Christology, Latin America; evangelization; Indigenous people; injustice; poverty; Spanish conquerors
Latin American Conference on Theology from the Perspective of Women, 1985, 65
Latin American Feminist Conference, 1983, 65
Law of Moses, Jesus' interpretation, 41
Lessing, G. E., 36
liberals, Latin American, 31, 31n11
liberation theology. *See also* Jesus, historical; women theologians, Latin American
    and concept of freedom, 47, 47–48n114
    emphasis on inclusion and relatedness, 79
    focus on the reality of poverty, 42–43, 46–47, 68, 156
    and the humanizing of marginalized women, 64–69, 76–77, 80
    and identification of sources of economic disparities, 63
    and the praxis of faith, 40–41, 44–46, 45n94, 47n112, 55, 55n160, 55n164, 65, 147–49
    and the rereading of Biblical texts, 45–46, 71–72, 72n62, 157
    and understanding justifications for oppression, 57–58
"The Life of Jesus" (Schleiermacher), 37

Lima, Peru
    Belen House, 144n52
    earthquake, 1687, 98
    impact of economic shock in, xiin4
    Inquisition in, 21–22
    as a modern city, 117–18
    role in Matto's novels, 118–19, 123–24, 127, 129–30
"Lord of the Miracles" painting, 110–11, 111n82
love. *See also* compassion
    God's, experiencing through faith, 55, 55n160, 76, 149–50
    as opposition to the anti-kingdom, 54
    and the reanimation of the crucified Christ, 99
    rethinking, through Queer Christology, 86
    and service to the suffering, xix, 41, 52n145, 66–67, 69, 75, 135
Luke 4:18–21, 43. *See also* liberation theology
Lumen Gentium, 42n68
Luther, Martin
    belief in salvation through faith, 142
    connection of ordinary knowledge and knowledge of Christ, xin2, 142–43
    focus on Christ's suffering and crucifixion, 143–44
    on humans as enslaved, 142–43
    on the institutionalized church, 141n37
    views of Christ as both human and divine, 141
Lutheran church, Lutherans, mission in Peru, 33, 144–48, 145n54

Margarita (character in *Aves sin nido*), salvation through assimilation, 127–28
Mariátegui, José Carlos
    on appropriate of Indigenous land, 13n49
    on education, 125n135
    on Spanish views of Indigenous peoples, 26n103

on survival of Indigenous beliefs, xiv
views on the woman question, 60
Marin family (characters in *Aves sin nido*), role as rescuers, transformers, xvii, 117–20, 118n14, 120n20, 122–23
Mark 15, 88
marranos, 3
marriage, 86–87, 86n124
Martha, confession of faith, 78–79, 78n88
Mary, Virgin Mary
    divinization of, 99–100
    focus on, among Indigenous peoples, 110
    as source of Jesus' humanity, 141n37
    and the Spanish concept of virginity, 97, 105
Marzal, Manuel, 111–12
Matilde (character in *Todos Las Sangres*), as faithful sufferer, 136–37
Matto de Turner, Clorinda
    on abuse of the mita system, 117
    background, education, historical context, 116, 125
    challenges to priestly celibacy/authority, 116, 116n9, 125–26
    Christology in novels of, xvii–xviii, 114–15, 122–23, 125–30
    controversies surrounding, 117–18, 126
    depictions of black women, 122
    directorship of *Perú Ilustrado*, xviiin22
    focus on moral action, 113–14, 116
    focus on the miraculous within the ordinary, 114
    love for Indigenous peoples and culture, 114–15
    savior motif, 122–23
    sensitivity to suffering, 127, 130
    solutions to Indigenous oppression, 117, 122–24, 125n34, 127, 158
    theme of abjection, suffering, excessive humility, 119–23, 127, 130, 152
Maurice, John, 32

Maya, spiritual understandings, 27
mayordomos, and religious celebrations, 110n79
mestizo, 31, 102–3, 121, 121n22, 136
metanoia concept, 52n148
miracles
    as concrete response to suffering, xvii, 110
    and the historical Jesus, xiv, 36, 38
    and mythic-religiosity, 114
    and Quechuan Christology, 109–11
missionaries, 26–28, 32–33. See also evangelization, Spanish approaches
mita system, xvii, 116–17, 116n7, 119
Moctezuma, xiii, 15–18, 23
Moncada (character in *El Zorro de Arriba y El Zorro de Abajo*), as a sane "madman," 138nn24–25
the *Mozarab*, 3
Muslims, Spanish, xiii, 1–6, 6n26
mythic-religiosity, xvii–xviii, 114. See also spirituality, Indigenous

names, Indigenous, change to Christian names, 14, 14n 55
Nassau, Protestant colonizers in, 32
nature, close Indigenous connection with, 27, 93–94, 104–5, 104n55
New Mexico, discovery of, 11

Olmendo, Bartolomé de, 14
Origen, 73
orthopraxis, and liberation theology, 46

Pacha (cosmos), 104, 104n54
"Pachacamilla Christ," Pachacamilla brotherhood, 110
Pachamama (Mother Earth), 104–5, 104n54, 135, 135n17, 145
Pacific War, 30, 125, 125n35
Papal Inquisition, 5–6
Paraguay, Mennonite missionaries in, 33
Pasión y Triunfo de Christo (Peralta), xvi, xvin17, 98–101
the passion, emphasis on, 98–100. See also the cross, crucifixion; resurrection

patriarchy. *See* feminism; Spanish conquerors; women
Penzotti, Francisco, 33
Peralta Barnuevo, Pedro de, xvi, xvin17, 98–101, 98n9, 98nn26–27
Peru. *See also* Christology, Latin American; Indigenous people; Quechua people
    changing status of the Catholic Church, 31n13
    Constitution of 1928, 103n52
    dialogue between Atahualpa and Pizarro, xiii
    dominance of the Roman Catholic Church in, 25, 144
    first Protestant church, 33
    Fujimori's financial policies, xiin4
    independence struggles, 102
    Indigenous languages in, xiii
    marginalized populations in, xii
    mythic-religiosity in, xviii
    Peruvian Christology, xvii–xix, xviin18, 92–93
Perú Ilustrado, controversy at, xviiin22
Peruvian Evangelical Lutheran Church (ILEP), xii, xvi
Peter, confession of faith, 78–79, 78n88
Pizarro, Fernando, 19
Pizarro, Francisco, xiii, 8, 18–20
Plática para todos los Indios (Domingo de Santo Tomás), xvi, xvin17, 93–94
Pope, authority of, 4, 19–20, 23, 31, 31n13, 34, 97
Porcile Santiso, María Teresa, 74, 74n74
poverty, the poor. *See also* faith; hope; injustice; Jesus, historical; liberation theology; women
    and the ability to receive grace, 50–51 151n72
    accelerating, in Latin America, xiin4, 34, 119–22
    addressing, multicultural approaches, 137–38, 137n22
    as austerity vs. exploitation, 49, 55
    and daily faith as basis for activism, 153–54, 153n79
    defined, xiin5
    as dehumanizing and marginalizing, 27, 27n110, 43, 45–46, 45n9877–78, 115, 119–23, 120n20, 127, 132, 153
    in Peru, xii, 147
    role of women, xii, xiinn4–5, 65–66, 74–75
    and the sinfulness of injustice, as a woman's burden, 68–69, 69n47
predestination, eschatological, 39
"The Problem of the Historical Jesus" (Käsemann), xiv, 40–41
progress, modernization, as solution to Indigenous suffering, 117, 122–24, 125n34, 127, 158
prophetic-Christly-community, 151
proselytism. *See* evangelization, Spanish approaches; Protestant missionaries
Protestants
    Christology, emphasis on spirituality and redemption, 34–35
    conflicts with Roman Catholics, 33
    and immigration to Latin America, 32–33
    in Latin America, xiv, 30–31, 34–35
    missionaries, approaches and ideas voiced by, 32–33
    and women theologians, 70
Providentialism, Spanish conquerors' belief in, 8

Quechua language
    lack of word for incarnation, 23, 23n89
    Matto's translation of Scripture into, 114
    as the noble language, 104
    translating Christian theological concepts, xiii, 13, 13n51, 93, 93–94, 93n6, 132
    words for the creator, 105n57
    word for heaven, 93–94, 93n6
    words for the Trinity, 13, 13n51
Quechua people. *See also* Indigenous peoples; resistance; spirituality, Indigenous

evangelization of, 93–94, 93n4, 97, 108
and the intermixing of African slaves with, 101–2
moral codes, 132–33
and the Peruvian Constitution of 1928, 103n52
resistance by, 104, 106, 106n65, 133
social and economic hierarchies, 102–3
Tahuantinsuyo, 18n76
unity of body and spirit, 105–6
world view and spiritual beliefs, xvi, 93, 93n6, 103–7
Quechuan church. *See also* Christology, Latin American
The Christian Doctrine for the Instruction of the Indians, xvi
Christology in, 108–10, 110n79
Plática para todos los Indios in, xvi
Queer Christology
and the concept of indecency, 85, 85n120
reinterpretation of gender and sexual categories, 86–87
reinterpretation of marriage and family, 86–87, 86n124
and *rejunte*, 86–87, 86n123
and rethinking meaning of love and sexuality, 86–88, 90–91
and transgressive reading of Scripture, 88–89
Quetzalcoatl, 15–16

redemption. *See* salvation, redemption
Reimarus, Hermann Samuel, xiv, 36–37
rejunte (re-joining) theology 86–87, 86n123, 146–47n56, 146–53, 158
relationship
chakana (relationality), xvi, 107–8
communal, in Quechua society, 93, 104
and communities of faith, 82–83, 82n108
familial, as experience of God's love, 76–77

integration of myth and Christian spirituality, 146–53
marriage, 86n124
oppressive, 152–53, 156
and the Quechua concept of Ayllu, 106, 106n65
and Queer Christology, 87
trueque practices, 29–30, 29n4
religious-patriarchal system, 60–61
Renan, Ernest, 38
repartimiento system, xiii, 13n49, 25, 116, 156
reproductive rights, 70–71, 70n54, 71n55
resistance, activism
daily faith as basis for, 152–54, 153n79, 154n81
as fundamental to Jesus' mission, 56
Luther's emphasis on moral action, 143
Matto's focus on, 113
as moral imperative, 139–40
myth as tool for, 152
and the myth of invisibility, 134
passive, among Indigenous peoples, 131, 134
struggle against, conversion as commitment to, 52–53
resurrection. *See also* the cross, crucifixion; Jesus Christ; salvation, redemption
in the daily lives of the marginalized, 54, 158
as difficult concept for Indigenous peoples, 132–33
evangelizers' emphasis on, 99–100, 153–54
women's stories as reflection of, 84
Revenholt, R. T., 71n55
Ritchie, Nelly, xin1, 77–78, 89
Roman Catholic Church. *See also* Christology, Latin American; evangelization; Spanish conquerors
emphasis on authority and dogma, 34

180 INDEX

Roman Catholic Church *(continued)*
  emphasis on Christ's suffering as tool for suppressing Indigenous culture, 131–32
  emphasis on religious unity, 8–9, 8n32
  and the expulsion of Muslims and Jews from Spain, 4–5
  hegemony of, Protestant challenge to, 156
  hypocrisy of, Matto's criticisms, 116n9, 126–27, 130
  imposition of, on Indigenous peoples, xiii, 25–26, 26n103, 132, 155–56
  and liberation theology, 42–43, 63
  as the official religion in Latin America, xii, 8, 8n32, 21–22, 144
  patronato real and the reinforcement of papal authority, 31, 31n10
  and papal authority, 4, 19–20, 23, 31, 31n13, 34, 97
  response to syncretism, xvi–xvii
  siting of churches/crosses in Latin America, 14
  status following independence, 31–32
  response to efforts of Latin American women theologians, 70
Runas (human beings), and the Quechuan world view, 104–7, 104n55

sacred-profane dualism, 149–50, 149n66
sacred spaces/texts, women as, 73–75, 83–85, 83n112, 84n115
salvation, redemption. *See also* the cross, crucifixion; faith; God
  and assimilation, 127–28
  as challenging concept for Quechua people, 22–23, 99, 132–33
  and Christ's presence among crucified people, 50–51, 51n140, 57–58, 149–50, 158
  and the concept of satisfaction, 23
  as a continuous daily experience, 51n140, 141n72, 142, 146, 151n72
  and God as Abba, 76
  Luther's views, 142
  as manifestation of God's love, 149–50
  Matto's views, 123–24, 127–29
Santa Hermandad (Holy Brotherhood), 5, 5n21
satisfaction, concept of, 23, 23n90
Schleiermacher, Friedrich, 37–38
Schweitzer, Albert, 38–39
Scorza, Samuel, xviii, 133–34, 134n10
scripture. *See* the Bible, Holy Scripture
Second General Conference of Latin American Bishops, 1968, 42–43, 42n70, 44
Second Vatican Council, introduction of liberation theology, 42–43, 42n68
see-judge-act approach to practice, 44
Segundo, Juan Luis, 46
"Señor de los Milagros," 110
service, active. *See also* injustice; resistance; women
  and the commitment to radical change, 52–53, 52n148
  and faith in an inclusive and relational Christ, xv, 30, 33, 79
  as key to achieving justice, 46n102
  and the praxis of faith, 45–46, 55, 147–49, 153–54, 154n81
  and the recognition of one's own experience, 153n77
  and the recovering of women's dignity, 84–85
sin, exploitation and poverty as, 45–46, 49, 45n98, 50, 50n135. *See also* injustice
Sobrino, Jon. *See also* liberation theology
  Christology of, xv, 35, 41n137, 53n153, 54n157, 57–58n167
  conversion to the reality of suffering, 51n140
  emphasis on Jesus' humanity, 48n117

on the experience of crucified
people, 49n129, 50n135,
51n138, 51n140
on idolatry, 53n151, 54n156
on liberation as a concept, 47–
48n114
methanoia, 52n148
on the praxis of faith, 47n112,
55n160, 55n164
punishment of, by the Catholic
Church, 57–58n167
social justice. *See* resistance; service,
active
Solberg, Mary, xin2, 55n161, 149n63
the Southern Cross, 104n54
Spanish conquerors. *See also* Atahualpa;
evangelization; Moctezuma
combining of spiritual and political
authority by, 132–33, 137
delegitimizing of Indigenous culture
and beliefs, 1–14, 27, 27n110,
136
divinization of by Indigenous
peoples, 12–14, 27, 136
as elites, 31, 31n11
expropriation of Indigenous land, 1,
13n49, 10
forced conversion, evangelizations,
3, 11–12, 14–15, 26, 93–98,
131–32, 152
importation of African slaves, 101
incorporation of Indigenous
traditions, 116
legal underpinnings of claims, 10
and the merging of church and state,
xii, 8, 8n32, 21–22
messianic view of conquest, xii–xiii,
7–8, 12–13
reaction to the arrival of Protestants,
30–31
and repression Christ-community
model, 82n108
siting of churches/crosses, 150, 14
subjugation of Indigenous peoples,
xiii–xiv, 11–12, 14, 24–28, 104,
131–32, 156
view of Indigenous peoples as
infidels, idol worshipers, xiii, 2,
11, 22, 24, 148n58, 155

Spanish language
communication barriers, xiii, 13,
13n51, 93, 93–94, 93n6, 132
use of to establish legal authority, 10
spirituality, Indigenous. *See also*
evangelization; Indigenous
people; idolatry; *rejunte* (re-
joining) theology
beliefs/worldview associated with,
24, 95, 103–7, 110, 132–33
and connections with the land,
27n111, 29, 92, 106n65
fusion with Christianity, 92–93,
101–4, 108–9, 124, 132, 140–41,
145
and Moctezuma's sin, 23
Spanish intolerance of, 1–14, 22, 24,
27, 27n110, 136
sterilization, mass, 70, 71n55
Strauss, David Friedrich, 38
suffering. *See also* the cross; injustice;
poverty
as the context for spiritual practice,
xi–xii, 43, 89, 98, 131–32,
133n5, 157–58
compassionate suffering, 135
conversion to the reality of, and
salvation, 51n140
education/modernization, as
solution to, 117, 122–24,
125n34, 127, 158
and the focus on the crucifixion/
Jesus' suffering, 48, 99–100,
111n85, 126, 132
and God's care and fidelity, 75–76
of Indigenous peoples, fictional
portrayals, xvii, 121–23, 135–36
of Indigenous peoples, and survival
skills, xii–xiv, xvii, 26, 50–51,
117, 152
role of the church in reinforcing,
125–26
and service to the suffering, xix, 41,
52n145, 66–67, 69, 75, 135
women as embodiment of, 90,
136–37, 147
syncretism, xvi–xvii, xix, 40. *See also*
idolatry; spirituality, Indigenous

Tahuantinsuyo (Quechua empire), 18–19, 18n76
Tamez, Elsa, 63, 84n112, 85n115, 152n75, 153
Tawantinsuyo, goal of religion, 27n111
Tayta Cristo (Vargas Vicuña), xviii, 134–35, 135n13
Tertullian, on women as sinful, 73
Third Council of Lima (Concilio Limense, 1582-1583), xvi–xvii, 108
Third World Women Doing Theology conference, 1986, 66
Thompson, Diego, 34n28
Thrumbul, David, 33
Todas las Sangres (Arguedas), xviii, 131, 131n1, 135–37, 146–47n56
transubstantiation, concept of, 97
transvestites, murders of, 88–89
the Trinity, Trinitarian theology. *See also* Christology, Latin American
 challenges of communicating to Indigenous people, 94–96
 feminist perspectives, 75, 75n78
 masculine and feminine aspects, 89
 Quechua words for, 13, 13n51
 relative disinterest in, among the Quechuan people, 112
"triple alliance," 30
trueque practices, 29–30, 29n4. *See also* relationship

Umayyad Caliphate, 3

Valverde, Vincente de, 13, 20, 23
Vargas, Virginia, 59–60, 59n1, 62n12
Vargas Vicuña, Eleodoro. xviii, 134–35, 158
virginity, as a Spanish concept, 97, 135. *See also* Mary, Virgin Mary

Wamanis, 135, 135n17
war, heightened impacts on Indigenous peoples, 125–26
War of Succession, 5n21
women. *See also* bodies, female; faith; feminism; poverty; suffering; women theologians, Latin American
 black women, 62n11, 70–73, 70n54, 71n55, 122–23
 daily suffering experienced by as embodiment of revelation, xv, xvn15, 70–71, 74, 89–90, 147
 dehumanizing of, as basis for pragmatic Christology, 77–78
 Jesus' valuing of, 80
 marginalized, survival skills, xii
 mass sterilizations, 70n54, 71n55
 Matto's focus on, xvii, 127
 as part of *imago Christ*, 73–75, 84n116
 peasant, special challenges faced by, 60–61
 and religious-patriarchal system, 60–61
 sexual abuse, xvii, 61
 as sinful and subordinate, 73–75
 in urban areas, impacts of modernization, 60–61
 and the womb as a symbol of God's creations, 75–76
women theologians, Latin American. *See also* activism, social action
 changing approaches to theological practice, 65–66
 and the disobedience of liberating faith, 81
 efforts to address impacts of imperialism and patriarchy, 64–65, 69–71, 83, 156
 exclusion from ordained positions, 61, 70
 and feminist Trinitarian theology, 75, 75n78
 and feminist views on poverty, 69–70, 69n12, 69n47, 72n62
 impact on praxis, 65
 and recognition of the Abba Father, 76–77
 and women as created in God's image, 73–75, 84n116
the Word. *See* the Bible, Holy Scripture

Yanahuanca community, 134
Yupanqui family (characters in *Aves sin nido*), as symbols of the oppressed, xvii–xviii, 115, 116n9, 122–24, 128–29

www.ingramcontent.com/pod-product-compliance
Lightning Source LLC
Chambersburg PA
CBHW051741230426
43670CB00012B/2113